Wm Dickinson (signature)

CUMBERLAND DIALECT DICTIONARY

Glossary of Cumberland Words and Phrases,
last published a century ago in 1905

Originally compiled by William Dickinson FLS (1799-1882)

Edited by Richard L. M. Byers

RICHARD BYERS
Cumbria

FIRST PUBLISHED in 1859.
Supplement issued 1867.
Second edition (revised and enlarged) 1878.
Revised editions (edited by E. W. Prevost) 1900, 1905.
This new edition (edited by Richard L. M. Byers) 2005.

RICHARD BYERS
Fletcher House, 136 Moresby Parks
Whitehaven, Cumbria CA28 8XH

www.richardbyers.co.uk

ISBN 0 9538447 7 3 (softback)

British Library Cataloguing in Publication Data
A catalogue record of this book is available from the British Library.

ACKNOWLEDGMENTS

The publisher wishes to acknowledge with grateful thanks the assistance, contributions and advice offered by Jo E. Byers, Amy M. Byers and
Natalie D. Byers, Andy V. Byers, Michael Burridge, Ted Relph and John
Holmes (both of the Lakeland Dialect Society), Whitehaven Record
Office, Carlisle and Workington Public Library. Furthermore access to
the works of the late E. W. Prevost and S. Dickson Brown and several
others have proved invaluable and essential inorder to do this work
justice.

ERRORS and OMISSIONS

Whilst the greatest care has been taken in the preparation of this book,
the publisher cannot be held responsible for any errors or omissions.

OTHER BOOKS FROM THE SAME PUBLISHER

Sugdens History of Arlecdon & Frizington (ISBN 0952981211)
History of Workington - Earliest Times to 1865 (ISBN 095298122X)
History of Workington - 1866 to 1955 (ISBN 0952981254)
Workington From the Air - Past & Present (ISBN 0952981246)
Bessemer Steel - Steelmaking at Workington (ISBN 0953844714)
Workington War Heroes (ISBN 0953844765)

INTRODUCTION

THE NATIVE FOLK-SPEECH of *'Oald Cummerlan'* has many of its roots in the Norse and Old English tongues, and is a peculiar language that once proved almost intelligible to people living beyond the borders of the county. Although many words are still commonly heard across Cumberland (which now forms the northern section of Cumbria) this book will reintroduce some of the old, lost and forgotten words and phrases to present generations.

William Dickinson's first *Glossary of the Dialect of Cumberland* was published in 1859. Twenty years later a second edition appeared with major additions and revisions. This dictionary is based very much on that edition and care has been taken to retain much of its original character. Also included is the work of E.W. Prevost who revised Mr. Dickinson's dictionary in 1900 and 1905. Over a century has now passed and copies of these original books are scarce and very much sort after.

Please do not view this dictionary as merely another studious book for the intellectual. It can and should be enjoyed by every member of the Cumbrian household. In a spare moment, either alone or with family and friends, reach for your copy and delight in its contents. Reciting just a few extracts will surely bring a broad smile to your faces.

I feel extremely privileged to have followed in the footsteps of Mr Dickinson almost a century and a half after his first dictionary was published. My task of editing this augmented work for todays reader presented me with a wonderful opportunity to fully explore his unique contribution to the study of Cumbrian etymology, linguistics and local history. The debt which Cumberland owes to William Dickinson is a heavy one, and it is my hope that this new edition will give his work the wider recognition it so richly deserves.

Richard L. M. Byers

READERS NOTES

ANYONE who has studied Cumberland dialect will be aware that many words often vary considerably in their pronunciation, spelling and even meaning, as we move from district to district across the county. Mr Dickinson reflected these geographic variations by adding a key letter to an entry where it had particular regional significance.

Basically he found that the county could be divided virtually horizontally into three distinct zones. The italic letter *C* following a word or phrase refers to the central area, essentially that part of the county lying between Aspatria in the north and Egremont in the south. Above this zone is the northern area, denoted by the letter *N*. Likewise the region to the south is referred to by the letter *S*.

Sometimes further variations occur across one of these three main areas and are indicated by using key letters such as *SW* and *NE*, which obviously refer to the South West or North East and so on. As the Borrowdale area has many of its own unique words or phrases, the letter *B* is used to highlight these entries. Where no italic letter follows an entry, that particular word or phrase is (or once was) in general widespread use across the county. The letter *G* is also used to indicate a general entry where appropriate.

Dialect however, has really no clearly definded boundaries and will often shade into and blend with its immediate neighbours. This occurs not only regionally, but also further afield. To the south of Cumberland, the words and the mode of pronunciation and expression gradually merges into those of the old counties of Lancashire and Westmorland. To the north into the Scottish regions of Dumfries and Liddesdale and to the North East into the distinctive Northumbrian dialect.

WILLIAM DICKINSON F.L.S

THE SON OF A FARMER, William Dickinson was born in 1799 at Kidburngill Farm, near Arlecdon in the west of the county. His parents were John Dickinson and Mary Fleming (of Wright Green). In 1824, he married Jane Norman (of High Dyke) and moved to nearby North Moses. Here he followed in his fathers footsteps and persued a career in farming. Later, he also held the adjoining farms of Moorside Hall and Moorside Parks, farming a total of about 600 acres.

Mr. Dickinson progressed to became a land surveyor and valuer, and a leading authority on agriculture in the county, winning several prizes for his essays on the *Agriculture of West and East Cumberland*. He was considered a knowlegdable botanist, an expert geologist and also had a keen interest in ornithology, history and local customs. He is credited with producing several books, many in dialect, as well as preparing the botanical notes for Harriet Martineau's 1855 *Complete Guide to the English Lakes*.

In his retirement he moved to Workington and built Thorncroft House on Park End Road. Here he further endulged his passion for knowledge and writing and in recognition of his achievements he was made a Fellow of the Linnaean Society. For many years, he was also a magistrate sitting on the Workington bench.

William Dickinson died at Thorncroft on 22 June 1882, aged 83. He is buried in the picturesque little churchyard at Arlecdon, almost within sight of his birthplace. The plot close at the chancel end of the church is marked by an usually large square gravestone. There is also an attractive marble plaque to his memory within the nave of St. Johns Church at Workington. But his lasting memorial is surely his books of Cumberland dialect. He considered that his study of local folk-speech was *'only for relaxation and not his serious employment'*. Yet over a century and a half later, his unique and invaluable books are still the definitive reference material for everyone with an interest in our native dialect.

THE WORDS OF OALD CUMMERLAN'

Ya neet aa was takkan a rist an' a smeukk,
An' snoozlan an' beekan my shins at t' grate neukk,
When aa thowt aa wad knock up a bit ov a beukk
    Aboot t' words 'at we use in oald Cummerlan'.

Aa boddert my brains thinkan some o' them ower,
An' than set to wark an' wreatt doon three or fower
O' t' kaymest an' t' creuktest, like 'garrak,' 'dyke stower,'
    Sek like as we use in oald Cummerlan'.

It turnt oot three-corner't, cantankeras wark,
An' keep't yan at thinkan fray dayleet till dark;
An' at times a queer word would lowp up wid a yark,
    'At was reet ebm doon like oald Cummerlan'.

John Dixon, o' Whitt'en, poo't oot ov his kist,
Ov words 'at he thowt to hev prentit, a list;
An' rayder ner enny reet word sud be mist
    Yan wad ratch ivry neukk ov oald Cummerlan'.

Than Deavvy fray Steappleton hitch't in a lock,
An' Jwony ov Ruffom gev some to my stock;
Than, fray Cassel Greystick a list com, fray Jock;
    They o' eekt a share for oald Cummerlan'.

Friend Rannelson offer't his beukks, an' o' t' rest
(O man! bit he's full ov oald stories - the best);
Aa teukk am at word, an' aa harry't his nest
    Ov oald-farrant words ov oald Cummerlan'.

Than naybers an' friends browt words in sa fast,
An' chattert an' laft till they varra nar brast,
To think what a beukk wad come oot on't at last -
    Full o' nowt bit oald words ov oald Cummerlan'.

Than who can e'er read it - can enny yan tell?
Nay, nivver a body bit t' writer his sel!
An' what can be t'use, if it o' be to spell
    Afoor yan can read its oald Cummerlan'?

William Dickinson, Workington, July 15th 1859.

Aa *C* I. *'Aa fell't ower the dog.'.*

A-bed in bed.

A-jar partly open.

A-jye on one side, awry, oblique.

A-lag *NE* a term used in calling geese together.

A-loddin not engaged, on offer. *'She's still a-loddin.'*

A-slew one-sided; out of truth; diagonal.

A-spar wide apart. *'He set his feet a-spar.'*

A-spole *C* asplay; wide asunder, with reference to the position of the feet.

A-swint aslant.

A-varst a vast deal.

Aa I.

Aa *N, SW* all; of; owe; own.

Aa'd I would; I had.

Aa'l I will.

Aa'z I is, I am.

Aad *SW* old.

Aakart *SW* awkward.

Aal *N* old.

Aalas *SW* always.

Aald *SW* old.

Aalwas *N* always.

Aamas *N* alms - a payment once given to support the poor.

Aan *SW* own.

Aapral *C, E, SW* April.

Aariddy *SW* already.

Aas *N, E, SW* ask; inquire.

Aas *SW* owns. *'Who aas tis?'.*

Aawgust *C, E, SW* August.

Aback behind.

Aback o' beyont no where, lost in the distance.

Abba abbey.

Abeun *C, E* above; more than.

Abe-nn *C* above.

Abe-nn wid his sel *C* rejoicing beyond reasonable control.

Abide *C, SW* to bear, stay, remain, suffer, withstand.

Abooan *SW* above; more than.

Aboon *NE* above; more than.

Aboot about.

Abraid *C* extended; spread.

Abreed *C* extended; spread.

Ac to heed. (see Neer ak).

Addle *SW* to earn

Adlins *SW* earnings.

Adveyce *NW* advice.

Afear't afraid.

Afeut *C, E* afoot.

Afe-tt *C* before.

Affwordance ability to pay for or meet an expence.

Afit *N* afoot.

Afooat *SW* afoot.

Afoor *C* before *'It'll rain afoor neet.';* in front of; in preference to.

Afoorhan beforehand.

Afore *N* before.

Afrea't *NE* afraid. (not often heard 1878).

Afword *C, E* afford.

Afwore *E, N, SW* before; in front of; in preference to.

Age *C* to grow old.

Ageann again; against. *'I's nut ageann yer plans to wed, but yer fadder is.';* before.

Ageann t'hand *C* inconveniently placed, interfering with progress.

Ageatt going, on the way, on foot again, progressing.

Ageaun t'grain *C* displeasing; contrary; literally - to plane wood against the fibre or grain.

Agin again.

Aglet *C, SW* the metalled end of a boot-lace.

Agreeable assenting to.

Agreen *N, NE* the ragwort plant, *Senecio Jacoboea.*

Agyan again.

Agyen *NE* again.

Ah I.

Ahint behind.

Air *NW* early.

Airk *N* a chest. (see Mealark).

Airm *N* arm.

Airs *C* humours. *'He's in his airs to-day'.*

Airt *N* point of the compass; quarter.

Airy breezy. *'It's rayder airy to-day.'*

Akkern acorn.

Akrike screech, scream.

Alang along.

Alean alone.

Aleann alone.

Aleb'm *C, E, SW* eleven.

Aleeven *C, N* eleven.

Allan a bit of land nearly surrounded by water; an island.

Alliblaster alabaster.

Allus *N* always.

Ally *B* see Taw.

Ally a narrow lane between houses; the aisle of a church.

Alongs *C* along (from old deeds).

Alongsides *C* beside.

Alongst *C* along (from old deeds).

Am him. *'Catch am an' hod am, an' whack am weel.'*

Amackily in some fashion, partly.

Amang among.

Amang hands among other things.

Ameasst almost.

Ameast *C, SW* almost.

Ameeast *N, E* almost.

Amess *C* a kind of oath; a note of verification. *'Amess it is.'*

Amex! oaths or affirmations.

Amiss used in slight (negative) approval. *'it's nut seah far amiss.'*

Amry *NE* a cupboard or place where victuals and other valuables are kept. (nearly obsolete 1878).

Amyast *C* almost.

An 'ing' - as a terminative. eg. *'Risan'* - Rising.

An *G* one, eg. *'baddan'* - bad one.

An' *C* and. *'Ham an' eggs fwoor oor teas.'.*

An' o' also, and all, too. *'We'd breed an' butter an' cheese an' o', an' o' maks o' drink.'*

An'all *W* as well. *'Dick's fray Cockermuth an'all.'.*

Ananters *E* in case. *'Or anters in yon mouldering heap.'* - John Stagg poems

Ancome *C* see Income.

Anenst *C, SW* opposite to; over against. (Anemst in some old writings).

Aneuf *C* enough. *'Ah knew Dick's oald fadder weel aneuf.'.*

Aneuff enough.

Anew enough.

Ane-gh *NE* enough.

Ang nails *C* jags around the nails; nails grown into the flesh.

Ang-ry vexed; applied to a sore it means inflammed or painful. *'That's an ang-ry bile on t'leg.'.*

Anger nails *N* see Ang nails.

Angleberries *N* excrescences, warts or growths on the under parts of cattle resembling raspberries or hineberries.

Angry inflamed and painful

Anither *N* another.

Anny *SW* any.

Anonder under; beneath

Anondyr under; beneath

Anoo *SW* enough.

Anters *NW* in case. *'Or anters in yon mouldering heap.'* - John Stagg poems

Anudder *C, E* another.

Apod *E, SW* uphold.

Applegarth *N* orchard.

April fe-ll *N* April fool.

April gowk *C* April fool

April noddy *C* April fool

Arbitry *C* arbitrary, applied to manorial customs.

Arch wool *C* a vent hole in the wall of a barn, etc.

Are ye middin weel? a greeting basically meaning *'How are you?'.*

Argify to debate.

Argy argue; signify. *'It doesn't argy'* - it does not signify

Ark a chest. (see Mealark).

Arls *NE* money given to confirm a bargain.

Arm *C, E* arm.

Armin chair an arm-chair or elbow-chair.

Arr *C, SW* a scar from a wound, a cicatrice.

Arridge an angular edge; arris, in architecture.

Arse abuett feass back to front; all wrong; topsy-turvy.

Arse end backside or bottom.

Arse-beurd *N* the end board of a cart.

Arse-breed a contemptible width or extent. *'His heall land's nobbet a arse-breed.'*

Arse-smart *C* the Pepperwort plant, *Polygonum Hydropiper.*

Arsewurts backwards.

Arsin abeutt to fool about; to turn around.

Arsin' see Arsin abeutt.

Art *C, SW* point of the compass; quarter.

Arvel *N* relating to funeral matters.

Arvel breed *N* bread prepared for a funeral.

As how *C* that. *'He said as how he wad nivver gang near them.'*

As-ley *E* willingly; as soon that way as the other.

Aside *C* beside; near to. *'Parton aside Whitten.'*

Ask a lizard or newt.

Ass *C* ask; inquire.

Ass ask; ashes.

Ass-beurd *N* ashes box.

Ass-grate *C* a garting through which ashes pass from the fire into a sunken cell or pit.

Ass-trug *C, SW* ashes box.

Assel-teuth one of the grinders or molars (teeth).

Assel-tree axle-tree

Ast asked; did ask.

Asteed instead.

Aswint one-sided; out of truth; diagonal.

At *C, SW* to. *'Gang at thresh.'.* (nearly obsolete by 1878, but common in the 18th century).

At that

At is 't that it is. *'It's gay bad wark 'at is 't.'*

At is aa that I am. *'Aa's cum to advise tha, 'at is e.'* - Robert Anderson.

At is e that I am.

Atomy *C* a skeleton. *'She's dwinnelt away til a atomy.'*

Attercrop *C* spider's web

Atween whiles at intervals.

Aumry *N, E* a cupboard or place where victuals and other valuables are kept. (nearly obsolete 1878).

Aw *C* our.

Away to go away or leave. *'I'll away to t' church.'*

Awivver however, *'Awivver, we knea yer fadder's nivver rang.';* indeed.

Awsom appalling, awful.

Awtagidder *C* all together.

Awtin *SW* a pleasure jaunt.

Awwer *SW* our; hour.

Awwt *SW* out.

Awwtin' *SW* an outing, pleasure trip or jaunt.

Ax *C, E* ask; inquire.

Ax't at church *C* having had the wedding banns published.

Ax't out *C* the wedding banns having been read three times.

Axin *C* asking. *'Find oot what udder fwokes are axin, before yer selt it.'.*

Ayder either.

Ayder syne mak *C* not a pair; differnt kinds.

Aydle *C* to earn.

Aydlins *C* earnings.

Ayga *C, SW, E* ague.

Ayont *NW* beyond.

Ayqual *SW* equal.

Aywas *C, N* anywise; always.

Baa *SW* ball.

Baal *N* bold, imprudent.

Baald *N* see Baal.

Babblement silly discourse.

Babby baby or small child.

Babby larkins children's playthings.

Bacca tobacco.

Bachelor buttons *C* the double white or yellow *Ranunculus* plant with bow-shaped flowers.

Back end *C* the autumn season. *'On about t' back end.'*

Back fling *E* a relapse. (see Back kest.)

Back kest a relapse. *'He was mendan' nicely but he gat a sair back kest i' winter.'*

Back nor edge *C* unmanageable; useless *'I can mak nought on him nowder back nor edge.'*.

Back rackonin' an unpleasant reference to an old grievance.

Back shift the second shift worked down a mine etc., generally 2pm to 10pm.

Back up just as an angry cat elevates its back, so an angry person is often said to set his back up.

Back watter't When the tail race of a water wheel is flooded the stream above is unable to keep the wheel moving.

Back-boord a board to roll dough upon; a bake board.

Back-bred bred late in the year or season.

Back-dyke *C* A fence or dyke faced in stone on one sided and backed up with earth and sods on the other.

Back-set a reserve; something to fall back on.

Back-set an' foor-set surrounded with difficulties.

Back-side the back yard.

Back-stick the rod connecting the foot board of the spinning wheel with the crank.

Back-stick *N* sword.

Back-word a countermanding or a change of mind. *'They ax't us t' tea yaa day, and than they sent us back-word.'*

Backa beyont *C, N* a far away, often isolated place.

Backen to retard.

Backins clippings of cloth etc., formerly used by tailors for stiffening coat collars etc.

Backstone *C* an iron plate or slate to bake cakes upon.

Bad bade, the past tense of bid. *'He bad ma come back.'*.

Bad beukks out of favour. *'I's in yer Mary's bad beukks, fwor doing nought.'*.

Bad bread *C* To be out of favour is to be in bad bread.

Bad fettle poorly or ill.

Baddan *C* bad one; the evil one.

Badder worse. *'Many a badder thing med happen.'*

Baddest worst. *'It's t' baddest thing 'at could hev happen't.'*

Baddin *N* bad or evil person.

Badger *C, SW* a person who buys corn and resells the meal ground at the mill to another; a travelling dealer in butter etc.

Badger body *N* a person who buys corn and resells the meal ground at the mill to another; a travelling dealer in butter etc.

Badly *C* poorly; ill; out of health.

Badly off poor.

Baffle *C* to confound; mystery; to defeat by stratagem.

Bag the belly; the udder of a cow etc.

Bag shakkins a short supply; the last of it.

Baggin' *C* provisions taken into the field for farm workmen.

Baggish luggage; also a term of reproach to a child or a female. *'a dirty baggish!'*

Bagwesh *C* poverty and destitute. *'He's gone to bagwesh.'*

Baily *C* bailiff or sheriff's officer. see Bumbaily

Bain *C, NE* handy, *'Yon's ti bainest way.'*; willing.

Bain near, nearest; shortest or soonest. *'It's a better to gang that way, for it's faraway t'bainer'.*

Bairn *N* a child, a term of familiarity.

Bait lunch, meal or snack; a feed for a horse while travelling.

Baith *N* both.

Balderdash nonsense.

Balky *B* an obese person.

Ball money *N* money given by members of a wedding party at the church gates to treat the children (often thrown).

Ballet ballad.

Bally cruds *B* milk from a newly calved cow boiled and turned to curd. (see Bull-jumpins).

Bally rag to scold or reproach; to rally contemptuously.

Baltute *C* the bald coot. an aquatic bird.

Bam *C* a jesting falsehood, trick, cheat.

Ban *NE* band.

Band *C* a boundary on high and unenclosed land.

Band did bind.

Bandylowe *C* a prostitute.

Bang to strike forcibly producing sound; a heavy blow.

Bang to beat; to excel; an act of haste. *'He was bad to bang.'* *'He com in wid a bang.'*

Banger anything great. *'It's a banger'*

Bannick *N* thick oat-cake usually made for the harvest-home or kern supper.

Bannish *N* banish; forbid the house.

Bannock a hard biscuit baked over an open fire.

Bannock feass't having a flat face and a short nose.

Bannock iron *B* a plate to fix on the grate of a open fire to bake bannocks upon.

Banty *C* the bantam; a dwarfish (small) person or animal.

Banty *N* a bantam.

Banty cocks *C* intermediate sized cocks of hay.

Bare gorps *C* unfledged birds.

Barfet *C* feet naked, without shoes or clogs.

Bark to peel the skin or bark off, to unbark. *'He bark't his nockles ower tudder fellow's skope.'*

Bark at t'heck stop or wait at the outside door or gate; a compulsory warning. (see Heck)

Barken't *C* dirt hardened on; to make crisp like bark; hardbound, stiff.

Barley play *C* a term used by boys bespeaking a cessation of their game.

Barn *C, SW* a child, a term of familiarity.

Barn time *C* pregancy, the period of fruitfulness in women.

Barnicles an old name for spectacles; irons put on the noses of horses to make them stand quietly.

Barnish childish.

Barns children. *'Oor lass is still at heamm wid t'barns.'.*

Barra wheel barrow.

Barra cwoat *C, B* a young childs under garment.

Barramouth see Beermouth.

Barrin' *C* except. *'You may hev any of my kye barrin' t' white an'.'*

Barrin' out schoolboys used to bar their teacher out of the schoolroom at Christmas and negotiate for holidays before re-admitting him.

Barryham *SW* a neck-collar worn by a horse when drawing a plough.

Bash to strike so as to disfigure; a blow on some soft yielding matter.

Bash *C* to spoil the appearance. *'Her bonnet was bash't in t' rain.'*

Bash away! *C, NW* work vigorously; strike hard.

Bash on *C, NW* see Bash away

Bask *C* see Baum.

Bassenthet *C* Bassenthwaite.

Bat a blow; a stroke; the sweep of a scythe; condition. see Oald bat.

Batch *C, N* a sack of corn prepared for being ground at the mill; a pack of cards.

Bateable lands *N* Debateable lands, land claimed by either English or Scottish Reviers in the Border Marches.

Batlin stick *B* a wooden mallet, often resembling a cricket bat, once used for beating linen clean.

Batlin' steann *B* a clean broad stone near a well or stream for washing and beating linen.

Batlin' steann *C* a stone used to beat the course hempen shirts of old times uopn, to soften them prior to being worn.

Batten to fatten; to thrive. *'Here's good battenin' to t'bam, and goo mends to t'mother,'* - a usual toast on the occasion of a birth.

Batter to slope; to incline; to beat; to attack with repeated blows. *'That girt lad batter't oor laal Jack.'.*

Battins *C* corn in the half-thrashed state.

Battleder *B* see Batin stick.

Baum balm.

Baum *B* a place in a dry bank or hedge where partridges bask and dust themselves.

Baum balm; to bask in the sun or by the fire, *'Baum in t' sun like a hagworm.'*

Baurgh *C* a horse-way up a steep hill.

Bawk *C* see Boke.

Bawnce *SW* bounce.

Bawnnd *SW* bound.

Bawty *B* a dog having a white face is so called.

Baww *SW* bow, bend.

Bawwnce *SW* bounce.

Bawwnd *SW* bound.

Baze to prize, or force, or lift with a lever.

Beaddless *C* impatient of suffering.

Beak *C* bake.

Beak *N* nose.

Beakk bake.

Beam see Baum.

Beann bone; person. *'He's a bad beann.'.*

Bear *C, SW* bore, did bear.

Beard *C* to lay short brushwood to project over the edge of a wall to prevent sheep going over. Sods or stones are laid on the wall to keep it firm.

Bearr bare.

Bearr *C* bore; did bear.

Beasst to baste a roasting joint or bird, during cooking; to sew loosely; to beat.

Beast milk the milk of a new-calved cow.

Beaste to thresh or beat with a cudgel or thick stick; a deliberate whipping judicially administered.

Beat to thresh or hit with fist or stick.

Beat t' yub'm *C* to supply sticks etc., to the oven while heating.

Beath both.

Beatin' stick *B* a stick kept for stirring the fire in the brick oven. By rubbing this stick on the arch of the oven after the flame has subsided, the proper heat is known by the sparks emitted.

Beatt abate; did bite. *'Our dog beatt a lump out o' t'oald busy bodys hand.'*

Beatth *C, SW* both

Beck *C, SW* brook, small stream or watercourse.

Beck dote *C* see Dote.

Beck grains *C, E* where a beck divides into two streams.

Bed bid or bade. *'They bed o't'parish to t'berryin'.'*. (see Bad)

Bed-gown *B* a long dress of this name, reaching to the feet, was in use at an earlier date than the short one (1878).

Bed-gown *C* a women's outside dress reaching only to the hips, common in the early 19th century and worn only by day.

Bee-bink *E* a stand for beehives.

Beeak *SW* bake; to heat hazel or other thin branches so they bend more easily for basketmaking; to bask or bake by the fire.

Beeal *SW* to bellow; to brawl.

Beeans *SW* beans.

Beeas *SW* beasts or cattle.

Beeast *SW* beast.

Beeath *N* both.

Beegle *C* beetle.

Beek *C, N* to heat hazel or other rods (thin branches) to cause then to bend more easily for basketmaking purposes; to bask by the fire.

Beel *C, N* to bellow; to brawl.

Beel *N* boil.

Beel *N* see Bile.

Beeld a shelter; a fox den.

Beeldin' *N* building.

Beer to bear.

Beermouth *C* an adit or level dig into a hill-side, a near horizontal entry into a coal or iron ore mine.

Beese *C, N* beasts, cattle.

Beestins *C* the milk of a new-calved cow.

Begon began.

Behadden *N* beholden, obligated.

Behint behind. *'I's nut far behint yer.'*.

Behodden *C, SW* beholden or obligated.

Bela' *SW* below.

Belangs belongs.

Beleev believe.

Belengs belongs

Belk *C, N* belch; an eructation or the act of belching.

Bellar to use bellows on a fire; to shout.

Bellars bellows.

Bellcute the bald coot, an aquatic bird.

Bellican *C* an obese person or animal.

Belliz bellows.

Bellt *N* bald.

Belluz bellows.

Belly flapper see Belly flopper.

Belly flopper a poor dive into water, landing almost flat with a blow to the stomach.

Belly kite *B* one who eats unwholesome things.

Belly rim *N* the membrane inclosing the intestines in cattle.

Belly rine *C* the membrane inclosing the intestines in cattle.

Belyve *B* if I live.

Belyve after a while. *'Aa'l pay thee belyve.'*.

Benk *C* a low bank or ridge of rock; a bank or finance house.

Bennert *C* the daisy, *Bellis perennis.*

Bennish *N* banish.

Bensal *B* violent motion. *'He com wid a bensal.'*

Bensal to beat. *'Aa'l bensal ta'* - I'll beat thee.

Bent *C* bleak. *'Yon's a bent pleass o' yours.'*

Benwort *C* see Bennert.

Berries *C* gooseberries.

Berry *C* to thrash corn with the flail.

Berryin' *B* a funeral.

Berryin' skin *C, SW* a dried horse skin used for thrashing upon to prevent the grain sticking to the clay floor of the barn.

Besom out a signal that open house is kept; a wife being from home.

Bessy blackcap *C* the blackheaded bunting.

Bessy blakelin *C* the yellow-hammer or yellow bunting.

Bessy dooker *E* the water-ouzel, a dipper or blackbird.

Best bib and tucker on *B* said of a female in a very fine dress (1878), later also used to refer to a well dressed male in his best suit or *'sunday best'* outfit.

Bet betted, did bet: did beat.

Better *C* more. *'Theer was better ner twenty.'*

Better it to improve it. *'He wad n't hev done 't if he could hev better't it.'*

Bettermer of the better sort. *'The bettermer swort sat snug in the parlour.'* - Robert Anderson.

Betterness improvement. *'Theer nea betterness in t' weather yit.'*

Between whiles at intervals.

Beuk *C, N, E* book.

Beukk book.

Beunn days days on which a customary tenant must work for the lord of the manor; boons or gifts of work to a new farmer when entering a new farm.

Beunnmest *C* uppermost.

Beunns see Beunn days.

Beur *C, N* bore, did bear.

Beurd beard.

Beus *C, N, E* cow stall.

Beuss *C, N* stall for a cow or horse.

Beut *C, N, E* boot.

Beutless *C* bootless.

Beutt jack an implement used in pulling off boots, often located just outside the door so dirty boots could be removed before entering the house.

Beutt money money given to equalise an exchange.

Beutt stockings *C* long upper stockings from foot to above the knee, much worn by elderly men on horseback around 1800.

Beutts boots.

Bever *E* tremble.

Bew bough or branch of a tree.

Beyble *NW* bible.

Beyd *N, NW* to abide etc.

Beyont beyond.

Beyout beyond.

Beyt *NW* bite.

Bicker *C, N* a small wooden vessel used for porridge etc.

Bid to invite.

Biddable obedient; tractable.

Bidden *C* occupied; taken.

Bidden weddin *C* A wedding custom (now obsolete 1878), at which subscriptions were collected for the newly married pair, and sports held for the amusement of all.

Biddy *C* nursery name for lice, differnt speices infest the bodies of humans, animals and plants; term often applied to a cantankerous woman. *'Yer Marys a oald vile biddy.'*.

Bide *C, SW* to abide etc.

Bield see Beeld

Big build.

Biggan *N, SW* the act of building.

Biggin' building.

Biggle *C* to blindfold.

Biggly *C* game of blindman's buff.

Bile *C, E, SW* to boil; a sore inflammation or swelling.

Bin *N* been.

Binch *C* bench.

Bindin' *C* a long rod or binder used in hedge making.

Bink *N* a low bank or ridge or ledge of rock; a row of peats etc. stacked up.

Binna *B* be not.

Binsh bench.

Bir any rapid whirling motion; the sound produced by motion.

Birk the birch tree, *Betula*

Birtlin' *C* a small and sweet apple.

Bishop't burnt in the pan.

Bisky biscuit.

Bit *B* small or little. *'A bit buoy.'* - a little boy.

Bit *C* but, *'Yon field grows nought bit bent and pry.'*.

Bit but; position or station life, *'He's pinch't to hod his bit.'*.

Bit *N* little.

Bit thing *N* small or insignificant.

Bite a mouthful; a hasty repast or snack.

Bitter-bump *C* the bittern bird, *Ardea stellaris*.

Bittock *N* a bit.

Biz'ness *C* business, *'A good stroke o'biz'ness.'*.

Bizzen *NE* ugly or ill-natured; shameful.

Bizzin' *B* buzzing as bees; busy at work.

Bizzom *N, E* besom.

Bla *N* blow.

Blaa *SW* blow.

Blaa out *N* a drinking session.

Blab to let out or reveal a secret or an indiscreet talker.

Blabberskite *NE* a vain-talking fellow; an indiscreet tell-tale.

Black Jack a leather tankard. (one existed at Eden Hall 1878).

Black an' white writing; a written contract or oath. *'Put it down in black an' white.'*.

Black bole to polish boots, shoes, etc. - polishing shoes was once called blackballing.

Black dog *C* the sulks.

Black feutt *C* a go-between in a love affair; one who courts for another.

Black kites *C* wild bramble berries.

Black-a-vyz't *C* dark complexioned

Blacklead a blacklead pencil (not very common after 1878)

Blacks *C* flakes of flying soot from a chimney etc.

Bladder *C* idle talk.

Blake pale yellow, *'Blake as May butter.'*.

Blare *C* to roar violently; to bellow.

Blash to splash.

Blashy poor, weak, *'That Workin'ton yal nut blashy.'* or *'Mary maks blashy tea.'*.

Blead blade.

Bleadd blade.

Bleaken blacken.

Bleakken blacken.

Bleam blame.

Bleamm blame.

Bleary *C* windy, cold and showery.

Bleatt *C, N* bashful; timid.

Blebbery *C* the bleaberry, *Voccinium myrtillus*.

Blebs *C* bubbles; watery blisters

Bleckon'd *B* blackened; the skin discoloured by a bruise.

Bledder the bladder; to talk nonsense.

Bledder *N* to roar violently; to bellow.

Bleeak *SW* bleak.

Bleeat *SW* bleak; bleat.

Bleet *C, E* blight.

Bleeze blaze.

Bleight *SW* blight.

Blenk *C, N* a gleam, *'A blenk o' sunshine.'*.

Blether *N* idle talk.

Bleud *C* blood. *'Sum o'them gat gay bleuddy feasses.'*.

Bleudd *C* blood

Bleum bloom.

Bleumm bloom.

Blin *N* blind.

Blin' mouse *B* the shrew mouse.

Blind man's holiday evening twilight; darkness.

Blinders *C* eye-shades for horses

Blink *C, N* see Blenk.

Blinnd lonnin' *C* a grass lane used as an occupation way.

Blish *E* an attack of purging.

Blishes *C* small blisters.

Bliss *G, N* bless.

Blitter't *C* torn by the wind.

Blob the best of it.

Blob nukkel't *C* newly calved and in full milk.

Block to strike or hit; the head, *'I'll knock thee block off.'*. - blocks are used in hat making.

Blocker *C* a butchers pole-axe.

Blonk *C* a blank, *'Jack's got duble blonk.'* - double blank at dominoes.

Blow to let out a secret; to spend money fast, often with little thought.

Blow it keep silence; do not publish it or tell others.

Blown fruit fruit blown down by the wind.

Blown milk milk from which the cream is blown. (a practice seldom used 1878).

Blue buttons *C* the *Scobiosa succisa* plant.

Blur blot; to defame.

Blurt *C* to tell or speak out something unexpected.

Bo *C, E* ball.

Bo the calf of the leg. *'T'bo' o't'leg.'*.

Bo man *C* an imaginary person used to frighten children, eg. bogeyman.

Boar seg a castrated boar.

Bob a pre-decimalisation shilling, legal tender until 1971 (equivalent to 5p).

Bob tail't *C* a waggish tail, and thickest at the end.

Bobberous *C* boastful; proud.

Boddam bottom; low ground; a small valley or hollow; to empty. *'He could boddam a quart at a wind.'*.

Boddamest the lowest.

Bodder bother. *'Yer lad bodders about nought.'*.

Bodderment perplexity, distraction, confusion or anxiety.

Boddersom troublesome.

Boddom bottom.

Body *C* person, *'This het weather*

an' hard wark fairly ups a body.'.

Boff *B* to strike with an axe and not make a clean cut; a stroke with a dull sound.

Bog onion *C* the flowering fern, *Osmunda Regalis*.

Bog trotter *N* During the the time of the Border Reivers, the borderers were sometimes called *Bog trotters*, as they had to ride in a gentle trot across the marshes and sands, a heavy tread would cause them to sink into the bog - moss trooper was also a general term

Boggin very dirty.

Boggle *C* ghost or bogeyman. see Dobby.

Bogie sledge on wheels, small cart.

Bogie whol *C* a small cupboard or store, often filled to the brim with seldom used items.

Boilies *C* food boiled for infants.

Boilin' the whole quantity. *'The heall boilin' o' them.'*.

Bok *C* the motion in the throat when attempting to vomit from nausea.

Boke *C* a ridge of land left for division of ownership.

Bokes *C* a hay-loft of rough poles with tturf or branches in place of boards.

Boly *C, SW* a horse having white legs and a white face.

Boly his leann *B* alone; the nickname for a dancing master noted for his well polished shoes.

Bond sucken an obligation of certain farms to use only the manorial mill to grind their corn.

Bonnily prettily.

Bonny beautiful, handsome, *'Ho er ye to-day, bonny wee Jack?'*.

Bonny burd-een the cuckoo flower, *Cardamine pratensis*; the primrose, *Primula farinosa*.

Boo *C, N, E* bow, bend.

Booak *SW* book.

Booal *N, E, SW* bowl.

Booal *SW* see Bool.

Booas *SW* cow stall.

Booat *SW* boot.

Booats *SW* boots.

Booer *N* a parlour; a house or shelter.

Boogle *NE* see Boggle.

Booin *C* ragwort, *Senecio Jacoboea*.

Book bulk.

Booksom bulky.

Booky bulky.

Bool *C, N* to bowl, as in cricket etc; boldly. *'Bool in lads.'*.

Boon service done by a customary tenant to the lord of the manor.

Boon days see Beunn days.

Boonce *C, E, N* bounce.

Boonmest *SW* uppermost.

Boor staff *C* the pin the handweaver turns his beam with.

Boot a bout; a turn; a contest; an entertainment.

Booze *C* a carouse or heavy drinking session; a drinking match; alchoholic beverages.

Boretree *N* the elder-tree, *Sambucus nigra*.

Borran *C* a cairn or heap of stones; ancient funeral piles.

Borst *N* burst.

Bosom wind an eddying or whirling wind.

Boss *C* a milkmaid's cushion for the head.

Botch to mismanage, make a mess of job or task. *'Thou has mead a botch on 't now.'*.

Botcher *C* a drink made by pouring water on honey-comb after the honey has been drained. *'Sweet as botcher'* was an old expression (proir to 1878).

Bottom wind *C* The waters of Derwentwater are sometimes considerably agitated even in a calm day, and are seen to swell into high waves rolling easterly, and this is called a bottom wind.

Bouk *B* to boil the linen web in water and ashes (of ashen wood) prior to beating on the batlin steann and bleaching it.

Bound days see Beunn days.

Bounder *C* boundary. (a term found in old deeds).

Bout a bout with a plough is twice the length of the field, or once about.

Bowel whol *N* a vent hole in the wall of a barn, etc.

Bowster bolster.

Bowt bought, did buy. *'Ah bowt yan off him.'*; a bolt.

Bowze *B* to rush out, as blood when a vein is cut.

Bowze *C* the recoil of a gust of wind against a wall, etc. *'T'wind com wid a girt bowze an'whemmelt ma.'*.

Brack *C* brine. *'This bacon's as sote as brack.'*.

Bracken dote *C* see Dote.

Brackin clock a small brown beetle, used as a bait for fishing in June.

Brackins bracken, the fern family.

Brae *N* a brow, or bank.

Braffam *C* a neck-collar worn by a horse when drawing a plough.

Braid *C* a cow is said to braid during the throws of parturition or labour. The Saxon meaning is to resemble; to favour.

Braid *NE* broad.

Braid *NW* to spread; to throw about.

Braith *N* breath.

Brak broke.

Brake *B* a break on a wheel; an instrument for breaking the dried stems of flax.

Brake *C* to beat.

Brake-sowt *C* inflammatory fever in young sheep.

Brakshy *B, N* inflammatory fever in young sheep; this name is also given to the flesh of sheep dying of this disease. see Brake-sowt.

Bran new having the maker's brand; new and unused.

Brandied *C* brindled or spotted, varigated with spots.

Brandreth *C* an iron frame for supporting the baking-plate or girdle at a proper distance above the open fire; a trivet.

Brandreth steann *C, B* a boundary stone at the meeting of three townships or parishes.

Brang *C, SW* brought.

Branglan' *NE* wrangling.

Brank *C* to hold the head proudly and affectedly. *'Brankan'like a steg swan.'*.

Branks *B* a game formerly common at fairs; also called *'hit my legs and miss my pegs'*.

Branks *N* a kind of halter, having an iron nose-band which tightens when the horse pulls.

Branlin' worm *C, B* a good bait, and so called from being attractive to the branding trout, or from its brindled markings.

Brannigan *C* a fat puffy infant boy.

Brannit *N* brindled or spotted, varigated with spots.

Brant *C, SW* steep. *'As brant as a hoose side.'*.

Branthet *C* Branthwaite.

Brash *C* rash, headlong. *'He's a brashan' body, and runs heid and neck still.'*.

Brash *E* a spell or turn of work. *'Kursty, come kurn a brash.'*.

Brashy *C* weak; delicate.

Brass copper money; riches; impudence; assurance. *'He's plenty o'brass in his feass.'*.

Brass pan the largest vessel once commonly found in the Cumbrain farm kitchen, used when the killed pig was to be scalded and drest or dressed.

Brast burst.

Brat *C* a contemptuous term for a troublesome child; a coarse apron. In Borrowdale they had a saying that *'when it rains on Maudlin (Magdalen) day, Jenny Maudlin is bleaching her brat.'*.

Brat noisy, cheeky or naughty child; to spay - a young ewe is bratted to prevent it having a lamb and thus promote fattening.

Brattit to spay (see Brat.)

Brattle the loud rattling noise of thunder, etc.

Brattle can *C, B* a noisy child. *'Mary's sec a la'al brattle can.'*; a kicking cow.

Brave superior; fine; of a good sort.

Bravely *C, NE* quite well. *'I's bravely, how's thou?'*.

Bray to beat or strike; chastise and bruise, mostly in reference to children.

Brayin' steann *C, N* a rounded stone used for pounding sandstone to produce sand, which was used to clean floors.

Braythet *C* Braithwaite.

Brayzent *C* brazen; impudent; excess of assurance.

Brazzle *C* to press into a crowd, etc.; to scorch or singe.

Brazzled pez *NE* scorched peas scrambled for by boys. A glorious feast for the youngsters! A sly urchin steals a sheaf of peas; notice of the fact spread quicker than the progress of the Fiery Cross in old times, and the village green is soon peopled by joyous faces.

Breaa *SW* brow, to its limit or boundary. *'T'beck's breaa full.'*.

Bread sticks *N* a wooden frame for drying bread-cakes upon before an open fire.

Breadd *SW* broad.

Break to beat with a stick (used chiefly as a threat), generally applied to boys.

Break *C* the portion of land ploughed out of ley in the year.

Breakk *C. SW* to thrash; to beat

Bree *B* in a great hurry, *'In a girt bree.'*; joyous or uplifted.

Bree *NW* good. *'He's no bree.'*.

Breea *N* see Breaa.

Breead *SW* bread.

Breeak *N* to beat.

Breear brier or any prickly plant, eg. the sweetbriar or wild briar.

Breeast *SW* breast.

Breed *C, NE* bread. *'Cut thy sel a shyve o'cheese an' breed.'*.

Breeght *N* bright.

Breekin' *C* the space behind the udder of a sheep; the fork.

Breeks breeches.

Breest breast; to breest a hedge is to face it with stone, or sod and stone alternately; The kiln breest is the horizontal part of a limekiln or drying kiln. Quarry breest and stack breest, the upright part.

Breet *C, SW* bright.

Breeth *C, E, SW* breath.

Breeze *N* bruise.

Breigham *N* a neck-collar worn by a horse when drawing a plough.

Brek *C* to break; fun; a practical joke. *'Sek breks!'*; a good story; the portion of land ploughed out of ley in the year.

Brek break.

Brek of a front a thaw.

Brekfast *C* breakfast.

Brekkan *C* breaking.

Breme *NE* to froth. *'It bremes ower'* - it froths over the brim.

Brent *N* steep. *'As brent as a house side.'*.

Brenth breadth.

Breuk't *C* A white sheep having the belly and legs black is a breuk't sheep in colour.

Breum broom or brush; the broom plant *Sarothammus scopari*.

Breuz *C, E* bruise.

Breuzz *C* bruise.

Bridewain *C* see Bidden Weddin.

Bridle rwoad bridle path or way, a track over which a horse may be led or ridden, but not for other purposes.

Brig bridge.

Briss *C* bruise.

Brist *C, NE* breast.

Brist burst.

Brither *N* brother.

Briz *C* bruise.

Brizled pez *NE* see Brazzled pez.

Broach *C, B* a wooden pin on which the ball of new-spun yarn of wool is placed to be wound on to the garn winnels.

Brock broke or broken, *'He fell off t'oald byre an' brock his leg.'*; a badger.

Brocken broken.

Brong *N* brought.

Broo *C* brow, to its limit or boundary, *'T'beck's broo full.'*.

Broon brown.

Broon leemers *C* nuts browned (and over ripe) and ready to drop out of the husks.

Brooy being on the edges or sides of hills.

Brossen *C, SW* burst.

Brossen hackin *E* a very fat or corpulent, gluttonous person.

Brossen kern This term is applied in ridicule when the harvest-home is held prematurely.

Brot *C* refuse corn; odds and ends.

Brot out *C* Corn is said to brot out when the grain is shed through over ripeness.

Browe *B* an impudent lad.

Browse *C* friable; mellow. *'You may begin to sow, for t'land's browse now.'*.

Browte brought.

Bruffle *B* excitement.

Brugh *NE* a halo round the sun or moon. *'A far off brugh tells of a near hand storm.'*.

Brulliment *N* broil or cook over hot coals; disturbance or noisy quarrel.

Brully *C* broil or cook over hot coals; disturbance or noisy quarrel.

Brumstan *C, E* brimstone, sulphur (inflammable lemon-yellow brittle substance).

Brunstan *N* brimstone, sulphur (inflammable lemon-yellow brittle substance).

Brunt burnt.

Brusey *C* an overgrown female.

Brushin' *B* small branches fixed on the top of steak and ryse. eg. in hedging.

Brussan *N* burst.

Brussel bristle.

Brussen *B* burst, overworked. *'Oald Jonty's brussen wi'wark.'*.

Brust burst.

Bruz *C* bruise.

Bruzled pez *NE* see Brazzled pez.

Bu bough, branch.

Buck i't'neucks *E* a rude game among boys.

Buck up *C* to subscribe; help or assist; to advance. *'Buck up till her, lad.'*.

Buckel't *C* A saw is *buckel't* when it is over-bent, or a wheel is *buckel't* when its rim is bent and bowed and does not revolve true.

Buckle *C* order; condition; health. *'He's I'girt buckle today.'*.

Buckle *C, SW* to marry; fasten upon; attack.

Buckle to attack and seize.

Buckle beggar *N* the Gretna Green parson. His office became extinct by Act of Parliament in 1857.

Buckle teah begin; take in hand. *'Buckle teah, men, ye're varra welcome.'*.

Budder brother.

Buff *C* to strike with an axe and not make a clean cut; a stroke with a dull sound.

Buff nakedness. *'Strip't into buff.'.*

Bule *C* the bow of a basket, or corfe, or pan. *(see Yetin).*

Bule pan the third smallest pan once commonly found in the Cumbrian farm kitchen, bigger than a *'shank pan'*, but smaller than a *'iron ub'n'*.

Bull feasses *SW* tufts of the *Aira cæspitosa* - a very coarse grass.

Bull fronts *N* see Bull feasses

Bull-grips iron claspers for leading bulls by the nose.

Bull-heed *C* a tadpole-like fish, about 100mm long, the *River Bullhead* was once common in fresh water, whilst the *Short-spined Sea Bullhead* was found in the Solway.

Bull-jumpins *C* the second day's milk of a newly-calved cow boiled till it curdles.

Bull-ring a ring put through the nostrils of a bull by which he is led; the ring to which bulls were once secured prior to being baited or slaughtered; also a place of public challenge.

Bull-stang the dragon fly, *Libelluloe*.

Bull-toppins *C* tufts of the *Aira coespitosa*, a very coarse grass.

Bullace the wild sour plum, *Prunus insititia*.

Bullens *N* dry stems of the kesh or cow-parsnip, or of hemp, once used to light candles.

Bullister *NE* the fruit of the bullace-tree (a wild sour plum) *Prunus insititia*.

Bully-rag to scold or reproach; to rally contemptuously.

Bultree *C* the elder tree, *Sambucus nigra*.

Bultree gun *C* a boy's pop-gun, a toy made of a young stem of the elder.

Bum to be furiously busy. *'Bumman about like a bee in a bottle.'.*

Bum *SW* see Bumbaily.

Bumbaily bailiff; a sheriff's officer. *Billy Bumley* house on Workington's foreshore was a Customs officers look out point.

Bumly *C* the humble-bee, *Bomba*.

Bummel *C* to bungle; blunder.

Bummel kites *N* wild bramble berries.

Bummelty kites *E* see Bummel kites.

Bump *C* a blow; a hump.

Bumper a large one.

Bun *N* bound.

Bunce *N* bounce.

Bunch berry *NE* the fruit of the stone bramble, *Rubus saxatillis*.

Bund *C, E* bound.

Bunnels *C* dry stems of the kesh or cow-parsnip, or of hemp, once used to light candles.

Bunsan cow *N* a cow given to attack people.

Bunstan *N* brimstone.

Buoy *B* boy. *'Johnny sec a la'al buoy.'.*

Bur *B* hinderer. *'He bur't me.'.*

Bur *C* a short run to gain impetus for a leap or jump; a wheel-stopper; the rough seed-ball of the burdock used by children to stick upon each other's hair or clothes.

Bur *C, SW* a halo round the sun or moon. *'A far off bur tells of a near hand storm.'.*

Bur see Bir.

Burk birch.

Burn *N* brook, rivulet, streamlet or watercourse.

Burn t'beck having taken or caught no fish.

Burnt his fingers applied to persons having failed in some object, or having been over-reached, lost money through careless investment. *'Tommy's burnt his fingers at shopkeepin'.'.*

Burnywind *N* burn of the wind; the blacksmith.

Burr *C* a sudden hurry *'He went off wid a burr.'.*

Burth birth.

Burthday birthday.

Burtree *SW* the elder-tree, *Sambucus nigra*.

Buryin't'cald wife the treat by an apprentice on attaining his freedom.

Busk *C* bush. (obsolete 1878).

Buss *N* bush. (obsolete 1878).

Busy body one who to enquires into others affairs and tells tales. *'Yer Mary's summat of a busy body.'.*

But and ben *N* the outer and inner rooms of the Border farmhouses.

Butch to slaughter cattle for the shambles (eg - butchers market).

Buts short ridges of land of unequal and decreasing lengths.

Butt welt to turn the butt-ends of corn sheaves to the wind to dry.

Butter Sleatt a slab of slate kept in the dairy for holding the pounds of butter, and keeping them cool.

Butter an' eggs *C* the Toadflax plant, *Autirrhinum Linoria*.

Butter bwoat *C* a small tureen or bowl having a handle at one end and a spout at the other, similar in design to a gravy boat.

Butter finger't having a careless habit of allowing things to drop through the hands.

Butter kits *C* square boxes used for conveying butter to market in a wallet (the bag or knapsack) on horseback.

Butter leaves the leaves of the mountain dock, *Rumex alpinus*, once used for packing pounds of butter in the market-basket.

Butter pats *C* used to pat fresh butter into shape, see Pats.

Butter shag *C* bread and butter spread with the thumb, and sometimes also called a thumb shag.

Butter sops *C, N* a meal of wheat or oat bread steeped in melted butter and sugar.

Button twitch *E* couch grass, *Holcus avenaceus.*

Butts *C* earthen mounds at bowshot or target distance for bow and arrow practice.

Butty bulky at the butt or lower end, *'like oald Bennett wife.'*.

Buzzert the buzzard or bustart; a coward or timid person. *'She's a fair buzzert at 'neets.'* - Probably named from the ghost moth, *Hepialus humuli,* which frequents churchyards in the evening and was formerly an object of superstitious fear.

Bwoat *C boat.*

Bwore *C, SW* bore, did bear.

Bworn *C* born.

Bworn days *C* *'In o'my bworn days.'* - in the whole course of my life.

By jing! see By jingo!.

By jingo! a rustic oath, often spoken to show suprise.

By-neamm nickname.

By-set *C* anything set aside till wanted.

By-wipe *C* an insinuation.

Bye by.

Bye-blow a bastard.

Byse-ful full of vice; mischievous, see Byse-pel.

Byse-pel full of vice; mischievous; by-spell or begotten by a spell, or by an evil spirit or demon. Byspel in Middle English means *'an example"* and by way of reproach *' a sad example.'*.

Caa *N, SW* to call; scold; proclaim. *'T'kurk clark co't'a seall.'*.

Caakers *N, SW* calkers (see Cockers).

Caald *N, SW* cold. *'It's parlish coald.' 'Ey, fit to skin a teadd.'*.

Caan't *C, E* cannot.

Caat *SW* cannot.

Caaw *B* to walk with the toes turned inward.

Caaw't twisted; said of shoes when worn down on one side.

Cabbage skrunt *C* cabbage stalk.

Cabbish cabbage; to purloin or steal. A plagiarist cabbishes.

Cabbish runt *C* cabbage-stalk.

Cad *C, SW* to mat or felt together. *'Her hair was caddit till it cud niver be cwom't mair.'*.

Cadge to beg or borrow.

Cadger *C* a hard biscuit, .

Cadger *N* a retailer of small wares having a cart. *'A peat cadger.'* - Robert Anderson.

Caff chaff.

Caird *N* card.

Cakum *B* a foolish person.

Calavine *N* a black-lead pencil.

Caleever *E* energetic and ungraceful action. *'He's a caleeveran' dancer is Jack.'*.

Callas't *C* hardened skin; calloused.

Caller *N* fresh, cool.

Cam *N* came.

Cammarel *C* the heel or hock-joint of animals; a wooden stretcher used for suspending carcasses by the hocks.

Campers persons who sleep in tents or camps; vagrants.

Cample *C* to reply pertly (briskly and boldly) to a superior.

Camps *C* hairs growing among sheeps wool.

Cams *C* the top stones of a rubble wall; coping stones.

Can *C* able or can, *'I'll nut can gang to-day.'* - I am unable to go.

Canker't ill-conditioned; rusted.

Canna *N* cannot.

Cannel candle.

Cannel stick Candlestick evidently took its name from a stick having a split side-branch wherein a lighted candle could be fixed or stuck.

Cannel-bark *C* a small box made of bark and used for holding candles - now made of tin or wood and retaining the name.

Cannel-leet candlelight. *'When harrows begin to hop, cannel-leet mun stop.'....'Efter oald Cannelmas neet ceukks find cannel-leet.'*.

Cannel-sieves *C* rushes used for candle wicks.

Canny a term of praise or encouragement. *'Canny Jack! lig at him till he nivver giz in.'*; pretty, nice, suitable, gentle; cautious. *'Be canny.'*.

Canny bit an uncertain term of comparison; as *'a canny bit better'...'a canny bit warse.'*.

Canny come off ludicrous, ridiculuous and unexpected turn of affairs.

Canstrips *B* unearthly and strange deeds or events, natural phenomena.eg. the Northern lights or *Aurora borealis.*

Cant to overturn; to lean to one side. *'It's gitten a cant to ya side.'*.

Canty merry, lively, cheerful.

Cap *C* a cloud on the mountain top; a weather presage or prediction. *'When Criffel gets a cap Skiddaw wots well of that.'*.

Cap to cap corn is to put better dressed grain at the top of the sack.

Cap't to surpass or better something, to overcome. *'He's fairly cap't now.'*; puzzled

Cape cut lugs *C* anything unexpectedly puzzling or droll.

Caper corner way *C* diagonally.

Capes *C* light grains of wheat with the husks on.

Capper one who excels.

Cappers something difficult. *'Aa'l set thee thy cappers.'.*

Cappin a patch of leather on a clog or shoe.

Car cart.

Car clout nails *C* broad-headed nails formerly in use for securing the tire of wheels.

Car end-board *C* the board closing the rear end of the cart.

Car kist *B, SW* the body of a cart.

Car rack a cart-rut or truck of the wheels.

Car reeght *N* cartwright.

Car reet *C* cartwright.

Car scut *SW* the board closing the rear end of the cart.

Car stangs *C* the shafts of a cart.

Car-hoos *C, E* cart-house.

Car-hoose *C* a house or shed to shelter carts in.

Car-limmers *SW* cart-shafts.

Car-stangs *C* cart-shafts.

Carf carve, *'Fadder, carf t'ham at t'teabbel.'.*

Carkish a corruption of carcase.

Carl coarse unmannerly fellow. *'A rough carl.'.*

Carl cat *E* a male cat, a master cat.

Carl hemp the coarsest of hemp.

Carlin'pez *NW* grey pease softened in water and fried in butter, and eaten on the Sunday next before Palm Sunday (seldom practised now 1878).

Carr *C* a rather extensive hollow place where water stands in winter; as *Brayton Carr, Eller Carr, Kirkland Carr* etc.

Carran *G, not E* carrion.

Carras *N* a house or shed to shelter carts in.

Carrier sark *C* see Top sark.

Carry *C* the movement or direction of the clouds. *'It'll be fair to-day because t'carry's i'west.'.*

Carry to drive or convey. *'He carry't his yowes to sell and hed them to carry back ageann.'.*

Carry on *C* see Carryin's on

Carry on the war! *C* continue the fun.

Carryin's on *C* to be playful or rompish. *'They'd fine carryin's on.'.*

Casebait *C, B* a bait used in angling; the larva of a *phryganea*.

Cash *C* friable shale in coal strata. *'A varra cashy reuff.'.*

Casly a spinning-top.

Cassel *G, not E* castle.

Cassen *N* cast, overturned. (see Cassen).

Castick *NE* cabbage-stalk. (see Cabbage runt.)

Cat collop *C* the spleen.

Cat galas two sticks set upright with one across in the form of a gallows; used for boys to leap over (eg - hurdles).

Cat geatt *C* a narrow space separating the buildings of adjoining owners; a space left around a corn harvest when stored in barns.

Cat lowp in near proximity; *'within a cat lowp.'* - within the jump of a cat.

Cat mallison *C, E* a cupboard which cats cannot rob; a dog given to worry cats.

Cat saddle *B* This and the following are forms in which boys arrange their fingers in a certain play. Castle; Dog saddle; Two men haggan a tree and laal Jack gedderan spealls (chips); Priest in his pulpit.

Cat skip *B* a cat-like leap.

Cat, an implement having six legs projecting from a central ball in a triangular form. It is so called from the impossibility of its being overturned or upset. Used in supporting the plate of toast before a open fire.

Cat-o'-nine tails *C* the earwig.

Cat-tails *C* the cotton grass. *Eriophorum vaginatum.*

Cat-talk *C* idle conversation; small talk. *'Jack talk't nought bit a heap o'cat-talk.'.*

Cat-whin *C* the dwarf whin, *Ulex nanus.*

Cat-wittit *C* silly and conceited.

Catascope *C* clay ironstone or iron ore, found in nodules.

Catch't *G, not E* caught.

Catchy *C* capricious, apt to change suddenly.

Catchy weather unsettled, liable to change quickly, freakish weather - when the crops are gathered in, in small quantities as they become dry between the showers.

Catscalp *C* clay ironstone or iron ore, found in nodules.

Catty *SW* see Scabskew.

Cause because.

Caw *SW* cow.

Cawm *G, not E* calm.

Cawn calm.

Cawt *C* called.

Caww *SW* cow.

Cawwas *SW* cow-house or byre.

Cawwer *SW* cower, crouch.

Cawwnt *SW* count; account. (see Count).

Cawwrse *SW* coarse, course.

Cawwrt *SW* court; caught.

Cawws *SW* cows, cattle; kine.

Cawwshin *C, E, SW* caution.

Cawwshious *E, SW* cautious.

Cayshin *G, not E* occasion. *'Nay, thank ye, I've neah 'cayshin.'.*

Ceakk cake.

Ceapman a chapman, a market seller or trader; the surname Chapman.

Ceapp cape.

Ceapps *C* light grains of wheat

with the husks on.

Cearr care.

Ceass case.

Ceass hardent case hardened; insensible or unfeeling to shame or remorse.

Ceestern cistern.

Cellar op'nin' a benefit night for the new occupier of a public house.

Cennel *C, G* cannel coal; a band of coal found beneath the West Cumberland coalfield.

Cessen *C, G* cast; overturned. *'Jack's car was cessen in a gutter.'.*

Cest cast.

Ceukk cook.

Ceull *C, G* cool.

Cha-waww *C* abundance of silly talk.

Chaffer *C* to tease in bargaining.

Chafts jaws.

Chalks marks. *'Better by chalks.'* - bets were sometimes made to determine who can reach farthest or highest, and there make a chalk mark.

Chammerly *E, SW* chamber-lye, water from a chamber pot; stale urine.

Champ *C* to bruise or crush. *'He champ't his thoom in a yat sneck.'.*

Chance barn an illegitimate child.

Chang the cry of a pack of hounds; the conversation of numbers.

Chap fo'en *B* disappointed, chop fallen; dejected or dispirited.

Chap't *SW* cracked skin from cold or neglect.

Charm words, actions or other things imagined to possess some occult or imagined powers; a charm was once professed for stopping bleeding and could only be communicated by a man to a woman, or vice versa, and only

to one.

Chase *NW* chase.

Chaser *C, SW* chaser. A defective male sheep much given to annoy the females. (see Humlin, Riggelt)

Chass *SW* chase.

Chats *C* small potatoes; ash-tree seedlings.

Chattees *C* potatoes

Chatter *C* to shatter *'Chatter't into splinters.'.*

Chatter hen *E* the wren, *Wrenna vulgaris.*

Chatter wallet *C* a talkative child.

Cheas *N* chase.

Cheass *N* chase.

Cheeap *SW* cheap.

Cheeat *SW* cheat.

Cheel *N* a droll, comical or farcical young fellow.

Cheelie *C* see Cheel.

Cheeny china ware.

Cheese band a linen hoop for supporting a newly-made cheese.

Cheese rennet *C* the plant *Galium verum.* The infusion has been used as rennet in cheesemaking.

Cheese sinker a circular wooden die fitting the top of the rim when the cheese is in the press.

Cheg *C* to pull sharply or suddenly; to champ or bite with the repeated action of the teeth; chew without dividing.

Chemmerly *C, N* chamber-lye, water from a chamber pot; stale urine.

Chennel *C, E* channel.

Chepiter day *B* visitation day by the Bishop or Chancellor.

Cheppel Sundays *C* Sundays set apart annually in August or September at Bassenthwaite, Thornthwaite, Newlands etc., when people assemble from a distance to attend a particular

church, dine with their friends and then adjourn to the inns to make merry in honour of the saint to whom the chapel is dedicated.

Chern *SW* churn.

Chern't milk *SW* butter-milk.

Cherts o'grass *C* the first blades of grass in the spring.

Chess *C, E* chase.

Chibies *N* onions.

Chickle-head *C* a stupid person.

Chiggle *C* to cut wood unskilfully.

Chillip the cry of a young bird.

Chillipers *C* nut coals.

Chilpers *C, B* young grouse or heath-cock, birds of the *Tetrao* genus.

Chimla *C, SW* chimney or flue.

Chimla boke *B* A beam built into and supporting the chimney flue above an open hearth fireplace. The hams were hung here to be smoked or *'reeked'* (see Rannle tree).

Chip *C* to trip; a term in wrestling; the first breaking of the shell by the young bird.

Chirm *C* to chirp; abundant female gossip, *'Chirman like as many sparrows.'.*

Chirrup *C, E* chirp; the noisy chatter of incipient inebriety or drunkeness.

Chist chest.

Chit a note used to call a cat.

Chitter animated whisperings.

Chitter chatter idle talking or chatting.

Chitter waaw *C* the amorous language or call of mating cats.

Chitters *C* the small entrails of the goose or sheep.

Chitty feast baby faced.

Chitty wretn the wren, *Wrenna vulgaris.*

Chock full *C* full to the top.

Chokes marks. (see Chalks.)

Chollers *B* the wattles or fleshy area under the throat of a cock.

Chollers *C* fatty jaws and double chin.

Chooaz *SW, E* choose.

Choop *C, SW* the fruit of the wild rose.

Chop to barter; to change. *'T'wind chops round t'north.'.*

Chop't 'taties *C* boiled potatoes mashed and mixed with milk and butter.

Chopper *N* a butcher's cleaver.

Choppers *SW* snuffers, an instrument for cropping the snuff of a candle.

Choppin' knife *SW* a butcher's cleaver.

Chops jaws. *'Aa'l slap thy chops for tha.'.*

Chowe chew.

Chowk *C, N, E* to choke or strangle.

Chowl *C* the fleshy part of the cheek.

Chowl *C, E, SW* jowl.

Chris'mas Christmas.

Chris'mas box a gift or present given at Christmas.

Chris'mas cannel a candle given by grocers to each customer at that season. Nutmegs or other spices are occasionally substituted.

Chris'mas shaf *C* the sheaf of corn given to each cow and horse on Christmas morning.

Chufty *C* a person having fat cheeks; chubby.

Chump *C* the first note of a hound on scenting game. *'We try't o't'day and niver hed a chump.'.*

Chuns *N* the sprouts of the potato.

Chunter *C* to reply angrily and weeping.

Chur *C* the subdued growl of the dog; the prolonged note of the night-jar bird, *Caprimulgus europoeus.*

Churchwarner *C* churchwarden.

Churry *C, E* cherry.

Chwose chose, did choose.

Citty the wren; a receipt or order, delivery note or similar note on a slip of paper.

Clabber *C* dirt in a pasty (like paste) state.

Clack a low, quick sound. *'She listened and heard the soft clack of the mill.'*- Blamire.

Clag to stick to.

Claggum *N* toffee, (see Taffy).

Claggy clammy, adhesive.

Claith *N* cloth.

Clam did climb. *'Jack clam out at t'fell heed like a crow fleean.'.*

Clam up *C* to satiate or fill up, feed to the full, to cloy or glut. *'Aa's fairly clam't up wi'sweets.'* Sullivan also says *'to starve'*, others suggest *'to pinch'*.

Clammer clamber or to climb.

Clammers *SW* a yoke round the neck of a cow to prevent her leaping hedges.

Clammersom *C* clamorous, loud and noisy.

Clamper *C* to make a clattering noise with the feet.

Clap to pat; to squat as the hare does. *'Jack clap't his sel down on t'settle without iver bein'as't.'.*

Clap bread *C* bread cakes beat and clapped out with the hands.

Clap on *C* put on a lid or hat, etc.

Clapper clowe *B* to give a severe scolding.

Clark clerk.

Clart adhesive dirt; anything clammy; a scrap. *'He still leaves clart on his plate.'.*

Clartan *B* getting dirty or messed up; wasting time. *'Yer Mary's just clartan on.'.*

Clash *C* to abuse; to weary; to throw or strike furiously; gossip.

Clash *N* news; a female newsmonger, gossip or tell-tale.

Clash't *C* fatigued and exposed in bad weather.

Clashy *C, SW* showery. *'Clashy weather.'.*

Clashy wet and dirty.

Clat *C* news; a female newsmonger, gossip or tell-tale.

Clatch *C* a brood of chickens.

Clatter clogs *C* a noisy walker in clogs or pattens.

Clatter clogs *E* the coltsfoot plant, *Tussilago farfara.* (see Clents.)

Clavver to climb

Clavver *N, E* clover, *Caryophyllus aromaticus.*

Clavver grass *C* goose grass - *Galium aparine.*

Clawt *SW* a blow; a patch; a rag.

Clawwt *SW* a blow.

Clay biggin' *NW, N* a house built of clay.

Clay daubin' *C* a house built of clay.

Clay daubs *B* home-made clay marbles.

Cleadd *C* to clothe, to cover or enclose.

Clean heel't active; and when a person runs away through fear, he shows *'a pair o'clean heels.'*

Cleanin' time the general house cleaning before Martinmas and Whitsuntide.

Cleath *C, E* cloth.

Cleavers *C* the plant *Galium Aparine.*

Cleaz clothes.

Cleazz *C* clothes.

Cleckin a shuttlecock. *'As leet as a cleckin.'.*

Cleckin *N* a brood of chickens, etc., or the set of eggs from which brood is produced.

Cled clad, clothed.

Cled score *N, E* twenty-one to the score, a score being the number or quantity - twenty. (see Double cled)

Cleea *SW* claw, hoof.

Cleean *SW* clean.

Cleeaz *SW* clothes.

Cleed *N* to clothe, to cover or enclose.

Cleek *N* see Click.

Cleekin *N* a brood of chickens, etc., (see Cleekin.)

Cleenin' the afterbirth of animals.

Cleet *C* a cross rib in carpentry; a batten.

Cleg *C* the sting fly, *Chrysops*. To stick like a cleg is a common expression for a good or close adhesion.

Clensin the afterbirth of animals.

Clents the coltsfoot plant, *Tussilago farfara*. The young leaf resembles the impression of the foot of a foal in outline.

Cleps *C* weedsticks - tongs or a stick often with a hook, used for pulling, cutting or removing weeds.

Clethe *N, E* to clothe, to cover or enclose.

Cleu *C* claw, hoof.

Cleugh *N* a ravine or cleft, *'Cleugh, a kind of breach downe along the side of a hill.'*- Verstegan.

Cleutt *N* claw, hoof.

Cliar't *C* the lungs adhering to the ribs of cattle; consumption or lung disease, *Phthisis pulmonalis*.

Click *C, SW* to snatch; a steep part of a road. *'It's a sharp click up Workiton Ho'brow.'*.

Click reel a reel or frame onto which yarn, thread etc. are wound. (see Knack reel).

Clim to climb.

Clinch to rivet the point of a nail, hammer and shape it board at the end.

Clincher *B* something that settles an argument or game.

Clincher a positive fact. *'Theer, that is a clincher.'*.

Clink a blow, a jingling sound.

Clip to cut with scissors; to shear sheep; the wool of a whole flock.

'Ned Nelson hes a parlish clip o'woo'Gasket.'.

Clip't *C* shortened. *'T'days is clip't in a bit.'*.

Clip't an' heel't in proper trim - like a game cock prepared for battle.

Clipper *C, SW* a clever one.

Clippin the annual sheep-shearing.

Clivver *C, N, E* clever. *'Jacks sec a clivver lad, fwor his age.'*.

Clock *C* a beetle; a head of dandelion seeds. Children pretend to tell the hour by the number of puffs required to blow off all the seeds from a ripe flower head.

Clock lound *C* very still, as a clock - probably stopped. (see Lownd.)

Clocker *E* a hen when disposed to sit.

Clog *C* shoe with wooden sole; a block of wood to hang to the neck of an uneasy cow or to the leg of a rambling horse.

Clog wheels *C* cart wheels of thick plank and without spokes. (common in the 18th century).

Cloggins *N E* snowballs or a build up of snow on the feet.

Cloggy fat and heavy. *'As cloggy as a fat su.'*.

Clom *SW* having climbed.

Clonk *C* a sounding blow.

Clonter to walk clumsily and make a clattering noise with the feet.

Clooas *SW* close, hot; to shut; an inclosure

Clood cloud.

Cloor heed *E* a sluice at the head of a mill-dam, to retain and control the flow in the mill-race.

Cloot *C, N* a blow; a patch; a rag.

Closs *C* the *Juncus lampocarpus* plant.

Clot *C* to strew, spread or scatter. *'Her cleazz and things is*

o'clottan about like hay and strea.'.

Clot *C, N, E* an idiot or silly person; a clod; to throw clods, etc. *'They clottit t'lasses wid apples and hed sec fun!'*.

Clot bur *N* the burdock, *Arctium Lappa*.

Clot heed a stupid person.

Clotch *C* to shake roughly.

Clotchin *C* a brood of chickens, etc., or the set of eggs from which brood is produced.

Clough see Cleugh.

Clout-nails *C* broad-headed nails used for attaching the iron hoop to the old clog (cart) wheel.

Clovven *C* when a sheep is fit for slaughter the fat on the rump is indented or *'cloven at t'tail heed.'*.

Clowe *B* to often scold or up-braid (reproach).

Clowe *C, SW* to scratch; to beat. *'She gev him a clowin.'*.

Clower *C* a quick worker. *'A clowan knitter.'*.

Clowk *C* to snatch.

Club nut two or more nuts united in growth.

Cludder *C* to crowd together; cluster.

Cluff *N* a blow.

Clum *C* having climbed; in Borrowdale - the fee as guide for the climb. A woman who acted as guide over a mountain said to a tourist on completing the journey, *'I claim t'clum,'*.

Clunch *C* a heavy stupid person or animal.

Clunter *C* to walk noisily in ironed shoes (pattens) or clogs.

Clwose close; hot; to shut; sultry.

Clwoze *C* close; an inclosure.

Co' *C* to call, scold, proclaim. *'I'th'kurk garth the clark co't'a seall.'*; come. *'Jack co'towert me and I said cuh naa narder.'*

Co'i'the court *N* customary

tenants were required to answer to their names when called in the old manorial court, and this is termed having a co'i' the court. It implies being a yeoman or his representative.

Co'in' scolding.

Coald *C, E* cold. *cold. 'It's parlish coald.' .... 'Ey, fit to skin a teadd.'.*

Coald pie *C* a fall on the ice.

Coave *C, E* to calve.

Coaves *C, E* calves.

Cob to kick; to beat; a loaf of bread, often round in shape.

Cobble steann a boulder stone. *'With staves or with clubs, or els with cobble stones.'*- Gammer Gurton's needle.

Cobble up to perform roughly and hastily.

Cobs *B* snowballs on feet of men or horses.

Cock *C, SW* to sit bashfully or unobserved.

Cock drunks *C* the fruit of the mountain ash, *Pyrus aucuparia.*

Cock dyke *N E* a mode of hedging; the same as *'Stower and Yedder'.*

Cock gard *C* a mode of hedging, the same as *'Stower an'Yedder'.*

Cock sure *C* confident; perfectly certain.

Cock tail't horse see Set tail't horse.

Cock walk during the rage for cock-fighting, young game cocks were sent out with one or two hens each among the friends of the owner, to be kept at some retired shed or hut till ready to be trained, and this was the *'walk.'.*

Cock web *SW* spider's web.

Cock-a-lilty *C* in a merry, noisy agreeable mood.

Cock-crow-land *E* superior croftland over which the cock exultingly leads his harem.

Cock-loft *C* top attic where cocks

may have once occasionally been kept in cock-fighting times.

Cock-me-dainty *E* a pert (forward, saucy, bold) and showily dressed girl or young man.

Cock-steull a kind of stocks for the punishment of female scolds (rude, clamorous and foul-mouthed women).

Cockan' cock-fighting.

Cockelty *SW* unsteady; on a precarious foundation.

Cocker a cock-fighter.

Cockermuth. Cockermouth.

Cockers *C* calkers, those employed to seal seams of ships; calkers - pointed part of a horse or ox shoe to prevent slipping); irons for clog bottoms.

Cockfeighters the seed stems of *Plantago minor*, once used by boys in play.

Cockly *C, N* unsteady or on a precarious foundation.

Cockly bur *C* see Bur.

Cockly-jock *E* a game once played among boys. Stones are loosely placed one upon another, at which other stones are thrown to knock the pile down.

Cocks dillies! exclamations of surprise.

Cockswunters! exclamations of surprise.

Cod a pillow; hassock; pin-cushion.

Codbait *C, B* a bait used in angling; the larva of a *Phryganea.*

Coddle to embrace.

Coddy *B* a young foal; a donkey or ass.

Codebeck *C* Caldbeck.

Codikel *C* a corruption of codicil - a supplement to a will.

Cofe calf.

Cofe heed *B* a foolish fellow.

Cofe lye *C* the womb of the cow.

Cofe lyer *C* a cow's womb.

Cofe trunnels *E* entrails of the calf selected and cleansed,

shred and seasoned, and made into a pie.

Cofe-lick't *C* when human hair grows perversely (distorted), it is said to be calf licked. The hair of a calf or cow remains for some time in the direction of the last licking by the animal's tongue.

Coff *C, E* cough.

Cogs *B* shoes with heavy wooden soles; snowballs on feet of men or horses.

Coitleth *B* cloth for a coat.

Col *N* cold. *'It's parlish coald.' .... 'Ey, fit to skin a teadd.'.*

Colfins *C* gun wads - soft material pushed down the barrel, to retain the charge in the gun.

Collaps scallops; slices of potato, usually pan fried in bacon fat or lard.

Colleckshun collection.

Collogue *C* to plot; to confederate or to unite.

Collop Monday the day after Shrove Sunday, when collaps are usually prepared for dinner.

Collops scallops; slices of potato, usually pan fried in bacon fat or lard.

Collorake see Scrapple.

Colrak *SW* a tool to scrape with; a coal-rake.

Colrake see Scrapple.

Colrik *B* see Scrapple.

Com *C, SW* came.

Com come.

Come calm.

Come ageann. pardon can you repeat what you said.

Come at *C* to obtain. *'I want it to hev't bit I couldn'come at it.'.*

Come on to prosecute. *'He come on Jemmy for brekkan a yat and gat sebm shillin'.'.*

Come t'time when the day or time comes. *'It'll be three year come t'time.'.*

Come thy ways an usual invitation. *'Come thy ways in, bonny laal barn.'.*

Come't *C* came. *'He's come't in.'* - He came in.

Comers an' gangers visitors, etc; coming and going.

Con *C, SW* a squirrel.

Conk *C* the nose or profile *'Oald Bob with t'howker conk.'.*

Connily *C, SW* prettily.

Conny pretty, nice, suitable, gentle, cautious. *'Be conny,'or cautious.*

Consate conceit, pride; to suppose, *'I consate you're a stranger hereaway?'.*

Coo *C* to intimidate; to place in subjection.

Coo *C, N, E* cow.

Coo clap *C* the dung of the cow as dropped in the field.

Coo skarn *C* cow-dung.

Coo struplin *C* the cowslip. (nearly obsolete 1878).

Coo swat *C* the semi-fluid dung of the cow as dropped in the field.

Coo tee cow tie or tether; a rope to fasten and secure the hind legs of a kicking cow during the operation of milking.

Cooas *C* cow-house or byre.

Cook *B* to imitate the call of the cuckoo.

Coom a hollow scooped out of the side of a mountain, eg. *Black Comb* etc.

Coom *B* the debris of coal; culm.

Coom cardins *N* wool once carded or combed prior to spinning.

Coom cards *N* the first and coarsest cards used in carding or combing wool.

Coomb a hollow scooped out of the side of a mountain, eg. *Black Comb* etc.

Coomins *N* wool once carded or combed prior to spinning.

Coont *C* count. *'Coont t'things ower agean.'.*

Coontit *C* counted.

Coop *C* a small fell-side cart.

Coop board *C* the board closing the hinder end of the cart.

Coor *C, N, E* cower, crouch.

Cooter coulter - the fore iron of a plough with a sharp edge that cuts through the earth or sod.

Cop *C* the top; a peak; a conical hill; eg. *Coulerton cop, Kinniside cop* etc.

Coppy coppice.

Copt *C* pert; set up; proud.

Copy steull *C* a child's stool, usually with three legs.

Corby *N* the carrion crow, one that feeds on the dead body or flesh of animals.

Corker something very good or appropriate. *'That is a corker!'.*

Corkin' *B* a severe beating.

Corlak *C* a tool to scrape with; a coal rake. *(see Scrapple).*

Cornage a rent paid by certain customary lands towards the cost of a person to watch and give notice, by blowing a horn, of the approach of an enemy.

Cornish cornice.

Corp *C, SW* to die.

Corp *N, E* corpse.

Cot a humble dwelling.

Cot did cut; has cut. *'He cot his thoom wid his sickle.'.*

Cot *SW* to wait on a sick person; to saunter or stroll around idly about home. *'Issac cots on about heamm.'.* (see Teutt).

Cotter *C* to entangle; to mat together. *'It was cotter't like an oald wig.'.*

Cotterel a pin for preventing the withdrawing of a bolt; a coin.

Cottit *C* short-tempered.

Count *C, N* count; account. *'I count nought o'sec wark.'* - I hold it in no esteem.

Countin' counting; arithmetic.

'Jack! git t'countin' dun.'.

Country side neighbourhood. *'Our country-side lads ageann o'Ingland.'.*

Courts small railed-in spaces in front of houses eg. forecourt.

Courtship an' matrimony *C* the plant, *Spirea Ulmaria*, has been so called from the scent of he flower before and after being bruised.

Covver to recover. *'He cover't five pund dammish.'.*

Cow band the cow band of the last century was made of tough ashwood, and D shaped (superseded by chains 1878).

Cow clog *C* a clog or block of wood to hang on the neck of a *'lowp-i-dike'* cow - a cow likely to jump over an hedge or fence.

Cow t'lowe *C* snuff or extinquish the candle.

Cow't *C* bare, without ornament or shelter; without horns.

Cow't cow *C* a cow without horns.

Cow't leady *E* a pudding made of flour and lumps of suet.

Cow't lword *C* a pudding made of oatmeal and lumps of suet.

Cowdy *C* better fed than taught; in high spirits.

Cowe a stem or branch.

Cowe *SW* to intimidate; to place in subjection.

Cowey *C* a cow without horns.

Cowgh *N* cough.

Cowk the core.

Cowl *SW* to rake together.

Cowp to exchange.

Cowp *N, SW* to upset; overturn.

Cowp *SW* a small fell-side cart.

Cowper hand *N* The upper hand; the advantage as of a practised chapman or trader.

Cowper word having the first word, or the word that gives the advantage.

Cowpress *C* the fulcrum.

Cowrak *SW* a tool to scrape with; a coal-rake.

Cowshin *C, N* caution.

Cowshious *C, N* cautious.

Cowt colt; a petted child, *'Mother's la'al cowt.'.*

Cowt't dyke *C* an earthen fence devoid of growing wood or hedge.

Coydls *C* quoits.

Coze hoose the house where a corpse is placed; mortuary.

Craa *SW* crow; to boast in truimph, to swagger.

Craa *SW, NW* crow, *Corvidae.*

Craa teazz *N* the early purple orchid, *Orchis mascula.*

Craal *SW* crawl.

Craawl *C, N* crawl.

Crack a conversation, gossip, news - *'Come Jack lad, give us thy crack.'*; to do quickly or succeed in a task. *'As will, in a crack.'*; to boast; to restrain. *'He's nought to crack on, for he set his dog on a bit lad and wad n't crack't off ageann.*

Crack't not in his right sense. *'Theyne dog's crack't in t'heed.'.*

Crackan *C* talking or chattering.

Crackers *C, B* silly or mad. *'Yer dog's gan crackers when he hurd tha'.'*; the air vessels of the *Fucus vesiculosus.*

Cracket *C* the cricket insect, *Gryllus domesticus.* A superstition used to prevail that prosperity comes and goes with the crickets.

Crad *C* a troublesome child; an inferior animal.

Craddagh *C* a troublesome child; an inferior animal.

Crag *C* the face; the neck or countenance. *'He hang a lang crag when t'news com.'.*

Crag starlin' *E* the Ring Ouzel, a bird of the thrush family, *Turdus torquatus.*

Crammel *C* to scramble; the walk as if with sore feet.

Crammelly *C* tottery, unsteady.

Cranch *C* to crush with the teeth. Coarse sand cranches under the feet.

Cranch craunch or crunch.

Crankelty *C* very crooked; zigzag; *'O'in's an'outs.'.*

Cranky crotchety; sickly and complaining. *'How's thy oald mudder?'.... 'Nobbet varra cranky to-day.'.*

Cranky sark *C, N* a shirt made of home-grown, home-spun hemp - The grandfather of WD (the compiler), was called out as a cavalry or yeomanry soldier in 1745; and, like his neighbours, all wore a check linen shirt with white frills on the breast - then called a *'cranky'.*

Crap *N* crept.

Crater *C, N, SW* creature.

Cravvik *N* see Crovvik.

Crawl *E, SW* crawl.

Crawwl *SW* to crawl.

Crawwn *SW* crown; the top of the head.

Creaanns *N* cranberries, the fruit of the *Oxycoccus palustris.*

Creapp *C* crept.

Cree to crush or break into fragments.

Creeak *SW, NW* crook.

Creean *SW* the subdued roar of the bull.

Creean trough *C* see Knocklin' trough.

Creean trough old stone troughs of circular or semi-globular form, in which barley was crushed or ground into flour for making bread.

Creeater *SW* creature.

Creein' crushing (see Creean' trough)

Creel *C* an ancient package for carrying goods on horseback; a wicker basket.

Creelin' *E* cowering, crouching.

Creeper *B* the larva of the May fly or insect.

Creeter *C* creature.

Creetur creature.

Creuk't axe an axe having the edge turned inwards; an adze.

Creukk *C* crook.

Creukt crooked.

Creunn *C, N* the subdued roar of the bull.

Creupp *N* crept.

Crib *C, N* curb; the curb of a bridle.

Crine *E* to overdo in frying or roasting. *'Thou's crine't it tul a cinder.'.*

Crinkelty *C* very crooked; zigzag; *'O'in's an'outs.'.*

Crippel *N* crupper or rump of a horse; leather strap of a saddle which passes under the horses tail.

Crippin *SW* see Crippel.

Crippy *B* a stool. *'La'al Jack sit tha' on thy crippy.'.*

Cro *C, E* crow, *Corvidae*; to boast in truimph, to swagger.

Croab't *C* drunk, *'Oald Jonty's naa croab't agin.'.*

Crob lambs *C, SW* see Crobs.

Crobbek *C* a disease in the stomach of cattle occasioned by want of change of pasture.

Crobs *C, SW* lambs, the worst of the flock.

Crock *C, SW* old; an old ewe - a *'crock yowe'*; To crock, grow feeble and decrepit with age.

Crockly *C* crumbly.

Croft a field next the house, usually level and of good quality.

Croft land a range of fields near the house, of equally good quality with the croft.

Croful *C* not much, a small amount, little or none - a very lean person is said to have not a croful of flesh on his bones.

Crones *C* cranberries, the fruit of the *Oxycoccus palustris.*

Cronk *C* the hollow note uttered by the raven when on the wing.

Crony *C, B, N* a comrade, friend, companion. *'Wudsworth and his gay cronys are out o' t'fells ageann.'.*

Crood crowd.

Croodle *C* to crouch.

Croon *C, N, E* crown; the top of the head.

Crooner coroner.

Croopin *C* crupper.

Croose *C, N* haughty; set up; elated.

Crop *C* crept.

Crop sick *C* disordered in the stomach.

Croppen *C, SW* crept. *'He was lang varra wankle bit he gat croppen out ageann.';* failing in bodily appearance. *'T'oald woman's sare croppen in.'.*

Cropt horse formerly it was considered a mark of gentility to be the owner of a crop-eared or a set-tailed horse for the riding.

Cross buttock a term in wrestling.

Crottelly *C* crumbly.

Crottels *C, N* small lumps.

Crovvik *SW* a disease in the stomach of cattle occasioned by want of change of pasture.

Crow an iron trivet for supporting a pan on the openfire when cooking.

Crowdy oatmeal mixed with the fat of broth; a horse's mess of seeds and meal, etc. (see Stick by t'rib).

Crowfeet the plant *Ranunculus repens.*

Crowk *C* a frog-like croak. The guts *'crowk'* when the bowels make a rumbling noise.

Crowkins greaves or sediment from melted fat.

Crowl *C, N, E* to crawl, *'La'al Jack crowl't onder t'teabbel.'.*

Crub *C* a crib or manger; the curb of a bridle.

Crub *C, N, E* to curb; restrain.

Crud curd.

Cruddle to turn into curd; to coagulate.

Cruel *C* cover a hand-ball with worsted or thread needlework.

Crum horn't horns turned towards the eyes.

Crummy horns turned towards the eyes.

Crump *C* brittle; crumbling; the sound of horse's teeth when eating.

Crunch *N* craunch or crunch; to crush with the teeth. Coarse sand cranches under the feet.

Crusty ill-tempered.

Cry *N* call, *'Cry the lad back.'* or *'Cry in as ye come back.'.*

Cry 't i' the kirk *NE* having had the wedding banns published.

Cryke *C* a crevice or ravine in the side of a fell or hill.

Cubbert cupboard

Cuckelty burs *C* the seed heads of the burdock, *Arctium Loppa,* which mischievous boys stick into each other's hair.

Cuckoo bread an' cheese *C* the leaves and flowers of the wood sorrel, *Oxalis Acetosella.*

Cuckoo spit *C* frothy matter seen on plants in early summer; the breeding places of the *Tettigonia,* a species of beetle.

Cud *C* could.

Cud nut two or more nuts united in growth.

Cuddent *C* could not, couldn't.

Cuddy an ass or donkey. *'As't thee 'iver sin a cuddy lowp a five bar geatt.';* an idiot or simpleton.

Cue *C* trim; temper. *'He's i'girt cue to-day.'.*

Cuff *C, N* the back or nape of the neck; a blow on the head.

Cuh *C* come. *'Mary co'towert me and I said cuh narder.'* (see Co').

Cum *C* come. *'I cum fra Workinton.'.*

Cum a useless expletive frequently preceding a remark, etc. *'Cum! What hes ta to say?'.*

Cum bye *C* reprisal. *'It'l cum bye him.'-* It will visit him hereafter.

Cum what cum may *C* whatever will be will be; let the consequence be what it may.

Cum yer ways in *C* come in and welcome.

Cum't milk *C* milk curdled with rennet and seasoned.

Cum-atable attainable.

Cum-mether *C* godmother. (seldom used 1878).

Cumman *C* coming. *'A reet storm's cumman, John.'.*

Cummerlan *SW* Cumberland.

Cummins *C, B* the rootlets of barley when malted.

Cummiter *C* godmother. (seldom used 1878).

Cun *C* come, *'T'dog's cun heamm.'.*

Cundert conduit; culvert.

Cundeth see Cudert.

Cup down *C* It was formerly the custom to turn the cup upside down or place the spoon across it when a person had done or finished drinking their tea.

Curl the ripple on water caused by a slight wind.

Curly kue a flourish or bold stroke in writing, etc.

Curly powe a curled poll or head of hair. *'Dainty Davie, curly powe.'-* from an old song.

Curr *C, SW* cower, crouch.

Currock *NE* a heap of stones used as land-mark, etc.

Cursen christen.

Cursenmas Christmas.

Cursmas Christmas. *'At Cursmas mery may ye dance.'.*

Cush! *C* exclamation of wonder; a kind of oath; a call not for cattle.

Cushat *E* see Wooshat.

Cushy *C* a pet name for a cow.

Cussin cousin.

Custa *C* comest thou? *'Gwordy, whoar custa frae?'*.

Cut a certain quantity of yarn used to castrate an cow or sheep etc.

Cut lugs short-ears; There is an old saying relative to any stroke of great cunning, that *'it caps cut lugs, and cut lugs caps the de'il.'*, but who *'cut lugs'* was is a mystery.

Cut'n has been cut; cutting.

Cute acute, clever. *'He's nit sea 'cute to wussel oor Jack.'*.

Cuthbert an ass or donkey; idiot or simpleton.

Cuts pieces of straw, etc., often once used in drawing lots.

Cutter to whisper or talk softly. *'I'the'pantry the sweethearters cutter't quite soft.'*- Anderson.

Cuttery coo *C* secret conversation; the note or cry of the male pigeon.

Cuttle *N* to chat or gossip.

Cutty *N* short. (see Skutty).

Cuvvins *C* periwinkle shell-fish, *Turbo littoreus*.

Cuz comes. *'He cuz ower to see us now and than.'*.

Cuze accuse.

Cwoam *C, E, SW* comb.

Cwoat cards *B* pictured cards.

Cwoat cards *SW* court cards.

Cwol *C, N, E* coal.

Cwol greuvv *C* an old name for a coal workings or mine.

Cwol greuvv law *C* the rule of turn, *'Furst come furst sarv't.'* - first come, first served.

Cwol sill clay shale or silt overlying coal measures.

Cwol skrat *C* a tool to scrape with; a coal-rake.

Cwolly *C, NE* the shepherd's dog; a colley or collie dog.

Cwoorse *C, N, E* coarse, course.

Cwoort *C, NE* court.

Cwoort cards *C* pictured cards.

Cwoort cards court cards.

Cworn oats, corn.

Cworn creak the corn-crake or landrail plant, *Crex pratensis*.

Cworn later *C* a person begging for corn. It was the custom till lately (1878) for a poor man beginning the world on a small farm, to go round among his neighbours soliciting for seed corn, when one or two gallons would be given him at nearly every farm-house.

Cwosty pin *C* a large brass pin used to fasten the cloak or coat collar with, below the chin.

Cwoze hoose the house where a corpse is within; mortuary.

Cyds *C* quoits.

Daab daub or bedaub, to besmear with anything visous, slimy or thick; gross flattery, play the hypocrite.

Daad *C* a slight covering of snow etc. *'A laal daad o'snow on t'grund.'*.

Daarent *C, E* dare not.

Daarentwatter Derwentwater.

Daarentwatter lets the *Aurora borealis* or northern lights. On the night of the execution of the Earl of Derwentwater the *Aurora borealis* was said to have flashed with remarkable brilliancy, and was locally since been so named in remembrance of him.

Dab an expert one.

Dabbin *B* a dam.

Dadder *C, SW* to shiver; to tremble.

Dadder grass *C* quaking grass, *Briza media*.

Daddle to walk or work slowly; to trifle; the hand. *'And give us a shak o'thy daddle.'*.

Daddy long-legs the *Tipula* or long-legs insect. (see Jenny spinner).

Dade *N* dada, daddy, father.

Dadge *E* to trudge.

Dady *N* dada, daddy, father.

Daffan' joking, bantering.

Daffy *C* the daffodil.

Daffy-doon-dilly *C* the daffodil. *Pseudo-narcissus*. *'Willy Wurdswuth reatt a grand poem aboot daffy-doon-dillys.'*.

Daft silly, wanton. *'Oor Jack's fairly daft about her.'*; idiotic. *'He's nobbut daftish.'* *'Ey, daft as a besom.'*.

Dag *N* to ooze; to flow gently and slowly like a moist ulcer or *'deggan sare.'*.

Daggy *N* wet and misty weather.

Dally *C* a wooden toy. *'Tee tak o', daily an'o'.'*.

Damp the inflammable gas in a coal mine.

Dancin' mad in a towering or high passion.

Dander passion, excitement; a blow. *'His dander's up.'*.

Dander *N* to hobble; to wander, *'danderan about.'*.

Dang *N* to push, to strike. *'Dang him for a feull! Aa'll ding him ower, and efter he's dung ower aa'll dang his silly heed off.'*.

Dansen *C* dancing.

Dar *C* dare; oaths - real or implied.

Dar-zonn! see Dar.

Darg *N* day's work.

Dark to lurk; to listen in the back ground; *'like a pig in a strea heap.'*.

Dark *SW* day's work.

Darkan' lurking; listening without appearing to do so.

Darken *C* to stand or be in the way. *'She sal niver darken my door na mair.'*.

Darknin' evening twilight.

Darna *N* dare not.

Darrak *C* day's work.

Darrat *C* see Dar

Darter *C* quick person.

Dash *N* a flourish in writing thrown by a free hand.

Dashers *C, B* the inside workings

of a barrel churn used in butter making.

Dass *N* cutting in a hay-stack.

Daud *C* daub, dot, a lump or rough quantity - *'lumps o'puddin' and dauds o'panceakk.'*; a flake of snow. *'It fo's i'girt dauds.'*.

Daur *N* dare.

Dawp *E* the carrion crow, one that feeds on the dead body or flesh of animals.

Dawted *C* doted, foolish.

Dawwn *SW* down. *'Let's ga dawwn to t'shooar an' hev a dook.'*.

Dawwt *SW* doubt.

Dawwter *SW* daughter.

Day mining tem for the surface.

Day by t'lenth *C* all day long.

Day leet'nin' morning twilight; daybreak.

Daycent *SW* worthy, favourable. *'A varra daycent man.'* *'A daycent swort of a day.'*.

Dayz't *C* pasty, half-baked, exhausted, stupid, dazed.

De'el bin! *N* a mode of oath.

Dea *C* do.

Deaa nettle *C* the dead nettle, *Lamium album.*

Dead ripe over ripe and ready to drop.

Deal very much; a great number or quantity.

Deall *B* a field near the house; croft.

Deall land land held in defined but unfenced parcels in an open field.

Deall meall *C* Dale mail, a tribute formerly paid by the customary tenants of the manor of Ennerdale for permission to put sheep and cattle on the forest.

Deamm *C, SW* dame; mistress of the house; wife.

Deary me! *C* an exclamation of lament. *'Deary me!' said Daniel Fidler, 'Three girt lasses and cannot o'mak a taty puddin'!'*.

Death come quickly *C* the

plant, *Geranium Robertianum.*

Deaz't *SW* see Dayz't

Decent *C* worthy, favourable. *'A varra decent man.'* *'A decent swort of a day.'*.

Deddy *C* dada, daddy, father.

Dee die; do.

Dee *N, E* do. *'Will ta ivver dee it agyan.'*.

Dee nettle *C* the dead nettle - *Lamium album.*

Deea nettle *C* see Dee nettle.

Deead *SW* dead.

Deeaf *SW* deaf; (see Deeaf).

Deean' *C* doing.

Deeath *SW* death.

Deeav *SW* to deafen; to stun with noise.

Deed *B* indeed.

Deed *C, N, E* dead.

Deed beat dead heat; when neither wins.

Deed drunk *C* dead drunk, a man who can *'nowther gang, ner stand, ner hod by t'girse.'*.

Deed horse wark *C* paying off an old debt by labour.

Deed lift *C* the moving of an inert body; a difficulty without assistance.

Deed tongue *C, SW* the poisonous water hemlock plant, *Cicuta virosa.*

Deef *C, N, E* deaf; applied to corn or crops, it means light grain; and to land, weak and unproductive.

Deef-nut a nut without a kernel. *'He cracks nea deef-nuts.'* - said of a well-fed person or animal.

Deeght *N* to separate; to winnow or dress corn, to separate chaff from com; to wipe or make clean.

Deel devil.

Deepness *C* depth.

Deer door.

Deet *C* to winnow or dress corn; to wipe or make clean.

Deeth *C, N, E* death.

Deetin' cleath *C* a cloth used to winnow or dress corn upon.

(see Deeght).

Deetin' hill *C* a hill where corn was dressed, by throwing the grain up against the wind. Some ancient barns had opposite doors, between which the grain could be cleared of chaff in the draught, when the weather was unsuitable for the use of the deeting hill.

Deetin' sheen *B* winnowing machine, used to separate the grain from the chaff.

Deeval *N, E* devil.

Deeve *C, N* to deafen; to stun with noise.

Deft *C* quiet, silent.

Deft *N* handy. *'Jonty's varra deft wid pleugh.'*; pretty in old times.

Deg *C* to ooze; to flow gently and slowly like a moist ulcer or *'deggan sare.'*.

Deil *N* devil

Dem a dam or weir.

Dench *C* squeamish; delicate.

Despart *C* desperate; inveterate; great. *'He's a despart fellow for drinkin'.'*.

Dess *C* to adorn; to build up as applied to cocks of hay, haystacks etc.

Deuh *C, E* do.

Deukt cattle blotched with white are deukt.

Deun done.

Deun out *C* fatigued. *'Yer mam's deun out wid hoose wark.'*.

Deun ower intoxicated. *'Yer fadder's deun ower wid ale.'*.

Deur door, *'Steukk that deur, lass.'*.

Dewe *SW* do, dew; (pronounced day-oo, quickly).

Deyke *N* hedge.

Deyl't *N* moped, made stupid; low-spirted or spiritless; with faculties impaired.

Dibble to plant seed; Sometimes applied to the burial of a corpse in hope to rise again.

Dibler *N* a large earthenware dish; a double-sized one.

Dickadee *C* the common sandpiper, *Tringa alpina*.

Dickey *C* the hedge-sparrow, *Accentor modularis*.

Dicky *B* short upper garment of coarse linen till lately worn by working men (1878).

Dicky not good; he's ruined, or dead. *'It's dicky wid him.'.*

Dicky bird a general name originally for a canary (1878), later also used to refer to other spieces of bird.

Dicky sark an additional shirt breast or front.

Didder *N, E* to shiver; to tremble.

Difficulter *C* more difficult.

Dig dog. *'Yer brudder's digs will feight yananudder.'.*

Dilly dally *C* to waste time; flighty. *'Yer Tilly nobbet a dilly dally lass.'.*

Din noise.

Din *N* dun colour, a dark and dull brown and black colour.

Ding dew *E* a person who walks with his toes much turned out; splay-footed.

Ding drive *C, N* full drive; full speed.

Ding drive in hard earnest.

Ding ower to upset; to knock or push down.

Ding! *C* a kind of oath or declaration; to knock.

Dinna do not.

Dinnel *C* to tremble with cold.

Dinnet *C* do not.

Dint *E* to indent or dent; vigour; energy; thrift. *'He hez some dint in him'* - he will make his mark.

Dintless *E* lacking in energy.

Dirl *B* tremulous motion.

Dirl *C, N* a trembling, shaking or quivering sound. *'Sek a dirlin' and a birlin' it meadd'.*

Dirty gully *B* a butcher's untidy assistant in slaughtering.

Dis does.

Dis ta does thou, do you. *"Dis ta think that's t'reet yan ta sell.'.*

Dis'nan' *C* distancing or leaving far behind.

Disgenerate *C, W* degenerate.

Dish feaast hollow-faced; feminine.

Dish't defeated, overcome.

Disjest *C, E* digest.

Dispart *N* desperate; inveterate; great. *'He's a dispart fellow for drinkin'.'.*

Dissenton *C* Distington.

Dista *G, not E* see Dis Ta.

Div *B, N, E* do. *'Div ye gang to Wigton market?'.*

Divent do not.

Diverna *C* do not.

Divval *C, E, SW* devil.

Divval 'munt *C* mischievous, mischief-making. *'Dinna fret lass, yer fadder diz it for divval 'munt.'.*

Divvent do not. *'Now, divvent liken me to hur.'.*

Divvern't *W* do not.

Dix *N, E* does.

Diz *N, E* does.

Dizzen *N, E* dozen; to bedeck or adorn, to decorate.

Do thee *C* a command. *'Do thee gang to thy wark.'.*

Dobbin *B* an old horse.

Dobby a dotard or man whose intellect is impaired by age; a doting fellow; a boggle - a mythical, scary person or creature from local folklore, eg. the *Branthet boggle.*

Dockin the dock plant, a common weed of the genus *Rumex*. The leaf of the dock is reputed to cure the sting of a nettle when rubbed on the place, repeating *'Dockin in, nettle out.'.*

Dod a round topped fell, generally an offshoot from a larger or higher mountain.

Dodder *N* the corn spurrey plant,

Spergula arvensis.

Dodder *N, E* to shiver; to tremble.

Doddy *N, NE* a cow without horns.

Dode *C* daub, dot; a lump or rough quantity - *'lumps o'puddin' and dodes o'panceakk.'.*

Dodlin' *B* sauntering.

Doff to take off; to undress.

Doffboy *C* a stiff pudding without any fruit.

Dog cheap very cheap; much within its value.

Dog daisy *C* the daisy, *Bellis perennis.* (see Benwort).

Dog dyke *C, E* a boundary without a fence, where dogs are used to hound back trespassers.

Dog flower *E* the ox-eye daisy, *Chrysanthemum Leucanthemum.*

Dog fo' an undecided fall in wrestling; a draw, the advantages being equal.

Dog nwose *E* an old drink of hot ale and gin, formerly once also made cold.

Dog pig a castrated male pig.

Dog trail a hound race or trail.

Dogdaisy *C* see Dog daisy.

Dogger't *C* beggared, reduced to extreme poverty.

Doldrums *C* low spirits.

Dollop *C* a lump; a large share.

Dolly an instrument to twirl or agitate clothes within the wash-tub.

Dolly tub the tub where clothes were once washed.

Don to do on; to dress.

Done out *C* fatigued.

Donky dank, damp, moist, humid or wet.

Donky weather *C* mist and rain. *'It's a donky day, Dick.'....'Ey, rayder slattery.'*

Donnat devil; an unruly person or animal; a doughnut; (see Dow).

Donnican *E* a privy. (see La'al hoose).

Doo *C* a feast or merry making;

something exciting. *'We'd a grand doo tudder neet wid yer mudder.'.*

Dooal *C, SW* dowel.

Dooer *C, E* door.

Dook to bathe or swim; to duck; to dive.

Dookers a male swimming costume or swimming trunks.

Doon *C, N, E* down.

Doon at mouth *C* dejected; dispirited.

Doon come *C, N* fall in price or station.

Doon fo' done for; the low parts around mountains where sheep shelter in bad weather; a fall of rain.

Doon him *C* knock him down.

Doon liggin lying in.

Doon thump honest, truthful.

Doon't knocked down; felled. *'Dick doon't him at t'furst bat.'.*

Doonbank *C, N* downwards.

Door steann the threshold, door step.

Doors *C* the fold or inclosed yard before the door into a barn or farm building.

Doose *C, N* a slap. *'Aa'll doose thy chops.'*; jolly, hospitable, open-handed; having a good appearance.

Doot *C, N, E* doubt.

Dootsam *C, N* doubtful.

Dope *C* a simpleton or fool.

Dopy *C* a simpleton or fool.

Dost does.

Dote *C* dealt or shared; a specified share in an open field, etc. - *a peat dote, a bracken dote, a hay dote; a tangle dote* - share of the sea-shore; and also of a fence or road etc. - *a dyke dote, a road dote, a beck dote.*

Dotherin grass *N* quaking grass, *Briza media.*

Dottle *N* the small portion of tobacco remaining unconsumed in the pipe; small excrement or

dung - eg. *sheep dottles.*

Dottles *C* the globular droppings of sheep.

Double cled *N, E* twenty-two to the score, a score being the number or quantity - twenty. (see Cled score)

Double or quits a betting proposal - double the winnings if you win or I'll owe you nothing from the previous bets or wagers.

Doughboy *C* a stiff pudding without any fruit.

Dour sour looking.

Dow doing, *'Mair din nor dow'* - more noise than work; to be useful or good. *'He's nought at dow'* - not reliable.

Dowdy slovenly, disorderly; negligent; not of neat appearance.

Dowly *C* downhearted, sorrowful.

Down *C* to knock down.

Dowp *C* a bay in a lake; a recess.

Dowter daughter. *'Ma new la'al dowters call't Emilly.'.*

Dowy *N* the threshold.

Dozen't *N* spiritless and impotent; stupified - made dull or stupid.

Dozzle *C, N* a shapeless lump.

Draa *SW* draw; to catch or overtake. *'He's off, bit we'll seunn draa him.'.*

Drabble draggle or make wet and dirty.

Draff brewer's grains; a team of horses or oxen used to pull a plough or cart.

Draft sheep *C, SW* a selection of the best annually.

Drag a three-pronged fork used for drawing or pulling manure from the cart.

Draik't wet.

Drammock *E* a mixture of oatmeal and water.

Draw *C* see Draa

Drayk't *N* saturated with water, see Dreuv't.

Dreak drake or male duck.

Dreak't *N* saturated with water, see Dreuv't.

Dreakk see Dreak.

Dreann *C* the gratified note of the cow during milking.

Dreav *C, N, E* drove, did drive.

Dree slow, lasting, lengthy. *'It's a dree rwoad 'at niver hes a turn.'.*

Dreead *SW* dread. (see Dreed).

Dreeam dream.

Dreeav't *SW* saturated with water, see Dreuv't.

Dreed *C, NE* dread. *'He niver dreedit sec a thing.'.*

Dreen *C* the gratified note of the cow during milking.

Dreesom' *N* tiresome, lengthy.

Dreuv *C, N* drove; did drive.

Dreuv't *C* saturated with water. This term was once commonly applied to slaked lime when very wet and watery. A former name was *muddy lime.*

Dreuvy *B* water is so called when not quite clear, especially from half-melted snow. (see Dreuv't).

Dreyve *NW* drive.

Driddle *C* a corruption of dribble; to fall in small drops or slow running; to slaver as a child or idiot.

Dridge dredge; to sprinkle.

Driek *N, E* see Dreak.

Drift road a way over which a person has a right of driving cattle, etc., through others field, but not for other purposes.

Drip brilliantly white as the driven or new dripped (dropped) snow. *'White as drip.'.*

Driss *C* dress.

Driss butter *C* to work up and make fresh butter into cakes and pats or pounds.

Drisser dresser - a table or bench where meat and other foods are dressed or prepared; the crockery shelf.

Drissin' *C* a whipping.

Drive force, action. *'Our hay-*

knife's square mouth't and hez nea drive wid it.'.

Dro' *C, E* draw.

Drook't *C* severely wet. *'Issac gat drook't in t'beck.'.*

Drooken drunken.

Droon drown.

Drooty droughty (weather).

Drop dry a waterproof roof is drop dry.

Droppy rainy; beginning to rain.

Drouth *C, B, N* thirst.

Droven *C, E* driven.

Drucken drunken.

Drufty droughty (weather).

Drukken drunken.

Drush down *C* to rush down; to fall suddenly.

Druss *N* dress.

Druv *C, N* drove; did drive.

Druvven *C, E* driven.

Dry *C, SW* thirsty.

Dry wo' a dry stone wall built without mortar.

Dryish *C, SW* thirsty; fine weather.

Du do or did.

Du *SW* do; a feast or merry making; something exciting. *'We'd a grand du tudder neet wid yon lass.'.*

Duan *SW* doing.

Dub a small pond or pool.

Dub-a-cock *C* to clip off the comb and wattles from a cock ready to fighting.

Dubersom' *C* dubious; in some doubt.

Dubler *C* a large earthenware dish; a double-sized one.

Dud did. *'Dud ta nivver see her ageann efter t'tansy.'.*

Dudn't did not. *'I dudn't see yer at t'fair, as i dudn't ga.'.*

Dud n't see Dudn't

Dud ta? didst thou?.

Duddy fuddiel *N* a ragged fellow.

Duds clothes. *'Bits o'duds'-* the scanty wardrobe of indigence.

Duer *SW* door.

Duffle a coarse woollen cloth, generally blue, much worn in the days of home manufacturers.

Duffy *C* spongy; soft and woolly; finest dust.

Dulbert *C* a dull person of the male sex; a dunce.

Dullbert *E* a dull individual, stupid, blockish, slow of understanding etc.

Dum dumb.

Dumbwife *NE* a fortune teller - formerly a dumb person was often believed to be psychic or have a knowledge of futurity.

Dummel heead *SW* a blockhead, stupid fellow or person deficient in understanding.

Dump *C* to butt with the head.

Dump to butt with elbow or knee.

Dumps in so bad a humour as not to speak. *'Will's down in t'dumps ower theyne lass.'.*

Dumpy *C* short and thick. *'La'al Mary's a dumpy wee lass, if ivver I saw yan.'.*

Dumpy cow *C* a cow given to attack people.

Dun *C* done.

Dun ower *C* done over; tired or finished.

Dunder heed a blockhead, stupid fellow or person deficient in understanding..

Dunnecan *E* a privy or toilet. Originally a fixed rail was used instead of a seat-board. The user would just squat or perch on this simple low beam.

Dunnet do not.

Dunsh to butt with elbow or knee.

Durdum disturbance, noise and dispute, has its origins from when the country was divided into districts, each answerable for the good behaviour of its inhabitants. Meetings were held at the doors of suspected wrong-doers to inquire into an offence.

Durs n't durst not or dare not.

Durt dirt.

Durtment anything valueless or despicable.

Dus does. *'Mind thoo nivver dus agean.'.*

Dust one of the provincial terms denoting money.

Dust uproar, disturbance. *'Kick up a dust.'*

Dust his jacket *C* thrash him.

Dust ta does thou, *'Dust ta wish t'wed oor lass?'*; thou does. (see Dis ta).

Dusta does thou, do you. *'What dusta think?'.*

Duv *C* do. Used chiefly in asking questions in the first person singular, as *'Duv I ?'.*

Dwalla *C* to wither; to turn yellow with decay.

Dwam *C, N* swoon. (rarely used in 1878).

Dwine to wither slowly; to dwindle.

Dwinnel see Dwine.

Dwoat doat.

Dwoted *C, E* doted, foolish.

Dyke *C, SW* hedge.

Dyke dote *C* see Dote.

Dyl't *B* worn down with toil and trouble.

Dyster a dyer.

E *C* the eye; I.

E *SW* in. *'He'll rin or feyt ivver a yan e' aa Cummerlan.'.*

E'bn even.

E'e eye.

Eals *SW* eels.

Ear the kidney.

Ear brig the bar across the hind end of a cart.

Ear fat *C* the fat surrounding the kidneys.

Earan errand; task to perform.

Easter-mun-jiands *C* the *Polygonum bistorta* plant, a common ingredient in traditional herb puddings.

Eb'm even; one of bad character

or habits - *'a bad eb'm.'*.

Eb'm anenst directly opposite. *'It's eb'm anenst t'oald steann byre.'*.

Eb'm endways even endwise, continuous, without interruption. *'He mendi't eb'm endways.'*.

Eb'm fornenst directly opposite. *'It's eb'm fornenst oald Jonty's hoose.'*.

Eb'n even.

Eb'n down thump *C* honestly and truly.

Ebn even.

Eck berry *C* the bird cherry tree, *Prunus padus*.

Eckles hackles.

Edder *N, E, SW* adder.

Edge *C* an elevated and narrow ridge. *eg. Striding Edge* etc.

Edge o'dark *C* evening twighlight, dusk.

Edge o' t'ib'nin *C* evening twighlight, dusk.

Eeals *SW* eels.

Eeast *SW* east.

Eeat *SW* eat.

Eeb'nin' evening.

Eebnin evening.

Een eyes.

Eernin *SW* earning.

Efter after. *'Meet me up t'lonnin efter t'fair.'*.

Efter a bit after a while.

Efter fetches *C* after thoughts or actions.

Efter-neun afternoon.

Efterneun afternoon. *'Gud efterneun ivrybody.'*.

Efterword afterward; a word or expression habitually repeated.

Eg on *C* to urge and encourage. *'Dunnet eg on oald Sam to sing ageun.'*.

Egbattle *C* a person who urges others to quarrel and fight.

Egg berry *C* the bird cherry tree, *Prunus padus*.

Elba' grease hard rubbing or polishing; using hands and elbows.

Elbas elbows.

Elba reel yarn or thread being wound over the elbow, and between the thumb and fore finger. (see Hand reel, Knack reel).

Eldin *N, E* the butter burr plant, *Petasites vulgaris*, once used to as a firelighter.

Eldin' *C* fuel.

Elebben eleven.

Ellar *G* the alder, *Alnus glutinosa*.

Elson a shoemaker's awl, a tool for piercing holes in leather.

Emmal *N* the elm-tree, *Ulmus compestris*.

En *SW* than. *'I's gittan mair en I want.'*.

En' *N* end.

End part. *'A girt end of its for t'oald lass.'*; to set upright. *'End him up, lads, were off heamm'*; the river Ehen was once often pronounced 'end'.

End lang *C* without interruption.

End nor side something so very puzzling *'he could nowder mak end nor side on't.'*.

End on *C* right away.

End whol *C* the ventilating hole in the peak or gable of a barn or other building.

Eneuf *C* enough.

Enny *C, E* any. *'Thay refuse't ta let oald Jwon hev enny mair yal.'*.

Enny way *C* every way. *'This is enny way as good as oor weddin day.'*.

Er *G, not E* are. *'Ho er ye to-day, bonny lass?'*.

Er *NW* nor.

Ern *NE* iron.

Ern fork *NE* a pitchfork or iron fork.

Err *N* a scar from a wound, a cicatrice.

Esh *C, E* the ash tree, *Fraxinus excelsior*.

Esp *B* fastening for a gate, etc; hasp; clasp.

Esp *C* the aspen-tree, *Populus tremulus*. *'He trimmel't like an esp leaf.*

Est *N, E* nest.

Et *C* at.

Et *C, SW* to. *'Gang et thresh.'*. (common in the 18th century).

Ether *N, E, SW* the adder.

Etlins *N* earnings.

Ettle *N* to intend; to aim; to earn.

Eustat' *SW* Easthwaite in Netherwasdale, *'thwaite'* is thus shortened in some instances, but not in all cases.

Ex *SW* ask.

Expect *C* to suppose. *'I expect it's reet.'*.

Ey yes, aye.

Ey an'away *N* right away.

Eyce *NW, SW* ice.

Eydle *NW, SW* idle.

Eye *C* yes. *'Eye, I's gaan to Workiton for a par o'new shun.'*.

Eye sare eyesore, unpleasing or a blemish that may be seen.

Eysh *SW* the ash tree, *Fraxinus excelsior*.

Ez *C* as.

Ezins eaves.

Faa *N, SW* fall; a turn or bout of wrestling.

Faal *N* fold.

Faald *SW* fold.

Faallen wrang *N* become pregnant.

Faan *N, SW* fallen; slaken as lime.

Faat *SW* fault.

Fadder *C, E, SW* father. *'Fadder, carf t'beef at t'teabbel.'*; a child having features resembling those of its father. *'fadder it sel,'* and *'t'fadder's oan barn.'*.

Fadderless stew *B* meal of potatoes stewed without meat.

Fadge *B* applied to a child as accompanying some one. *'Come on, leyl fadge.'*.

Fadge *C* a slow trot. *'Fadge-te-fadge, like t'market-trot.'.*

Faff to mess about or waste time; to work ineffectively. *'Stop faffin abeutt.'.*

Faff *N* fallow.

Faffle *C* to trifle; imperfect fallow.

Faffle *E* a spring fallow for a barley crop.

Fafflement *C* trifling and unnecessary work.

Fag fatigue, *'Fadder was sair fag't efter wark'*; to hang back.

Fag end the worthless remains; the last.

Faggit *N* a term of contempt, usually addressed to a woman.

Faggot a term of opprobrium or reproach. *'An oald faggot!'.*

Faikins *C* a kind of oath.

Fail to be unsuccessful in business, *'Tommy's fail't at shopkeepin'.'*; to die.

Fain glad, anxious, eager.

Fair positive. *'It's a fair sham.'.*

Fairday dyke *C* a boyish attempt to extort gifts from people returning from the fair by obstructing the road with a rope or brushwood.

Fairin's sweets, etc., bought at or brought from a fair for presents.

Fairish tolerably good or moderately satisfactory.

Fairly positively. *'It's fairly good ta nowt.'.*

Fairy rings the dark green rings observable in grass lands - caused by fungi, once believed to be the dancing rings of fairies.

Faith a most binding oath among boys, now an obsolete word.

Faix a most binding oath among boys.

Fal-lals *C* trumpery or trifling ornaments of dress, etc.

Falderment *C* trumpery or trifling ornaments of dress, etc.

Fallops *C* rags hanging about a dress; the dress of an untidy woman.

Fallopy *C* untidy.

Fally like *C* untidy.

Famish famous; notable, *'Wudswurth was a famish poet fray Cockermuth.'.*

Famish'd hungry or starving

Fan *N* found.

Fancical abounding in fancies; fanciful or whimsical; subject to change.

Fand *C, E* found.

Fanticles *SW, NE* freckles on the face, etc.

Far away by much; by far. *'This is far away better than last neet.'.*

Far the weel *C* farewell. *'Fares to weel. Willy! tou's a wag amang t'lasses, an'I'll see the na mair.'.*- Robert Anderson.

Far-ish far, sometimes said when there is a degree of uncertainty over exactly how far. *'Cockermuth is a far-ish lang way fray Ulveston.'.*

Farder farther or further.

Fardest farthest.

Fardin farthing. *(see Farthin').*

Fares taw eel *N, E* farewell. *'Fares taw eel fayther! am off to Workiton.'.*

Farlies *C, N, E* wonders.

Farmaticles *C* freckles on the face, etc.

Farnticles *SW, NE* freckles on the face, etc.

Fart an anal escape of wind, breaking wind.

Farthin' a farthing coin, its value being a quarter of an old penny.

Fash trouble; inconvenience; to get annoyed or exasperated. *'I'll nivver be fash't any mair wid it.'.*

Fashious become annoying or troublesome through intoxication.

Fashy see Fashious.

Fassen *C, E* fasten.

Fasten eve *C, E* Shrove Tuesday evening or the eve of the feast before Lent.

Fat's in t'fire the mischief has begun; all is in a fury or blaze as if fat were thrown on the fire. *'Fat's in t'fire! wid that lass hev'in his barn.'.*

Fatter *N* to hummel (or separate) the awns of barley from the seed.

Faugh *N* fallow.

Faugh! *N* an exclamation of contemptuous dissent.

Fause *E, N* cunning, sly; artful; false.

Faver *C* family resemblance. *'He favers his fadder mair than t'others.'.*

Faver *C, N* fever.

Favver *SW* see Faver.

Fawwnd *C, E, SW* found.

Fawwthy *N, E* kind, liberal.

Fawwthy *SW* bulky; hospitable.

Faymish famous.

Fayther *N* father. *'Oor Fayther forgat t'oald lass's burthday.'.*

Feale *N* fail.

Fearfo' *N* extraordinary. *'They're fearfo' kind fray Kiprangill.'.*

Fearful *C, SW* extraordinary.

Feass face; assurance or boldness. *'He hez a feass for ought.*

Feasst cards court cards.

Feck *N* the main part. *'T'feck o't'wark's deun.'*

Feckless feeble, unsub-stantial.

Fedder *C, N, E* feather.

Feeast *SW* feast.

Feeaver *SW* fever.

Feed *C* provender (or dry food) for cattle; to fatten for slaughter.

Feek *C* to be uneasy or anxious. *'In a feek.'.*

Feel *N* smooth.

Feels *N* fields.

Feester *C, E* fester.

Feg *C* fig; not a care, contemptuous, *'He duzzent care a feg.'.*

Feght *N* fight.

Feight fight. *'Oor digs will nivver feight yan anudder.'.*

Fek *C* eke, enlarge or lengthen, to prolong; to help or aid.

Fell an *N E* one able to fight his way.

Fell heed *C* the top of a mountain not distinguished by a pike.

Fell in wid *C, SW* met with by chance; joined a gang or group.

Fell thrush *N* the missel thrush, *Turdus viscivorus*, a song bird.

Fell yat the gate opening onto the common land upon a fell.

Fell-fo the field-fare.

Fellies felloes, the curved pieces of timber forming the rim of an old wheel.

Fellon grass *C* the plant *Imperatoria Ostruthium*.

Fellon wood *C* the plant *Solanum dalcamara*.

Felt felled; thrown or cut down.

Fend to be able to provide or make a livelihood. *'Sam's a gay fendly laal body.'*; used as a salute. *'How fend ye?'* - how fare you?.

Fendan' an' preuvvan' defending and proving; arguing and debating; criminating and recriminating.

Fent faint.

Fess *C* to send cattle and other livestock to other farms to be grazed.

Fest *C* to send cattle and other livestock to other farms to be grazed.

Fetch a dodge. *'That was a queer fetch, bit it dud n't help him.'.*

Fetch to bring or get. *'Fetch that chair this way.'*; an indrawn breath.

Fettle *B* to beat. *'Aa'l fettle his lug for am.'.*

Fettle to fit; put in order; health or condition. *'What fettle's thy fadder in today?'.*

Feull *C, N, E* fool.

Feur day *E* the dawn or break of day.

Feutloth *E* one-eighth of a stone (fourteen pounds) weight, equates to approx 0.8kg.

Feutt *C* foot, speed, pace. *'He went a parlish feutt ower t'moor.'.*

Feutt axe an axe having the edge turned inwards; an adze. (see Creukt axe).

Feutt bo *C* the game of football; *'Uppies and Downies'* played in Workington every Easter.

Feutt cocks *C, B* the first and smallest of hay stacks, the foot being used in their formation.

Feuttins *B* two turves or turfs set up together to dry.

Few a number or quantity undefined. *'A girt few.'* *'A laal few.'.*

Fewe *SW* few or quickly; *'How does he fu?'*- How does he offer or seem to do? *'I can't fu,'*- I cannot for shame do so; or, I cannot begin it.

Fewl *C* fowl.

Fewsom' shapely, becoming.

Feyne *B* fine, good, handsome, not a problem. *'Jack's a fine laal lad in skeul.'.*

Feyne *N, NW* a term of comparison; as, *'a feyne girt an.'* ....'a feyne laal an.'.*

Feyt *C, E, SW* fight.

Feytin *C* fighting.

Fic-fac *C* the tendon in the neck.

Fidgetty uneasy, impatient.

Field keall *C* wild mustard, *Sinapis arvensis*.

Fiffle-fafflement *C* trifling and unnecessary work.

Fift fifth.

Fig-fag *C* the tendon in the neck.

Figsue *E* a posset of bread, figs, and ale (see Posset).

Fill bow *C, B* a hoop of whalebone used in filling sausages.

Filly fair *C* Palm Sunday was once a day of recreation for young people at Arlecdon, after the children of the parish had attended church. It was referred to as Filly fair day.

Filly fwoal female foal.

Filthment dirt; anything inferior or offensive; low characters.

Fin *N* find.

Fine *C, SW* see Feyne.

Finely *C, SW* healthy. *'I's finely, and fadder's finely an'o'.'.*

Fing-er finger.

Fingers *C, B* the nursery names for the fingers of the hand - *thumpkin, lick pot, lang man, ring man, laal Tommy tidy man.*

Finnd find.

Fir't *C* fired. *'He fir't his gun at the cro.'.*

Fire edge energy of person or animal. *'He gallop't his laal nag till t'fire edge was off.'.*

Fire eldin *C* fuel for the fire.

Fire fang't over-heated.

Fire hoose the dwelling, as opposed to the out-buildings of a farm etc.

Fire smatch't *E* having a burnt smell or flavour.

Firtle *C* to trifle and appear busy.

Fish belly *C* the *Cnicus heterophyllus* plant. The underside of the leaf is white, and turns up in the wind.

Fit disposed.

Fit *N* foot, speed, pace. *'He went a parlish fit ower t'moor.'*; fought.

Fitch the vetch, the leguminous plant, *Sutiva*.

Fiz a hissing noise.

Fiz bo' the puff-ball fungus, *Lycoperdon bovista*.

Fizzer *B* fiz; only it expresses a stronger hissing. Green wood fizzes on the fire; a drop of water on the heated stove - *fizzers*.

Fizzer *C* to punish; to give pain to; to put in a fix.

Fizzle *C* to work busily but ineffectively.

Flacks *C* flakes. *'A strinkle of sna flacks all ower t'yard.'.*

Flaggen *C* slowing down or labouring. *'T'oald horse seemed ta be flaggen a bit.'.*

Flail *C* a wooden instrument once used for trashing or beating grain from the ear by hand; to hit; to beat with a down stroke.

Flail cappin' the leather attached to the upper end of the flail soople. *(see Soople).*

Flail hingin' the leather thong or strap connecting the parts of the flail.

Flailin' a beating.

Flaitch *C* to flatter; a flatterer.

Flak *C* tired or exhausted, liable to go to sleep. *'T'oald lass just flak'd out by t'ingle.'.*

Flake *C* a barred water-heck.

Flakker *C* to laugh heartily as a child does; to flapper.

Flaks *N* turf. (see Toppin peats).

Flam to carjole, flatter grossly, blamey; falsehood told jestingly, not in earnest.

Flan *C, N* flat, shallow. *'They gave us fry't eggs and collops in a flan dish.'.*

Flang did fling; having flung.

Flange *B* to extend in a sloping direction.

Flannin flannel.

Flap *C* a blow scarcely in earnest.

Flap *E* a rude and boisterous girl (or hoyden); to wander or work without a purpose; agitated or disturbed, *'She's just flappan' up and down an' o'about nought.'.*

Flap-daniel *E* a careless and untidy person.

Flapper a young wild duck, *Anus of linn.*

Flapper't *C* nervous, frightened.

Flate afraid.

Flay to frighten.

Flay speadd a spade for paring (cutting or shaving) turf.

Flay-crow *C* a scarecrow.

Flayscarl *E* a scarecrow.

Flaysom' frightful.

Flayt frightened.

Flaytly timidly.

Fleaa to flay; to peel, shave or take the skin off.

Flear floor.

Fleck't marked with large spots or blotches.

Flecky flocker *N* the chaffinch, *Fringilla coelebs.*

Flee fly.

Flee blown maggots newly deposited.

Fleea flay.

Fleean flying.

Fleear *C, N, SW* floor.

Fleece woo' *C* cut, shorn or sheared wool as distinct from pulled or skin wool. To fleece wool is to wind the fleece.

Fleek *C* a frame horizontally suspended from the ceiling joists, on which flitches of bacon, etc., are hung or dried.

Fleek *E* a barred water-heck; a frame horizontally suspended from the ceiling joists, on which flitches of bacon, etc., are hung.

Fleek *N* flitch, a side of salted or air cured bacon.

Fleer *C, B, N* the floor. *'Oor lass has wesh'd the parlour fleer.'.*

Fleer't *B* floored, *'Willy fleer't him in t'ring'* - threw him down on the floor at wrestling.

Fleet *C* the lot; the whole number or quantity. *'Thou's can't t'heall fleet o'them.'.*

Fleet *C, SW* flight.

Fleet *N* to flee or remove, and especially when in debt. *'They mead a moonleet fleet on 't.'.*

Fleetin'dish *C* a craming-dish or skimming-dish.

Fleght *N* flight.

Fleke *E* a barred water-heck; a frame horizontally suspended from the ceiling joists, on which flitches of bacon, etc., are dried.

Fleud flood.

Fleudd flood.

Fleukk *B* feather.

Fleukk *C* the web of the plough sock; a one off; a very lucky win against the odds.

Fleukk the flounder or fluke-fish; the small flat parasitic worms found in a diseased sheep's liver.

Fleur floor.

Fleuss *E* a loose heap of straw or hay, etc.

Fleuterment ridiculous talk.

Fleuzz *C* An unhooped walking-stick is said to be fleuz't when the end is worn (or fringed) by use; bruised.

Fliar to laugh heartily; to laugh and talk loudly.

Flick *C, E, SW* flitch, a side of salted or air cured bacon.

Flinders *C* fragments; broken pieces. *'I'll knock tha o'to flinders.'.*

Flinish *C* the finch.

Flipe *B* to remove quickly. *'He flyp't off his pint, and he flyp't o't'rest off t'teabble, and than he flyp't his sel off.'* (see Flipe).

Flipe *C, SW* the rim of a hat.

Flit *C, N* flight; to flee or remove, especially when in debt. *'They mead a moonleet flit on 't.'.*

Flitches *C* sides or cuts of bacon, etc., hung to air dry.

Flitter *C, N* fritter; fruit cake baked on girdle.

Fllakker *B* applied to the fluttering of the heart. (see Flakker).

Flodder *C* froth; half-dissolved snow.

Flodderment *C* see Flodder.

Floff *C* the lightest of chaff.

Flooar flower; flour.

Floor to knock down; to defeat.

Flother *N* a miry bog.

Flowe *C, N* wild. *'Our filly's varra flowe yet.' 'It's flowe weather.';* bleak and cold.

Flowe *NW* a large, unsheltered

peat bog, as *Solway flowe, Wedholme flowe* etc.

Flowk   the flounder or fluke-fish; the small flat parasitic worms found in a diseased sheep's liver.

Fluer   *SW*   floor.

Fluet   *C*   a stroke. *'Hit him a fluet ower t'lug.'.*

Fluffy   *C*   very light and loose.

Flummery   flattering abundance of words (verbiage or verbosity).

Flummox   *C*   to defeat; to confuse; to put hors de combat (disable to fight).

Flung   deceived; defeated. *'He was fairly flung.'.*

Flush   *B*   equal to the surroundings, an architectural term.

Flush   *C*   to spring a woodcock; to seek out.

Flyte   *N*   to jeer; scold.

Fo   fall; a turn or bout of wrestling.

Fo o'wood   the extent of wood cut in one season.

Fo'en   *C, E*   fallen; slaken as lime.

Fo'out   to quarrel.

Fo'through   *C*   When a arrangement, deal or project fails it is said to fall through. *'Sellin t'farm as fo'through.'.*

Fo-en   *C*   fallen, slaken.

Fo-en skin   *C*   the skin of a domestic animal dying of disease or accident.

Fo-en woo'   *C*   wool pulled from the skins of sheep dying of rot or disease, said to be more liable to be worm-eaten than clipped wool when worked into yarn or cloth.

Foak   *C*   folk.

Foald   *C*   fold. *'Side t'teabbel an' foald up t'cleath.'.*

Foald   to impound stray cattle in a pinfold.

Foaldin'bit   *C*   a triangular piece cut from the edge of a sheep's ear as a mark of ownership.

Foat   fault.

Fog   aftermath.

Foggy   *C*   spongy.

Foil   *B*   following former courses or routes; *'Runnin' oald foils'* - a hunting term.

Foil   *C*   to defile, make filthy or unclean; to corrupt or violate.

Foisty   having a musty scent.

Fole   *N*   fold.

Foll'et   followed.

Followers   store cattle or sheep which follow the fatting stock in turnips; a breeding mare pony has sometimes two or more of her offspring with her on the mountains, and these are called her followers.

Font   *E*   silly.

Foo   *N*   drunk; to fill. *'Foo that cup.'.*

Fooal   *SW*   fool.

Fooat   *SW*   foot, speed, pace. *'He went a parlish fooat ower t'moor.'.*

Foomart   the pole-cat or foul-mart.

Foond   *C*   to purpose; intend. *'I foond to build a house.'* (nearly obsolete in 1878).

Foor   *SW*   furrow.

Foor deer   *B*   front door *'T'foor deer's pent't rid.'.*

Foor dooer   *C*   front door.

Foor doors   *C*   the yard or area directly in front of the house.

Foor-elders   ancestors.

Foor-hand   beforehand.

Foorberin   *C*   fore-warning.

Foormest   foremost.

Foorseet   foresight.

Foorsett   to anticipate; to way-lay.

Foorside   foreside.

Foothy   *C*   bulky, hospitable.

Foothy   *N, E*   kind, liberal.

Footstart   head start or to start before the rest.

For   going. *'Whoar is ta for to-day?'...'I's for Whitten.'.*

For bye   *N*   besides; over and above.

For o'   *G*   although, notwith-standing.

For-dwined   dwindled or vanished away. *(see Dwine).*

For-gat   forgot, forget.

For-git   forgot, forget.

For-ivver   forever; very much or many. *'Theer was for-ivver o'fwok at t'fair.'.*

For-nenst   *C, N*   opposite to. *'Their hoose is eb'n for-nenst ours.'.*

For-nent   *C, N*   opposite to.

For-ther   *N*   farther, further; to forward or promote.

Forder   *C*   to forward; to assist; to promote.

Fore-bears   *N*   ancestors.

Forgat   forgot.

Forgit   forget.

Formable   *C*   properly arranged; in due form.

Formel   *C*   to bespeak. *'He formelt a par o'shun wi'steel cokers and girt heedit nails at t'boddam.'.*

Fornenst   *NE*   opposite to: over against. *(see Anenst.)*

Forra   *SW*   forward, straight.

Forrad   *SW*   forward.

Forrat   *C, N, E*   forward, straight.

Forseakk   forsake.

Forter   *C*   to hummel (or separate) the awns of barley from the seed.

Forth-neet   *C, NW*   an annual merry-making. When flax-spinning by the line (or lint) wheel was in use, the young women would assemble at their neighbours' houses and spend the evening in spinning and singing till bed time. Frequently their sweethearts would call to walk them home.

Forthman   *C, N*   the person in charge or control of a stinted pasture, who directs when the cattle, etc., are grazed.

Fortneth   *C, E*   fortnight.

Fospel whol   *C*   the impression of a horses hooves, or other footprints on soft ground.

Fote   *C, E*   fault.

Foter   *C*   to hummel (or separate) the awns of barley from the seed.

Fots *B* woollen booties, substitutes for shoes in infancy. (see Beutt stockings).

Fots *N* see Beutt stockings.

Fotter *N* to hummel (or separate) the awns of barley from the seed.

Fourt fourth.

Fouthy hospitable; free in giving; ample.

Fower four.

Fowt fought.

Fowt *N* a fondling or foundling. Brockett says, an indulged or spoiled child; any foolish person.

Fox feet *C* the *Lycopodium selago* plant.

Foxy *B* crafty, sly or cunningly.

Foz bog *B* a shaking bog. (see Totter bog).

Fozzy *C* soft as a de-frosted turnip.

Frain't marked with very small spots.

Frap *C* to snap the finger and thumb; the noise of a sudden crack or report.

Fratch a quarrel or disagreement; a noisy quarrel. *'He aye snapt his thooms for a bit of a fratch'.*

Fratchy argumentative.

Frath'an *C, N* quarrelling.

Fray from.

Freckled sky *C* mackerel-like patterned sky.

Fred *E, SW* freed; cleared out.

Free *C* see Tine.

Free *SW* to keep untouched, to remove livestock from a grass field; under no promise or obligation. *'I's free to sell my horse to anybody.'.*

Freedom *B* cease play. (see Barley play).

Freeght *N* fright.

Freelidge the freehold privileges belonging to the burgage tenure.

Freen *N* friend.

Freend *N* friend.

Freet *C, E, SW* fright; fret.

Freet *N* to grieve; to tear.

Freeten frighten.

Freh *N* from.

Frem'd *B* dry cold, and ungenial; applied to weather.

Fremd *SW* strange. .

Fren *C* friend.

Fresh *C* partly intoxicated; the flood of a river as it flows to the sea.

Fresh weather *N* a thaw in cold weather.

Fret *C* to grieve; to tear.

Frev *C, N, SW* from.

Frey *N, NW* from.

Freysh *SW* partly intoxicated; the flood of a river as it flows to the sea.

Frind *C, N, E* friend.

Frizzle fry or roast.

Froff *C* easily broken. *'Froff as a carrot.'.*

Frosk *C* a frog (obsolete 1900).

Frostit *B* frosted; applied to window panes encrusted with frost.

Frostit spoiled by frost; frosted.

Frough *N* easily broken. *'Frough as a carrot.'.*

Frowe a fat and morose woman.

Frowsy *B* an overgrown woman.

Frozen out *C* In a long-continued frost the surface of the ground becomes dry and the roads dusty, and the moisture is then said to be frozen out.

Frudge *N* to press; to brush past or against in a rude manner.

Fruggam *C* a dirty, lazy woman.

Frummety *C* barley or wheat boiled and mixed with milk.

Frush *N* very brittle; crumbly.

Fry pig's liver. *'Mudder sent us a fry o' t'killin' day.'.*

Fu *C* offer. *'How does he fu?'*- How does he offer or seem to do? *'I can't fu,'*- I cannot for shame do so; I cannot begin it.

Fudderment *C* excess of clothing.

Fudderson' *C* troublesome;

annoying.

Fuffy *N* very light and loose.

Full *C, SW* drunk; to fill. *'Full that cup.'.*

Full bump *C* very forcibly.

Full drive very forcibly; in hard earnest. *'This bargaine is full drive.'.*

Fulley *C* ample; large. *'That's a fulley mead gown, Tibby.' 'Ey barn, it's t'fashion to leukk broad now, thou.'.*

Fullins small stones to fill the inside of a wall with; ashes; refuse material.

Fummel a blundering attempt; a fumble.

Fummellan' feast *C* When a married couple are dilatory in producing issue, a few sly neighbours assemble, unbidden, at the house of the barren pair and invite themselves to tea and make merry, and to wish better success.

Fun see Fand.

Fun *N* found.

Fund *C, E* found.

Funk *C* to become frightened or cowardly.

Funny beann *B* the funny bone, the point of the elbow over which the ulnar nerve passes.

Fur *C, E* furrow.

Fur fir.

Fur apples fir-cones.

Furkin firkin.

Furm a long stool or bench; a form.

Furst first.

Furst feutt *N* the person who first enters the house on New Year's day.

Fusom' shapely, becoming.

Fuss bustle; parade; mock business.

Futterson' *C* troublesome; annoying.

Fuz bo' the puff-ball fungus, *Lycoperdon bovista.*

Fuzzen strength; pungency;

briskness.

Fuzzenless insipid; wanting strength or spirit. *'Dud ta nut give her a kiss?'.... 'Nea, kisses is nobbet fuzzenless things.'.*

Fuzzy *E* soft as a frosted turnip.

Fwoal foal.

Fwoal feet the coltsfoot plant, *Tussilago farfara.* The young leaf resembles the impression of the foot of a foal in outline.

Fwok folk. The men say *'woman fwok'* and *'woman body.'* The woman say *'men fwok'* and *'man body.'.*

Fwoor for.

Fwoorarm forearm.

Fwoorneun forenoon.

Fwoorseet foresight.

Fwoorsuer *C* foreshore.

Fwoortelt *C* foretold.

Fwoortin *C* fourteen.

Fwoortun *C* fortune.

Fwor'ge *C* forgive. *'He'll nivver fwor'ge yer.'.*

Fworce *C, SW* a waterfall; as *Scale Force* etc.

Fworce force.

Fwore-elders ancestors.

Fwore-hand beforehand.

Fworeivver *C* forever.

Fworemest foremost.

Fworivver forever.

Fworsuer *C* for sure; a certainty.

Ga *C, SW.* go.

Ga'me *C* gave me.

Gaan going.

Gab the mouth; idle talk. *'Mary gabs on fworeivver an' tells yer nowt.'.*

Gabble to talk quickly and not wisely.

Gadgee person (usually male) *'Look at yon gadgee fra Wigton.'.*

Gadwands *E* see Yadwands.

Gaffer *C* governor; master. Thought to have been introduced with the railways.

Gah *C* go. *'I's gah t'toon this efterneun.'.*

Gaily fine, merry, jolly, jovial, in high spirits. *'I's gaily. How's thou?'.*

Gain *N* handy; near. *(see Bain).*

Gaird *NW* guard.

Gairn *N* yarn.

Gallas a person of evil conduct; the gallows.

Gallases *C* braces; suspenders.

Gallon *C* an old English measure for both dry and liquid goods. For liquids this was equivalent to eight pints (4.546 litres). The 'corn gallon' equated to 268.6 cubic inches in volume, a little less than the imperial gallon introduced during the late 19th century.

Galloway a stout pony or cob.

Gally balk *N* the beam on which the chimney crook hangs.

Gally boke *N* see Rannel boke.

Galoor *C* abundance.

Galore *C* abundance.

Gam *NW* a game of cards.

Gam *NW, E* game.

Gamashers *E* gaiters.

Game leg a lame leg.

Gamish the flavour of meat, etc., too long kept. (pronounce the a as in game, not as in famish.).

Gamman *B* not in earnest; making fun or game of.

Gammel gamble.

Gammerstang a tall and awkward person.

Gammy *N* sore; lame.

Gan *N* go.

Gang *B* turn to play or go. *'Its thy gang noo.'.*

Gang go.

Gang thy ways *C* This merely signifies 'go,'and is becoming obsolete (1878). *'Gang thy ways and fetch watter.'.*

Gangan going.

Gangan forth *C, NW* see Forth-neet

Gangan time *C* a course of free living; a busy time.

Gangin's on proceedings, events. *'Ey, theer was fine gangin's on at t'weddin'.'.*

Gangs *C, E, SW* goes, *'He gangs out iv'ry neet to t'inn.'.*

Gans *N* goes, *'He gans iv'ry day to see t'oald lass at yem.'.*

Gantree a clumsy stool or frame for resting ale-casks upon; a wooden bridge or scaffold structure.

Gap rails round poles let into stone or wooden posts in place of gates.

Gap stead the entrance to a field closed by gap rails.

Gar to compel. *'A'll gar tha gang.'.*

Garn *C, SW* yarn.

Garn winnels *C* a wooden cross from which yarn is wound off.

Garrak *C* awkward. *'As garrak as a unbroken cowt.'.*

Garron *C* a tall and awkward horse.

Garron *N* anything high or tall and ungainly.

Garth garden; a small enclosure near the house, as the *Calf-garth, Hemp-garth, Stack-garth, Apple-garth,* etc.

Gas *C* goes.

Gat got. *'Our taty tops gat a snapin' wi'frost.'.*

Gatin's sheaves of corn set up singly to dry.

Gaut a male or castrated pig.

Gavel-dyke *C* a section of fencing liable to be maintained by a farm not adjoining to it. *Gavel-dykes* were mostly adjoining commons lands, and the origin seems to have been for relieving the farms next the commons from the cost of repair and trespass occasioned by sheep newly turned out onto the common.

Gawky *N* a staring idiotical person; awkward; ungainly.

Gawvison *N* a noisy and foolish

person; a simpleton.

Gawwn *SW.* gown or dress.

Gay fine, merry, jolly, *'A gay fine day.'*; jovial, in high spirits, slightly intoxicated. Now all above superseded by a homosexual of either sex.

Gayly fine, merry, jolly, jovial, in high spirits, slightly intoxicated. *'We hed a gayly fine time last neet.'.*

Gayshen *N* an emaciated person, one reduced almost to a skeleton; a silly-looking person.

Gaz *C, N, SW* goes. *'She nivver gaz to see yer mam.'.*

Ge give. *'Ge me that.'.*

Ge'en given. *'He's ge'en tul't'- he is disposed to it.*

Geaa *C* go - a hunting term. *'Hoo geda hark to Towler!'.*

Geall *C* to ache with cold; to grieve or pain (formerly 1878).

Gealls *N* the cracks and fissures in seasoned timber.

Gean *C, N, E* gone.

Geann gone.

Geann wid it in the way of recovery.

Geap gape, yawn.

Geapp gape; to yawn.

Geapps a disease among fowls.

Geatt gate, path, foot-trod, way. *'Git out o'my geatt.'.*

Geavlick *N* see Geavlock.

Geavlock *C* an iron crowbar.

Gedder gather.

Gee *C* offence, *'He's teaun t'gee.'.*

Gee give. *'Gee me that.'.*

Gee's *N* gives; give us.

Geer wealth; cart and plough-hamess, *'He talk't about car geer an' middins, An't'reet way to mannish a farm.'.*

Gees *N* gives; give me.

Geggin *C* a small tub having a long stave for a handle. (see Hanny).

Geggles *E* a game something like nine-pin or ten pin bowling). Geggle alleys existed in many villages within living memory (1878).

Geggles a giddy girl; a careless horse with a high and unsteady head.

Geh *N* gave. *'He geh t'hoose to mither, when t'berry'd fayther.'.*

Geld cows not in calf.

Geld grund *C* a mining term signifying ground devoid of minerals.

Gemkeeper *C* gamekeeper.

Gemlek *N* gimlet. (see Gimlek).

Gentle an' semple *C* the upper and lower classes of society.

Gentles maggots of the bluebottle fly, used for bait.

Gether gather.

Geud *N* good.

Geudd *N* good.

Geus *C, N, E* goose.

Geuss *C, N, E* goose.

Geuss beuk *E* the goose book or register - which recorded the foot and other marks of each flock of geese kept in the parish of Kirkland, whereby each may be identified in case of being mixed with other flocks, or of straying.'.

Geuss bow bow hung round a goose's neck to prevent it creeping through hedge.

Geuss flesh a roughened state of the skin occasioned by a chill.

Geuss grass *C* the plant *Galium Aparine.*

Gev *C* give. *'She gev a knattle on t'flags wid her heel.'.*

Gev *C, E, SW* gave. *'He gev sek a shout!'.*

Geyde *NW, SW* guide.

Gez *SW* goes. *'He gez wid her to church iv'ry sunday.'.*

Gezlin *C, E* gosling.

Ghem *C* game.

Ghyll a ravine.

Gi 'them 't give thee, give thee it, give it to them.

Gi'tha give thou; give thee, give thee it, give it to them.

Gi'the 't give thou it; give thee, give thee it, give it to them.

Gi'thee *C* give thee or give you.

Gidder gather.

Gif *N* if.

Gifts white specks on the fingernails, once said to indicate certain events in life.

Gildert *C* a number of snares attached to a hoop for catching small birds on the snow.

Gill a ravine.

Gilt *C, SW* a young sow intended for breeding purposes.

Gimlek *C* gimlet, a bradawl-like instrument with a pointed srew end for boring holes in wood by hand.

Gimlik *SW* gimlet. (see Gimlek).

Gimmer a female sheep not exceeding two years old.

Gimmer clout *C* cloth sewed on the ewe's hind quarters to prevent procreation or reproduction.

Gin given. *'He's gin yer hoose t'lad.*

Gin *N* if. *'Gin ye'll gan I'll gan.'.*

Gin keass *C, B* a building to shelter horses when drawing machinery, as in a horse gin.

Ginnel lane or narrow passage.

Ginners the gills of fish.

Girdle a circular iron baking plate.

Girn *C* grin or pull a face.

Girse *C, SW* grass, *'Theer laal girse in our girsin' field t'year.'.*

Girse cocks *C* small cocks of newly-cut grass.

Girt *C* great; friendly.

Girt *NE* great.

Girt bees *C* drone bees.

Girt goods *C* the larger domestic animals, such as cattle and horses.

Girtin's *N* girthings.

Giss nor sty *C* When a person does not speak or answer, it was often said *'He nowder says giss nor sty.'.*

Giss! call notes for swine.

Gissy! call notes for swine.

Git get; offspring. *'They're o'his oan git.'.*

Git it *C* get it; receive it. (see Thou'll git it).

Git shot *C* get rid of; dispose of. *'They wantit to git shot on him.'.*

Git'n got, gotten, *'He's git'n his crowdy.'.*

Gittan *G, not E* getting. *'He's gittan it iv'ry whoar.'.*

Gitten got, gotten.

Give mouth to speak out; to give tongue - a hunting phrase.

Give ower stop or leave off. *'Is 't gaan to give ower sno'an think ye?'.*

Giz *C, E, SW* gives; give us or me.

Gizzern *C* gizzard. *'It sticks in his gizzern,'-* he remembers it with unpleasant feelings.

Gizzin *N* gizzard. *(see Gizzern).*

Glad *C, SW* working smoothly.

Glasser glazier.

Glasses spectacles.

Glaz't *C* varnished or covered with dirt.

Glazener glazier.

Glead a kite, *Falco milvus* - now a scarce bird (1878) but once common.

Gleb *N* sharp, quick. *'He's gleb at that job.'.*

Glee *C, N* to squint.

Gleg *N* sharp, quick. *'He's gleg at that job.';* working smoothly.

Glenderan' *C* looking earnestly.

Glent *C* glance.

Gleuv *N* glove.

Gleuvv *N* glove.

Gleym *N* to look sidewise.

Gliff a transient view. *'I just gat a gliff on't.'.*

Glime *C* to look sidewise.

Glint *N* glance.

Glisk *C* glance in the sunlight; a flash of reflected light. *'It'll rain afoor neet, it's seah glisky this mwornin'.'.*

Gloer *C, SW* to stare.

Gloor *N* to stare.

Gloot *SW* lout.

Glop *C, SW* to stare; to look wildly.

Gloppers *SW* see Blinders.

Glore *N* soft dirt.

Glower *N* to stare or glare.

Glowt *SW* a clumsy fellow.

Glum gloom, gloomy; to frown.

Glump't *N* gloomed or sulked.

Glwore *C, SW* to stare.

Go bon! *C* a sort of oath.

Goam *N* to regard; take care of.

Gob *C, N* mouth. *'Shut yer gob, or I'll shut in fwor yer.'.*

Gob the mouth; idle talk; to spit.

Gobstick *N* a wooden spoon.

Gocks dillies! an exclamation of gladness.

Goddy *N* a sponsor.

Godspeed *C* a wooden screen within the door.

Goe *E* a weak spring in an arable field (see Keld).

Goff *C, SW* a fool.

Gok sonn! an exclamation of surprise.

Goller *C, N* to shout; to bark or talk loudly.

Gollick *E* see Gullock.

Gommarel *N* an awkward and silly person.

Gone back *C* declined in health or substance.

Gone bye his sel *C* gone deranged.

Gone wid it *C* having accomplished it; recovered.

Gooas *SW* goose.

Good *C* congratulate. *'He may good his sell' on't, for he'll git na mair.'.*

Good an' with spirit; ener-getically. *'Jack set to wark like a good an'.'.*

Good an'o' entirely. *'He's gone for good an'o'.'.*

Good eb'n good evening.

Good few a fair number. *'A good few fwolk was ter last neet.'.*

Good for yan, Good for another applicable to all alike.

Good man the husband.

Good to nought *C* good for nothing.

Good to ought *C* good for anything.

Goodin' *B* indulging. *'Yer faythers goodin' his sel.'.*

Goodish goodly. *'A goodish swort of a fellow.'.*

Goodlike good-looking; handsome.

Goon *C, N, E* gown or dress.

Goose gogs gooseberries.

Gope *C* to shout. *'A girt gopan geuss! thou's hov nin on him.'.*

Goppers *SW* see Blinders.

Gorlin' *C, N* an unfledged bird. *'As neakkt as a gorlin'.'.*

Gormow *N* a clownish fellow; sometimes applied to a groat eater.

Gorps See Bare Gorps.

Gorrish *C* gross; over-luxuriant.

Gowan See Oppen gowan and Lockin gowan.

Gowd *C, N* gold. *'Gowd I'gowpius,'* - gold in handfuls.

Gowe *C* go.

Gowk *C* the cuckoo; a fool; the core.

Gowk the core. *'It's badly burnt lime - it's nought bit gowks.'.*

Gowl the howl of a dog; to weep.

Gowpin a handful; or the two hands full.

Gowze *C* to burst out suddenly; a rush or gush of fluid. *'Water com' gowzan' out.'.*

Goyster *C, N* to vociferate; to bully. *'He's a girt goysteran' foul.'.*

Grab *C* to snatch at; to lay hold of quickly; grasp.

Graft *B* a grave.

Graidly *SW* proper; good. (seldom

heard 1878).

Grain't forked; divided.

Grains prongs, eg. *Fork grains, Otter grains* etc.

Graith *N* wealth; horse-gear.

Graith't *N* dressed, apparelled, accoutred.

Grally *B* disturbance. *(see Skrowe).*

Gran *N* grand, *'Yer granfadder's varra old.'.*

Grane *N* groan.

Granfadder grandfather.

Granky *E* crotchety; sickly or unwell and complaining, *'Nobbet varry granky.'* (see Cranky).

Grape *N* grope, feel.

Grape *N* grope; to feel.

Grapple *C* to catch fish by hand in a brook; to wrestle.

Grass cocks *C, B* the first and smallest of haycocks or stacks, the foot being used in their formation.

Grass nail *C* a small iron hook connecting the scythe blade with the shaft.

Grassom a ancient manorial rent in lieu of fines.

Grat *N* wept.

Grater feast *C* much marked with small pox scares.

Grave *C, SW, N* to dig with a spade.

Grawe *C, E* grow.

Gray beard *C* grey stone bottle.

Gray feass *C* grey stone bottle.

Gray hen *N* grey stone bottle.

Gray yoads grey mazes - a circle of stones near Cumwhinton.

Grayseunn *C* Greysouthen village and township - anciently *Crakesothen.*

Greamm the surname - Graham. This has probably originated from Græhame.

Grean *C, E* groan.

Greane *N* groan.

Greann *C* groan, *'Greannan' like a snerp't fox.'.*

Greap *C, E* grope, feel.

Greapp *C* grope; to feel.

Greapp *N* grope; to feel; a dung-fork.

Greased shun greased shoes - time was when *'weel greas't shun'* was the prevailing mode with common people, before a time when they were polished.

Greath't *N* dressed, apparelled, accoutred.

Greav grave.

Greavv *C, SW* to dig with a spade.

Gree agree. *'They're about 'greeax for a horse.'.*

Greean *SW* groan.

Greeap *SW* grope; to feel; the space behind the cows in stalls; anciently a sink; a privy.

Greeas *SW* grease.

Greeat *SW* great; greet; friendly.

Greeaz *SW* grease.

Greeaz *SW* to apply grease.

Green side up arable land in grass.

Greenhew a payment once made to lords of manors for the privilege of cutting underwood in the lord's forests for flails, scythe and pitchfork shafts, swill wood, besoms, snow-poles, fell-poles, pea-sticks, etc.

Greeny *C* the green finch or linnet.

Greet *C, N* to weep; to deplore.

Greet great; greet; friendly.

Greg *C* to mortify the mind.

Grend *SW* ground, grind.

Grend *SW* ground.

Gret *N* wept.

Greunn *C* a swine's snout; a projecting upper lip.

Greupp *C* the space behind the cows in stalls; anciently a sink; a privy.

Greuvv hoose a hut on a coal-pit bank.

Greuvvs places from whence coal, slate, etc., have been dug.

Greymin' *N* a thin covering of snow, etc. (see Lymin).

Greymy *N* sooty, begrimed.

Greyp *N* a dung-fork.

Grimes flakes of soot.

Grimin' *C* a thin covering of snow, etc. (see Lymin).

Grimy *C* sooty, begrimed.

Grin *N* ground, grind.

Grip *C* a narrow and shallow gutter.

Grip to take firm hold of. (see Grip).

Gripe *C* a dung-fork.

Grissle *C, N, E* gristle, cartilage.

Groats shelled oats.

Groo *N, NE* a cold state of the atmosphere.

Groop *N* the space behind the cows in stalls; anciently a sink; a privy.

Groosam' *N* grim; dark and morose; coarse-featured.

Grosers *NE* gooseberries.

Grosk *C* freely grown; gross; fat.

Grosser grocer.

Grossers *NE* gooseberries.

Grout thin mortar.

Grouty *C* rather muddy.

Groven dug with the spade.

Growan growing; grown. *'H's growan int' a reet pleesant la'al lad.'.*

Growe *C, E* grow.

Gru *N, NE* a cold state of the atmosphere.

Grumfy *C* complaining, ailing or believing to be so.

Grummel grumble.

Grumpy *C* complaining, ailing or believing to be so.

Grun *N* ground, grind.

Grund *C, E* ground, grind.

Grundswaith *C* the ragwort plant, *Seaecio Jacobæa.*

Grundswathe *C* the ragwort, *Senecio Jacoboea.*

Grundwark foundation of a wall; the groundwork.

Grunsel *N* see Grundswathe.

Grunstan' grindstone.

Grup *N* the space behind the cows in stalls; anciently a sink; a privy.

Grussle *C, N, E* gristle, cartilage.

Gryke *C* a crevice or ravine in the side of a fell or hill.

Grype *C* to mortify the mind.

Gud *C* good.

Gudge *C, B* a scooping chisel; a gouge.

Guff *N* a fool.

Gull *C* the corn marigold, *Chrysanthemum segetum.*

Gullock *E* a deep gully or ravine; a deep cut or slash.

Gulls *E* mosses given to sick cattle; gruel prepared for calves.

Gully *C, SW* a butcher's knife; a large knife used for slicing bread and cheese; a hollow or slack between hills.

Gumption sense. *'He's nivver gat the gumption to see it's 'rang.'.*

Gumption *C* spirit, wit, sense, shrewdness.

Gurdle *N* a circular iron baking plate.

Gurn *C, N* grin or pull a face. *'Give ower gurnin' lass or thou'll git it.'.* (see Set a feass).

Gurse *N* grass.

Gurt *C* great.

Gurt *N* great; friendly.

Gurth *C, E* girth.

Gut a glutton; one who endulges of anything in excess.

Gutlin' *C* a gormandiser - a greedy or voracious eater.

Gwoat goat.

Gwol *C* a deep pool.

Gwordy *C* the name George; people from the North East of England (Geordies).

Gworge *N* the name George.

Gyverous *C* eating greedily; very anxious.

Gyversom' *G, C* eating greedily; very anxious.

H'ard heard. *'He niver h'ard tell on't.'.*

HInmest o'three *B.* a game played on village greens.

Ha-way *SW* go along; come on.

Haa *N, NE, SW* hall.

Haa *SW* a word used in guiding ⸱orses to the left; come hither.

Haa *SW* the fruit of the hawthorn, *Oxyacanthra.*

Haak *N, E, SW* hawk.

Haak an' spit to clear the throat and spit out; to expectorate forcibly.

Haald *SW* hold; shelter. *'T' hev and t' haald.'.*

Haapenny *N* halfpenny.

Hack a pickaxe having points about an inch in width; a hackney horse.

Hack't *C* cracked hands from cold or neglect.

Hackin *C* a pudding of mincemeat and fruit - until lately eaten for the family breakfast on Christmas day (1878).

Had *N* hold; shelter.

Had bye *N* stand out of the way.

Hadder *N* to drizzle; small rain or showers. *'It hadders and rains on.'.*

Haddit *N* held.

Hae *C* hare; hair.

Haf *N* half.

Haf thick *N* foolish person; a half-fatted animal.

Hafe half.

Haffets *N* locks of hair on the temples or upper forehead.

Haffle *N* to be undecided.

Haflins half-done; half-witted; half-shares.

Hag *C, E* a woody place intermixed with grass land.

Hag hack, to hew or chop with an axe.

Hag clog *C, N* a chopping-block.

Hag stock *C* a chopping-block.

Hagg an old or ugly woman; a derisive term for a female. *'Toald hag knaa's nowt n'summat.'.*

Haggan'at it *C* persevering or persisting to hardwork or labour.

Hagger a coal-hewer.

Haggis *N* see Hackin.

Haggis *NE* a pudding of mincemeat for eating with potatoes on Christmas day.

Haggle *C* to tease in bargaining; to overwork; to fatigue.

Haggle *N* to cut with a blunt knife which requires a sawing motion. (see Hassel).

Hagh ye! *N* hark ye; listen. (seldom used 1878).

Hagworm *C* a snake.

Hail *W* see Hale.

Hain *N* to preserve grass, etc.; untouched.

Hainch *N* haunch; the hip.

Hairly *N* hardly; scarcely.

Hake *C* a convivial assembly or dance; to tire; to distress. As applied to land, it indicates exhaustion from over-cropping.

Hake *N* a lean horse or cow; to butt with the horns or head.

Hakes *C* doings, happenings or events. *'Sek hakes at t'fair last neet!'.*

Hakker *C* to stammer. *'He hakkers an'gits nin on wid his talk.'.*

Hale *C* to do forcibly; to drive the ball to the winning-post. *'T'Uppies haled the ball at Workiton t'year.'. (see Feutt bo).*

Hale *W* the goal at Workington's Easter football. The *'Uppies or Downies'* need to hail or throw the ball in the air at a certain point to win the contest.

Haler *C* one who works or does anything energetically and effectively. *'Dick's a haler at it.'.*

Hallan entrance.

Hallan *C* the division between two horse or cow stalls.

Hallan *N* the partition within the entrance of an old-fashioned farm-house.

Hallion *N* a long hungry-looking

fellow. *'A girt lang hallion.'.*

Ham sam *C* promiscuous; all in confusion.

Hammer-band *C* up-hill work, constant pull on the shoulders; Hammer-band yoking -In old times the horse was yoked to the cart by ropes from the shoulders to iron, willow or hazel rings sliding on the shafts, held by a pin.

Hammer-bleat *C* the snipe. In the breeding season the note of the male bird resembles the bleating of a goat.

Han' hand.

Han'clout a towel or hand cloth.

Hanch *C* to snap as a dog does when it bites suddenly.

Hand direction. *'He's gone toward Ireby and that hand.'.*

Hand breed a hand's breadth.

Hand reel hands are held apart so yarn, thread etc. *can* be wound into hanks. a count was often made by repeating *'yan to yan, two to yan, thou's yan; yan to two, two to two, thou's two'* and so on.

Hand runnan' quickly and continuously; successively.

Hand's turn any sort of hand labour, digging etc. *'He will n't set to ya hand's turn!'.*

Handstaff the first half of the flail, used for threshing corn etc.

Hang leet get down; let go. *'Hang leet o'tha for mischief!'.*

Hangarel see Hanniel.

Hangarel *N* a long hungry-looking fellow. (see Hallion).

Hangment *C* devil or hangman; an exclamation of surprise. *'What the hangment 's you?'*;be very severe. *'He'll play the hangment wid ye.'.*

Hank *C* an evil habit. *'He has a hank o'gangan out at'neets.'*; to fasten with a hoop or loop.

Hank efter *C* a wish, longing or desire. (see Hankeran').

Hankeran *C, E, N* a wish, longing or desire. *'He still hez a hankeran' for yer lass Jonty.'.*

Hankisher *C* handkerchief.

Hankle *C* to entangle.

Hanklin *C, E, N* a wish, longing or desire. (see Hankeran').

Hankutcher *N, E* handkerchief.

Hanless *C* making free use of the hands or handsfree.

Hannel handle; a large pail or bucket.

Hanniel *C* a long hungry-looking fellow. *'A girt lang hanniel.'.*

Hanny *N* a tub having a long handle.

Hannykit *N* see Hanny.

Hansel to use for the first time; the price of the first article sold or the first money received.

Hant haunt.

Hantel *N* a large quantity; a number of.

Hap to cover. *'She hap't o't'barns at bed-time.'.*

Hap'm *C* happen. *'Hap'm I see thee in t'mwornin'.'.*

Happins *C* thick woollen bed-covers woven carpet-wise.

Hapshy rapshy at random, haphazard.

Har *C* the stronger end of a gate.

Hard *C* hardy. *'He's as hard as a fell teadd.'*; turning sour - said of beer, etc.

Hard heard. *'I hard whiff of thy news last neet.'.*

Hard heeds *SW* a large trout found in the streams of Esk, Irt, Mite, Bleng and Calder.

Hard laid on much oppressed.

Hard tell heard of. *'I nivver hard tell o'see a thing.'.*

Hard-faver't coarse-featured.

Harden jacket *E* a loose and light jacket worn over the shirt when stripped for work; a top shirt, commonly of linen.

Harden kytle *E* a loose jacket once worn by girls when employed in attending cattle or in outdoor work.

Hardfully *C* industriously. *'Bob gits his leevin reet hardfully.'.*

Harns *N* brains.

Harp on complain excessively and repeatedly; to often refer to an unpleasant subject or event.

Harrial *C* heriot, an ancient tribute or fee payable on the death of an owner, landholder etc.

Harrish harass.

Harrishin' *N* violent invasion; harrying.

Harrow bulls the ribs of a wooden harrow.

Harry to harry; to rob.

Harry *N* to rob.

Hartree *C* the strong end of a gate.

Hartsom' lively, cheerful.

Harvel *N* a foolish fellow.

Hash *C* harsh.

Hash a term seldom used except to signify defeat. *'Settle his hash.'.*

Hask *C* dry and cold weather; unkindly. *'Your cow hez a hask hide on her.'.*

Hassle *C* to cut with a blunt knife which requires a sawing motion.

Hat did hit.

Hat-shave the two covering sheaves of a cornstook or stack.

Hath ye! *N* hark ye; listen. (seldom used 1878).

Haugh *N* flat alluvial land by the riverside; a holm.

Havver *C, SW* oats.

Havy Skavy *C* all in confusion.

Haw *C, E* the fruit of the hawthorn, Oxyacanthra.

Hawbuck *C* a forward and vulgar young fellow.

Hawse a mountain pass.

Hawwnd *SW* hound.

Hawws *SW* house; the apartment

into which the front door opens.

Hawwse *SW* house.

Hay hey, often spoken to grab someones attention; what did you say?.

Hay *N* have. *'I hay'the noo.'* - I comprehend.

Hay bay disturbance.

Hay bote the right of cutting a specified quantity of hay-grass from the property of another.

Hay dote *C* see Dote.

Haygang *C* the gangway leading from the barn or hayloft to the cow-stalls.

Hayness *C* heinous - great, monstrous, extraordinary etc. *'Hayness fine.'* or *'Hayness dirty.'.*

Haypenny *C, SW* halfpenny.

Hayster to starve; An animal severely pinched by hunger and cold is hayster't.

Hazed extreme hoarseness.

Head head; hid.

Headd hid.

Heaf the part of the mountain or moor on which any flock is accustomed to depasture.

Heaf gangan' *C, SW* mountain sheep let along with a farm and depastured on a particular part of the common termed their heaf.

Heal whole.

Heall whole. *'Now giz us t'heall story, nut just yer side of gangin's on.'.*

Heall watter an extremely heavy rain. *'It com down heall watter.'.*

Heam home.

Heamly homely.

Heamm home.

Heamm comin' returning. *'I whope thou'll hev a hearty heamm comin'.'.*

Heamm spun *C, SW* linen or woollen spun at home; unpolished. *'He's a real heamm spun an.'.*

Heamm teuny *E* a stronghold or place of security.

Heammly homely.

Heams *C, E, SW* hames.

Hear hair; hare.

Hearr hair; hare.

Heart abeunn always hoping, never despairing. *'He hez a sair tue on't, bit he's heart abeunn still.'.*

Heart's wind *C* at the very top speed. *'They wrought at heart's wind o't'day.'.*

Hearten to comfort, to encourage.

Hearth ceakk a cake baked on the hearth.

Heasst haste.

Heast *C, E* haste; hasten.

Heat hot.

Heather cowe *N* a stem of heather.

Heather-bleat *N* the snipe. In the breeding season the note of the male bird resembles the bleating of a goat.

Heatt hot; rather hot.

Heck *C* a half-door, a small gate; the short passage way and partition at entrance into the living quarters of an old through-passage Cumberland farmhouse.

Heck an' ree ancient terms used in guiding horses to right or left, and now (1878) only used in reference to an obstinate person or horse who will *'nowder heck nor ree.'.*

Heck board *N* the board closing the back end of the cart.

Heck-berry *N, E* the bird cherry tree, *Prunus padus.*

Heckles a hackles; the neck feathers of a cock.

Hed had.

Hed n't had not.

Hedder heather.

Hedder-feass't rough-faced, unshaven. *'Yer fadders still reet hedder feass't.'.*

Hedge bote the right of getting hedging wood from the property of another.

Hedn't *C* had not.

Hee *C, N, E* high.

Hee leet day *C* broad daylight. *'They drank and sang till hee leet day.'* - from an old song.

Heead *SW* head.

Heeadlin' *SW* head rig or head land.

Heeals *SW* heels.

Heeap *SW* heap, a good many. *'Heeaps o'things.'.*

Heeard heard. *'I heeard about yer weddin' fray t'curate.'.*

Heed *C, N* head.

Heed-yak *SW* headache.

Heed-yik *N* headache.

Heedam acrossam *C* all in disorder, like hay and straw.

Heedlin' *C, N* head rig or head land.

Heedstan' head stone, a memorial or gravestone.

Heedwark *C* headache.

Heedy heady, intoxicating. *'This beer's varra heedy.'.*

Heemest highest.

Heemm *C, SW* home, *'Expect we'll soon git heamm to bed.'.*

Heerin herring.

Heese *N, SW* hoist.

Heet height.

Heffle *SW* to be undecided.

Heft haft; the handle of a small tool; have it.

Heft *N* to prevaricate. (see Heaf gangan').

Hefted *N* see Heaf.

Hefter *C, N, E* an effective speech or operation, such as driving the dagger up to the haft or hilt.

Heftin' a beating.

Heid *C, SW* head.

Hekkap hiccup.

Helliday *C* holiday.

Helm wind *E* an atmospheric phenomenon prevalent on the west side of Crossfell.

Helpsom' *C* ready and willing to help. *'Oor Mary's nut varra help-som.'.*

Helse *C* a rope to loop round a horse's neck in place of a halter.

Helter halter.

Helter for helter *C* swopped or exchanged. Among the lowest class of horse-dealers this term denotes an exchange of horses without any money being exchanged.

Helter-skelter hurry and confusion.

Hemmer *N* hammer.

Hemp dub a small pond used for steeping green hemp.

Hemplin *C* the red or brown linnet, *Fringilla linota*; a headrig sown with hemp seed.

Hempy *N* a mischievous character, one who bids fair to deserve hanging.

Hen bokes the attic of a shed where poultry are accustomed to roost.

Hen cawwer *SW* to cower or sit down as the hen sits.

Hen coor *C, N* to cower or sit down as the hen sits.

Hen drunks *C* The fruit of the mountain ash, *Pyrus aucupariia* is reputed to possess the property of intoxicating fowls.

Hen pen *C* the yellow-rattle plant, *Rhinanthus crista galli*.

Hen scarts *E* a peculiar form of cloud indicating wind.

Hen shun *C* cloth shoes put on the feet of poultry to prevent them scratching in gardens.

Hen silver *E* money begged at the church door after a wedding.

Hench *C, E, SW* haunch, hip.

Hennet *N* have not.

Hensegam *C* the village of Hensingham, near Whitehaven.

Hensigem *C* the township and village of Hensingham.

Hensigem fortune was a pair of pattens and a white apron. (100 years ago in 1878).

Hent to plough up the bottom furrow between ridges.

Herd *C, SW* hoard.

Herd up *C, SW* to hoard. '*Weel may he be rich, for he's been herdan'up o'his life.*'.

Herdwicks *C* the mountain sheep of the west of Cumberland. These are reputed to have originated from about forty which swam ashore from a wrecked Norwegian vessel. They were taken possession of by the lord of the manor, and on their increase, being found hardy an

Hereabouts *C* in this neighbourhood.

Hereaway in this neigh-bourhood.

Herensew *C* the heron.

Herple *C* to walk lame; to limp.

Herrinsho *N* the heron.

Herry *N, E* harry, rob.

Hes has.

Hes ta has thee or has thou?, have you? '*Hes ta come fray yer teas.*'.

Hesp *C* fastening for a gate, etc.; hasp; clasp.

Het hot; rather hot; to heat; heated.

Het feutt *C, SW* in a great hurry. '*He's het feutt'd it ower theer to see her.*'.

Het trod *N* in close pursuit. '*He follow't the reivers on the het trod.*'.

Het yal and a stick in't *C* hot ale with spirits in it.

Hettish hot; rather hot.

Heud hid.

Heudd hid.

Heudds the two covering sheaves of a cornstook or stack.

Heugh *N* a dry dell; a grassy ravine without water.

Heukk hook; the crest or point of the hip-bone.

Heukster *C, E* a huckster or small trader.

Heupp hoop, a six-quart (or 12 pint) measure, formerly made of a broad wooden hoops.

Heusins *C* the husks of nuts.

Heuzz *C, N* a dry cough.

Hev have. '*I hev'the noo.*'- I comprehend.

Hev at to set to or begin a task.

Hevvent have not.

Hevy Skevy *N* all in confusion.

Hey *C, SW* high.

Hey howe ham! unmeaning exclamations, often used when yawning.

Hey howe! unmeaning exclamations, often used when yawning.

Heyde *N* hide.

Heyde *N* hide; to beat.

Hez has, hath '*He hez tha noo*'- he is thy master.

Hezzel hazel, to beat or thrash. '*I'll hezzle thee.*'.

Hezzle hazel.

Hezzle mowd the fine powdery soil around the roots of the hazel. Sick cattle are fond of this soil when re-covering.

Hide *C, E, SW* hide; to beat.

Hidlins anything hidden or put out of sight.

Hiffle *C* to be undecided.

Higgelty piggelty *C, N* intermixed or mixed about; heads and tails.

Hikkelty pikkelty *SW* see Higgelty piggelty.

Hills ageann slacks to set hills against slacks is to equalize matters by giving and taking.

Hilth health.

Himmest hindmost.

Himsel' himself.

Hin en' *N* hinder, opposite or back end.

Hinch *N* haunch, hip.

Hinder ends *C* refuse or light corn blown out of the hinder end of the winnowing machine.

Hindermest hindmost.

Hindersom' *C* anything that retards, prevents or hinders. '*Yer

Mary's reet hindersom' ower the weddin.'.

Hine hind; a manager of an off-lying farm.

Hine berries N raspberries, Rubus idoeus.

Hing hang. *'Hing on Jack, lets gaa heamm by the beck.'*.

Hing lock C a padlock.

Hing on hang or hold on; wait or hold up; continue; stick to it.

Hingan' hanging, sloping. A hingan' field is one on the side of a hill.

Hingan' his lugs crest fallen; hanging his ears in shame or disappointment.

Hinge hang.

Hingy C poorly; dull through incipient illness. *'Fadder's o'hingy to-day and nin reet at o'.'*.

Hinmest C hindmost or hindermost, behind all others or the last; furthest away; at the back.

Hinney N honey; a term of endearment (see Honey).

Hipe a term in wrestling.

Hippins underclothes for infants.

Hirple A person having corns or tender feet hirples as he walks.

His-sel himself.

His-stigh! C, N terms used in driving pigs.

Hishoo! terms used forcibly to drive away fowls.

Hisk C to grasp; used with reference to the difficulty a person experiences in breathing on plunging into a cold water. *'He hisk't when he went in.'*.

Hit on to agree *'They don't hit on about it.'*.

Hitch B a spring from one foot.

Hitcht C contributed or gave willingly.

Hitch steppin' C hop, step and jump. (see Lowp).

Hitten hit.

Hitty missy C chance; not clear or sure; The sign of an old inn at Pardshaw was a sportsman firing at a bird, and the words *'Hitty missy, luck's o'.'*.

Hiz N us.

Hizzle N hazel, to beat or thrash. *'I'll hizzle thee.'*.

Hizzy N huzzy, a housewife's pocket case for needles and thread; hussy.

Ho how, *'Ho er ye to-day, bonny lass?'*.

Ho C hall.

Ho C, N, E a word used in guiding horses to the left; come hither.

Ho buck C a noisy and turbulent young fellow.

Ho bye stand out of the way.

Ho'penny C, SW halfpenny.

Ho'penny heed an' a fardin' tail C the different parts do not correspond; one part much better than another.

Ho-way C go along; come on.

Hoaf C half.

Hoaflins half-done; half-witted; half-shares.

Hoald C, E to hold; shelter. *'They've nowder house nor hoald to draw teah.'*.

Hobblety hoy an ungainly lad; a boy appraching manhood.

Hobthrush B a celebrated fairy, also once referred to as *Robin Goodfellow* or *Puck*.

Hocker to scramble awkwardly.

Hod C, E to hold; shelter. *'Keep hod of t'beukk, till Setterday neet.'*.

Hod hold; a shelter for fish in a stream or pond.

Hod bye stand out of the way.

Hod his bit C to retain health, station, or position. *'Hoo's Peggy?'.....Nobbet waikly and pinch't to hod her bit.'*.

Hod pot the one who detains the circling bottle or drinking vessel.

Hod te tail i' watter persevere, stick to it. A phrase of encouragement, but how originated we do not know.

Hod te watter be silent; shut up and keep quiet. *'Hod te watter lass, dunnet tell iv'ry yan.'*.

Hod thy bodder be silent (see Hod te watter).

Hod thy jo be silent (see Hod te watter).

Hod to dea C useless employment. *'It's fair had to dea.'*.

Hodden C held. *'Lampla' club's still hodden o't second Friday o'Joon.'*.

Hodden holden, held.

Hodden gray cloth made from a mixture of undyed black and white wool.

Hoddenly frequently, continuously, without interruption.

Hoddin C holding.

Hoddit C, E hold it; held. *'Hoddit and dunnet let it gaa.'*.

Hodfash annoyance. *'He's a fair hodfash, for he niver lets yan aleann.'*.

Hofe half. *'Hofe a shillin' is a tanner.'*. (see Tanner).

Hofe reet C half-witted.

Hofe thick C a foolish person; a half-fatted animal.

Hofelin half-way; a simpleton.

Hog lamb for twelve months after weaning.

Hog gap a covered opening in a wall for sheep to pass through.

Hog meann the mane of a horse clipped so as to stand upright like the reeds of a bog or marsh.

Hoggas C a sheep house; a house for wintering lambs in after weaning.

Hoggast E a sheep house; a house for wintering lambs in after weaning.

Hoggers N, E upper stockings without feet. (see Beutt stockings).

Hoity toity assuming airs above their station.

Hollin the holly, *Ilex aquifolium*.

Holme *C, SW* alluvial land by the river side.

Honey *C, SW* a term of endearment. *'Cum on honey, give yer oald dad a kiss.'*.

Honk *C* a lazy fellow. *'Yer lad's honkan about heamm when he sud be at wark.'*.

Hoo how, *'Hoo ur ye?'*.

Hoo that? *C* hows that; why was it so.

Hoo-way *C* go along; come on. *'Hoo-way! I'll nut stop here forivver.'*.

Hooas *SW* house; the apartment into which the front door opens.

Hood *C* the hob at the side of the fire.

Hooivver *C* however.

Hoolet *N* the owl.

Hoomer *N* shade; to shade..

Hoon *N* hound.

Hoond *C, E* hound. *'Jwon Peel an' his hoond's come fray Coadbeck.'*.

Hoor *C, E* whore.

Hoose *C, N* house; the apartment into which the front door opens.

Hoose *SW* a dry cough.

Hoose warmin' *C, B* an entertainment or party on taking possession of a new dwelling.

Hoosin' *C* a set of buildings..

Hoosomivver however.

Hoot! exclamations of unbelief. *'Hoot! it was nea sek things.'*.

Hoot! *C* expressions of dissent, or denoting contempt or inferiority.

Hop *C* a spring from one foot.

Hop term used to direct horses to the right.

Hopple *C, N* to fetter or tie up a cow or other large animal. (see Langel).

Horn hard *C* very hard. *'He wink't horn hard when he fir't his gun.'*.

Horndoon *C* lunch about ten in the morning. (now in disuse 1878).

Horned nowey *C* cattle with small loose horns attached to the head, but not fast to their skull.

Horse knop the knap weed - Centaurea nigra.

Horse mallison *C* a person who abuses his horse.

Horse mezzer a measure used for serving out oats, etc., for horses.

Horsin' steann horse block; a stone, block or low flight of steps to mount horses from.

Hot see Muck hot.

Hotbrush a hobgoblin having the repute of doing much useful work unseen and unheard during the night, if not interfered with, but discontinuing or doing mischief if crossed or watched, or endeavoured to be coaxed or bribed to work in any way but his own.

Hotch *C* to trot slowly and clumsily; market day trot.

Hotch *C, SW* to shake excessively or roughly; A fat or large person *'hotches and laughs'* when his sides shake with laughter.

Hote *C, N* a limp in the walk.

Hote halt; limp in walk.

Hotter *C* totter, to walk feebly.

Hotter dockin' *C* a nursery term for a busy child learning to walk.

Hottle *E* totter, to walk feebly.

Hough band *C* a strap or band sometimes fastened round the hough of an unruly cow or a wild sheep to restrain its movements.

House *C, SW* the living-room of the older farmhouses. The ground-floor consisting of house, parlour, kitchen, and milk-house.

Hout tout! *N* expressions of dissent, or denoting contempt or inferiority.

Hovrel *N* a foolish fellow.

How fend ye? a greeting meaning *'how are you?'* - similar to *'how goes it?'*.

How goes it? a greeting basically meaning *'how are you?'* - similar to *'how preuvv ye?'* or *'are ye middlin' weel?'*.

How preuvv ye? a greeting meaning *'how are you?'*.

Howdy *N* midwife.

Howe *C* a hoe; hollow, empty; a gentle hill or eminence, or knoll; spoken to a cow it means - *'go'*.

Howe hoe.

Howe meal seeds *C* the inner husks of oats.

Howe neet *E* the silence of the dead of night.

Howe strowe *C* all in disorder.

Howk to dig; to scratch in the earth etc; to punish.

Howker *C* a large one.

Howney *C* dismal, empty - applied to a house depleted of furniture.

Howry *C* hollow, empty.

Hoyden *C* a romping girl (rude and boisterous).

Hoyder *C* injury, mischief. *'Stop! you're gaan to play hoyder wi' me.'*.

Hoyse *C* hoist.

Hoyty toyty *C* haughty, proud or distainful; arrogant; flighty.

Hubble *C* a crowd. *'A hubble o'fwok at church for t'berryin'.'*.

Hud *C* the hob or side of a fireplace.

Hudden *C, N, E* hidden.

Huff to despise; pet, peevishness or fretful discontent. *'He went away in a huff.'*.

Huff't despised. *'They huff't it as if it hed been dirt.'*.

Huggaback *C* a climbing vetch - *Vicia cracca*; a coarse kind of towelling.

Hugger mugger *C* to act in a clandestine or unfair manner; to spend time unprofitably - *'Hugger muggeran'* about heamm.'*.

Hulet *C* the owl.

Hulk *C* a tall, lazy fellow. *'A girt lang hulk.'.*

Hull *B* to drive a trout into its hold.

Hull a small shed for calves or pigs, etc.

Hullet *SW* the owl.

Hum and haa *C, SW* to hesitate in speaking; to prevaricate.

Humlin' *C* a ram etc; having both testicles in its loins.

Humlock *C* hemlock, *Conium maculatum.*

Humly cowers *N, E* sliding in a sitting posture.

Hummel *SW* a ram etc; having both testicles in its loins.

Hummel jummel *C, N* confusedly mixed up.

Hummel mittens *N* woollen gloves having only the thumbs divided.

Hummelty cour *N, E* sliding in a sitting posture.

Hun *N* hound. *'Jwon Peel's huns are out on yon fell.'.*

Hun *NE* a hound; to hound.

Hung in t'bell reapp. *C* having had the wedding banns published.

Hunkers *C* the haunches.

Hunsup *C* to scold.

Hup up. *'Hup wi' tha' git out o'yer bed.'.*

Hur her.

Hurd herd; heard.

Hurl *C* a tempest or violent storm. *'Storm's cumman, John.'.....'Ey, an' it'll be a hurl.'.*

Hurple *N* to walk lame, to limp.

Hurry skurry *C* impetuously.

Hursle *C* hustle.

Hush *C* gush; to wash away soil from mines etc., using water.

Hut! *C* expressions of dissent, or denoting contempt or inferiority.

Huvvel *C* a cap for protecting a sore finger.

Huz *C, SW* us. *'Ham an' eggs fwoor huz teas.'.*

Huzzaf *C* a pocket-case for needles, thread etc. (see Hussy).

Hysta *C* hi thee.

Hyty-tyty *N* haughty, proud or distainful; arrogant; flighty.

Hyvin *C, N, E* ivy, *Hedera helix.*

I watna *N* I know not; I with not.

I' a contraction of *'I'* or *'in'.*

I's I am. *'I's to hev her.'*

Ianberries *C* excrescences on the under parts of cattle resembling raspberries or hineberries.

Ib-nin' evening.

Ibnin evening.

Ice shockle *C, E* icicle.

Ice shoggle *N* icicle.

Ider either.

Idle hizzy *N* whore.

Ilk *N* each; every.

Ilka *N* each; every.

Ill to degrade or slander. *'Don't ill a body if you can't say weel o'yan.';* bad or evil. (see Ill teull).

Ill gi'en given to evil deeds; ill-given; bad-tempered.

Ill teull *C* a bad boy or man; a tool of evil. *'He's been an ill teull o'his life.'.*

Ill thriven not having prospered; stunted; puny or weak.

Ill turn an injury or sickness.

Illfarrant *N* ill-favoured.

Illify *C* to defame or scandalise.

Illmite *N* very bad tempered.

Ime *C* a thin scum or covering.

Imin *C* a thin scum or covering.

Imma in me.

Immead'tly *SW* immediately.

In friendly; accepted by others. *'He gat in wi't'oald fwok, and he keeps in.'.*

In a twitter *N* soon, quickly.

In anonder under; beneath.

In av *NW* in. *'He leevs in av Aikton parish.'.*

In roads to progress with a task. *'Oor lass is makin' in roads with the cleeanin'.'.*

In-fair see Bridewain.

In-geatt an inroad; an attack.

Inam in him.

Inbank down-hill.

Income *C, SW* a swelling or other bodily infirmity, the origin of which is not apparent.

Infield land ancient inclosed land, and commonly the best.

Ing a common name for meadow land in a low or moist situation.

Inglan *C* England.

Ingle the fireside.

Inhill down-hill.

Inkhorn this term is used for any pocket vessel holding ink, originally made from cow or sheep horn.

Inkle *C* coarse woven tape.

Inklin' a slight hint or intimation; a thought or feeling. *'Jack hed an inklin' he was reet efter all.'.*

Inma in me.

Inman in him.

Ins an' outs the whole of the matter. *'He telt ma o't'ins an' outs about t'feyt.'.*

Ins and outs zigzags; reasons for and against - pros and cons; details of an event or arrangement. *'Mak sure you kno t'ins and outs of iv'rything, afwore you gaas aheed.'.*

Insense *C, N* to make a person comprehend or understand.

Inshot a recess.

Inside the stomach and bowels. *'He's bad of his inside.'.*

Insteed *N* instead.

Insure assure.

Intack an inclosure area of land taken from the common.

Intake see Intack.

Inteutt *N E* into it.

Intil't *N E* into it.

Intul *C* in too. *'He coonted t'money intul my fist.'.*

Intul't *C* into it.

Ir *C, N* are.

Ir are, *'Ir ye gaan away?'.*

Iron ub'n the middle sized pan once commonly found in the Cumbrian farm kitchen, bigger than a bule pan, but smaller than a keall pot.

Iron ub'n C, B a flat bottomed pan for baking in, a fire being placed on the lid as well as below the pan. Now superseded by cast-iron and sheet-iron ovens (1878).

Irrant are not.

Irrant are not.

Is are, *'Hey Jonty, how is ye to-day?'*.

Ish a ending often added to other words, may suggest a degree of uncertainty. eg. *goodish, badish,, fairish, hee-ish up, far-ish away.*

Issols C flakes of soot.

Ister is there. *'Ister enny churry ceakk fwoor the vicar?'.*

Ither N other.

Ittal It'll or it will, *'Ittall hev to do, theer's nin left!'.*

Iv C, N in. *'He's lishest lad iv o'Brumfell parish.'.*

Iv'ry C every.

Iv'ry like every now and then.

Iv'ry whoar C everywhere.

Iv'ry whup while every now and then.

Iv'rything everything.

Ivin C, N, E ivy, *Hedera helix.*

Ivry C every.

Ivver ever.

Ivverly E frequently; continuously.

Ivvery C every.

Ize I is. I am.

Izels C flakes from burning straw etc.; dead fire of wood in an oven.

Izzert the old name of the letter Z (zed).

Jaa SW bad language.

Jab C to spill. *'She brought milk in a can and job't it ower at iv'ry step.'.*

Jack durnill N the earth nut, *Bunias flexuosum.*

Jackalegs C a pocket clasp-knife.

Jacky steanns a game among school-girls played with small pebbles, and sometimes with plum or cherry-stones.

Jam to squeeze. *'T'lads and lasses war all jam'd up in yan la'al car.';* to press against; to wedge.

Jamers C see Jammers.

Jammers SW small cupboard hinges.

Jamp jumped, leapt.

Jams SW James - St. Jams' fair was held at Ravenglass on the 5th August.

Janglement angry disputations.

Jannick N See Jannock.

Jannock C right, fit, true.

Jant C an outing, pleasure trip or jaunt. *'I's been on oaldfwoks church jant to Seaskeall.'.*

Jarble C to bespatter. (see Slopper).

Jaw C bad language.

Jayls C cracks and fissures of timber in seasoning.

Jayvel C to stagger; to walk loosely.

Jedder C to shake; to jar; discord.

Jee a word used in directing horses. eg. *'Jee up.'.*

Jee-wa-awe twisted; all awry.

Jeelas N jealous.

Jeelas N, E jealous.

Jeest joist.

Jemmers SW see Jammers.

Jenny red tail E the common redstart, *Sylvia phoenicurus.*

Jenny spinner see Jinny Spinner.

Jenny spinner C, B a teetotum or childs toy resembling a top but twirled by the fingers; the Tipula or long-legs insect.

Jenny whol the ventilating hole in the gable of a barn, often used by the owl.

Jert C, SW jerk; to pitch a stone with the hand from the hip.

Jew trump C jew's harp or jaw harp.

Jew't cheated.

Jeybe NW jibe.

Jeyk C to creak like machinery requiring oil; the creaking noise made by new shoes.

Jiffy C in an instant. *'In a jiffy.'.*

Jillet N jilt.

Jimers B small cupboard hinges. (see Jamers).

Jimmerly E weak or ill-jointed - commonly applied to carpenter's work.

Jimmers N see Jammers.

Jimp tight; too little; tucked up in the flank as greyhounds are.

Jing C a rustic oath, often spoken to show suprise.

Jing-el jingle.

Jo C bad language.

Job an event. *'It's a bad job for us o'.'.*

Job-jurnal C a spinning play-thing.

Jockylegs N a pocket clasp-knife.

Joggle C to push; to disturb the elbow of a person writing.

Jollop N, E the jalap plant, *Exogonium purga,* its root was once used in medicine.

Jome C. E jamb; the side stone of a door or window.

Jonas C, E, SW jaundice.

Joo trump C jew's harp or jaw harp.

Jook C a long and tiresome journey on foot

Jook N to elude or avoid; an attempt to escape a missile.

Jookery packery N larking, romping.

Joon C June.

Joop B a short upper garment or jacket worn by females.

Joop't B to be domineered over by a woman.

Jope to splash; to bespatter. (see Slopper).

Jopins anything spilled.

Joram *C* a large mess; abundance.

Jordy *N, NW* the name George; Geordies, the people from the North East of England.

Jossy *C* Joseph.

Jowat *NW* a term of effeminacy. *'He's a feckless jowat.'.*

Jowl *C* the jaw; to jumble; This word often relates more particularly to the disturbing of a vessel containing fluid.

Jud *E* a game played with a hazel nut bored and run upon a string.

Jull See Joggle.

Jull *C* to shake; to jar; discord.

Jum wid *C* to fall in with; to meet accidentally.

Jummel jumble.

Jumper *C, N* the skipping maggot of the small flesh-fly - *Piophila*; a chisel for boring stone with.

Junk *C* a coarse joint of beef; a thick piece.

Jur *N* to shake; to jar; discord.

Jurnal *C* journal, diary or record book.

Just now shortly, soon. *'I'll come just now.'.*

Jwoke joke.

Jwon *C* John. *'D'ye ken Jwon Peel.'.*

Jworam *N* a large mess; abundance.

Jyst joist.

Jyste *C* to agist or feed or pasture the cattle of others; to put cattle out to grass upon another's farm.

Ka bye stand out of the way; come by.

Ka he quoth he; say he.

Kack hand'd left handed. *'Yan of ma dowters kack hand'd.'*; clumsy when performing a task using the hands.

Kange *E* to flog severely. *'I'll give him a kanjin.'.*

Kanjy *C* cross-grained; untoward.

Kay key. *'I seen him throo t'kaywholl.'.*

Kaybittit a sheep's ear marked by having a square piece cut from the edge.

Kayk *C* to wander listlessly; *'Kaykan' about like a pet geuss.'.*

Kayk *C, NE* a twist to one side. *'She hez a kayk in her neck.'.*

Kayk the cry of a goose.

Kaym't *C* ill-disposed, contra-dictious, crooked; to bend.

Kayte *C* kindly, friendly.

Ke *C* a small spring.

Keadd *C* the sheep's ked or louse, *Pediculus*.

Keagh! go, get away.

Keah *SW* key.

Keak *C, N, E* cake.

Keall *C* see Field keall.

Keall kale, broth;

Keall *NE* kale; greens; porridge of oatmeal.

Keall pot the large pan in which the meat and puddings are cooked in a farm-house kitchen; the third largest pan once commonly found in the Cumbrian farm kitchen, bigger than a *'iron ub'n'*, but smaller than a *'set pot'*.

Keall runts *N* cabbage-stalks.

Keall stick *N* a stick used for stirring a boiling pot.

Keam see Cwoam.

Keam *N, E* comb.

Keamm *NE* comb.

Keamms *E* hair sieve.

Keap cape.

Kear care.

Kearr *C* care.

Keas case.

Keavv *B* to pass a knife in all directions through newly-made butter to extract air, etc.

Keavv *C* to paw with the foot; to kick the straws out of a heap of undressed corn with the foot and rake.

Keb feuttit *E* a person who walks with the toes turned inward.

Kebby stick *C, SW* a hook-headed stick.

Keck *N* cackle, to laugh.

Keckle *C, E, SW* cackle, laugh.

Keeak *SW* cake.

Keek *N* to peep; to pry.

Keen cuts *N* see Keens.

Keen on fond of. *'Yer chap's keen on yer fadder's churry ceakk.'.*

Keens *N* cracks in the hands caused by frost.

Keep sustenance. *'He hez five kye and hes n't keep for two.'.*

Keep't kept.

Keld *C* a small spring.

Kelk *C* to hit roughly; a severe blow. *'An ugly kelk.'.*

Kelker *C* a heavy blow.

Kelkin' *C* a beating.

Kelly *C* land containing small springs which partly dry up in summer.

Kelt cwoat *C, B, E* a home spun coat of coarse cloth of mixed white and black wool.

Kelter *C* money, riches.

Kelterment useless trumpery or decorations.

Kemps *C* hairs intermixed in the growth of wool.

Ken to know; to see; to remember.

Kengeudd *N* something to remember; an example of good.

Kengood *C* something to remember; an example of good.

Kennel cannel coal.

Kennin' knowing. *'That youngster's growan'out o'ken-nin'.'.*

Kenspec't *N* conspicuous.

Kenspeckl't *C, SW* conspi-cuous.

Kent feasst *B* well known by the countenance or facial appearance.

Kep to catch anything in the act of falling.

Kep jope *C* a child's pinafore.

Kerb see Crib.

Kerb *C* the curb of a bridle.

Kerb *SW* to curb; restrain.

Kern churn. (see Quern).

Kern supper *C, SW* harvest-home.

Kern't milk butter milk.

Kernwinnin' *N* harvest-home.

Kersen to christen. *'Efter t'weddin, we'll hev t'kersenin'.'.*

Kersenmas Christmas. *'At Kersenmas mery may ye dance.'.*

Kersmas Christmas.

Kesfab *E* a cheese vat.

Kesh *C* the cow-parsnip, *Heracleum spondylium*; also any hollow stem.

Kesk *E* see Kesh.

Keslop *C, SW* the cured stomach of a calf used for making rennet.

Kessen *C, B* twisted; wood made untrue by rapid drying.

Kessen cast. *'T'sky's ower-kessen.'.*

Kessen metal *C* cast iron.

Kessick *C* Keswick.

Kest a swarm or nest of bees; to overturn sheaves of corn for drying.

Kest cast. *'T'Beerpot warks ner Workiton maks owt fray kest metal.'.*

Ket filth; carrion.

Ket-Kite *E* a person of mean actions.

Ketment filth; carrion.

Ketty dirty, mean, worthless.

Keud cud.

Keuddm cud; the inside of the mouth of a cow etc.

Keuk cook.

Keul cool.

Keull cool.

Kevvel *C, N* to kick or leap awkwardly.

Key *C, N, E* key.

Keye *N* cows, kine, cattle.

Keyn' *NW* kind.

Keynd *NW* kind.

Keyp *N* see Kyp't.

Keyte *N* the belly. (see Kyte).

Kick *C* the top or height of the fashion. *'The varra kick.'.*

Kill kiln.

Kill coo *C* no great object; nothing wonderful. *'Neah girt kill coo.'.*

Kill dry 't feass *C* a parched and withered face.

Kill ee the fireplace of a drying kiln.

Kill't killed.

Kill't t'crack stopped a conversation by adding an irrelevant or foolish remark, generally out of context.

Kilp *C* a sharp bend or angle. *'O kilps and creuks.'.*

Kilt up *N* to fasten up the skirts of the dress.

Kin kindred, family, ancestors or relations.

King cough *C* the whooping-cough.

Kink *C* the peculiar sound of the whooping-cough; a curling twist in a rope or cord.

Kinnel kindle, ignite.

Kinnellin' *C* materials to light a fire with.

Kins cracks in the hands caused by frost.

Kinsfwok ss Kin.

Kipper *C* a salmon out of season.

Kipper't *C, N* fish partially pickled or smoked.

Kipple *B* couple, *'They mak a fine kipple.'*; Two rams chained together by their horns are *kippl't.*

Kirk a church.

Kirk garth churchyard.

Kirk-gaan church-going; regular in attendance at church.

Kirkmaister *SW* churchwarden.

Kirkwarden *N* churchwarden.

Kirrock *N* a circle of stones. The large circle of stones on the summit of Carrock fell would seem to have given the mountain its name.

Kissin' crust the piece of crust adhering to a loaf, and which has been broke from another loaf, the two having been in contact whilst baking.

Kist a chest.

Kit *C* a small wooden pail or tub; a term of contempt. *'The heall kit '*- the whole set or company.

Kites berries (see Black kites).

Kith *N* see Kin.

Kitlin *C* kitten.

Kittle *C* to tickle; to bring forth kittens; active. *'Kittle as a mouse-trap '*- easily acted upon, quick, excitable.

Kittle to tickle trouts by grappling them with the hands.

Kitty cwoat Peggy *B* a woman who tucks up her clothes to work; a careful one.

Kizzen't over-roasted, shri-velled.

Knaa *SW* know.

Knaanat *SW* know not. *'I knaanat if t'berryin' ower yit.'.*

Knack *C, N, E* to talk quick, and attempt fine language. *'She knacks and talks like rotten sticks.'.*

Knack method. *'Dick hez t'knack to do iv'ry job.'.*

Knack reel a reel or frame onto which yarn, thread etc. are wound. Turned by a handle and giving a click when a certain number of threads had been wound; these were bound together forming a *'cut'*, and so many cuts make a *'hank'*.

Knackered worn out; tired.

Knacks *C* nothing beyond ordinary or special. *'He's neah girt knacks.'.*

Knaggy crochety; short-tempered.

Knap *C* to strike gently and quickly.

Knattle to tap gently.

Kneav knave.

Kneavv knave; a boy; servant; dishonest man.

Kneavv shyve *C* the first cut off

the loaf.

Kneaw *SW* knew.

Kneaww *SW* knew.

Knep *C* to bite in play as horses do.

Kneudd *C* to butt with the head as a calf or lamb may do when sucking.

Kneuls *C* small loose horns attached to the heads of cattle.

Kneyf *NW* knife.

Knidgel *C* to castrate by ligature.

Knifel *B* to pass away time in an idle manner. (see Knyfel).

Knock *C* a hard blow.

Knock on *C* continue, go on.

Knock onder *C* to resign; give precedence.

Knockin' trough *NW* a stone trough used around Wigton for bruising moistened barley in with a wooden pestle, for making barley-milk or frumerty.

Knodden *C* kneaded.

Knonnot *C, E* know not. *'I knonnot why he's gaan.'*.

Knop *C* a small tub having two longer staves for handles.

Knoppy *C* knotty; lumpy. *'It's a knoppy rwoad'* - as the man said when he stumbled over a cow.

Knot a rocky-peaked hill.

Knowe a rounded hill.

Knuckles knuckles.

Knur't *C* stunted; not freely grown.

Knyfel *C, N* to steal trifles.

Kurk a church.

Kurk louse *B* the wood louse, Oniscus.

Kurn stofe *B* the staff fitted for working up and down in a hand churn.

Kurn supper *C, SW* harvest-home.

Kurnel kernel.

Kursty Christopher.

Kye *C, E* cows, kine, cattle.

Kyp't *C* bent. A saw is said to be *'kyp't'* when buckled or permanently bent or twisted.

Kype *C, SW* to jibe; to insinuate; to die. *'T'oald horse is gaan to kype.'*.

Kysty squeamish.

Kyte *C, SW* the belly. *'T'Squires gat a greet kyte on him.'*.

La'al small.

La'al pan the name for the smallest pan once commonly found in the Cumbrain farm kitchen. *(see Shank pan).*

Laa *N, SW* law; low.

Laa man *SW* man of law; an attorney or solicitor.

Laaf *SW* see Lofe.

Laal *C* little, or small *'Fray la'al acorns, greet oaks grawe.'*.

Laal house *C* a privy or outside toilet. (see Donnican).

Laal set by a little saved; of small esteem or repute.

Laan *N* land.

Laatha! *E* look thou; listen thou.

Labber *C* to splash in water.

Ladder *B* See Lalder.

Ladder lather.

Laddie *C, N* a lad. This word was applied to a person having a particular strong habit or propensity. *'He's a laddie for o'maks o'spwort.'*.

Lag-ma-last *C* always behind.

Laggin the end of the stave outside the cask or tub.

Laggy last *C, B* behind; the one who lags behind.

Laghter *C, N* a brood of chickens or other fowls.

Laird *N* lord: landowner, yeoman.

Laith *N* loth.

Lake *C, SW* play.

Lakers *C* players. *'At lanter the caird lakers sat i'the loft.'*- Robert Anderson.

Lakin *C* a child's toy.

Lal *C* to loll or hang out the tongue derisively.

Lalder *E* to gossip.

Lalder *N* loud and foolish talk.

Lallup *C* see Lal.

Lam *E* to beat.

Lammin' *E* a thrashing.

Lampers *C* lamprey-eels; a swelling in a young horse's mouth.

Lampla' *C* Lamplugh.

Lampla' hokeys *C* an old breed of brown and black cattle with white faces, peculiar to Lamplugh. (now extinct 1874).

Lampla' puddin' *C* toasted biscuits steeped in hot ale with spices; a posset.

Lan' *N* land.

Land *C* an estate in land. *'Willy Fisher o'Winscales hed three lands.'*. - or separate estates.

Land *C, SW* to arrive. *'He landit in yester neet.'*; to receive; to find.

Lang long, tall, high. *'He'll be six feutt hee, and as good as he's lang.'*; to long or wish for; along.

Lang back't settle *C* an uncushioned sofa or bench.

Lang creukk *B* the crook hanging from the chimla boke, was usually from four to six or seven feet in length (1.2 to 2.1 metres). (see Chimla boke).

Lang end the final end.

Lang hundred six score - a number amounting to 120.

Lang last *C, N* at last.

Lang last at length; the end of. *'He's gitten a wife at lang last.'*.

Lang ligger *C* an uncushioned sofa, settle or bench.

Lang man *C, B* the middle finger - in nursery play (see Fingers).

Lang on *C* because of. *'It was o'lang o'him 'at I fell into t'beck.'*.

Lang sen *C, SW* long since.

Lang streak't laid at full length.

Lang ten a full ploughing-team made up of ten individuals - two pairs of long-horned oxen, one pair of horses, a ploughman, a person (often a woman) to hold down the beam, and two

'Plu'co'ers'. (more common in the 18th. century).

Lang windit prolix; a long speech, argument or converstaion. *'Yer Mary's reet lang windit an' nivver shuts up.'.*

Langel *C, N* a woollen fetter for sheep.

Langer longer.

Langer east shorter west *C* a deficiency in one part is compensated by abundance in another.

Langket *SW* a woollen fetter for sheep.

Langseyene *N* long since.

Langsom tedious. *'It's a langsom rwoad ower Hutton moor.'.*

Langsyne *N* long since.

Langways lengthwise. *'T'fleur's ten feútt langways an' six across.'.*

Lanky long and thin.

Lant the card game of loo. A distinction is made between Lant and Lanter. Five cards are required for the latter. The proper designation may be three-card loo and five-card loo. The rule of playing are also different.

Lant lakers *C* players at loo.

Lanter *N* the card game of loo. *(see Lant and Loo).*

Lantern leets *C* horn substitutes for glass in windows etc.

Lanters *N* players at loo.

Lantit defeated, disappointed.

Lap *N* leapt.

Lap sidit *C* unequally balanced.

Lap up *C* to desist; to give up.

Lapstan' *C* the stone held on the shoemaker's lap for beating his leather upon.

Larn learn - also to teach. *'He lams his scholars to read an' write.'.*

Larrop *C* to beat.

Lash to comb; a comb; an attack of diarrhœa; to whip; the sharp cord at the end of a whip.

Lash away! a common exclamation of encouragement applied indifferently to work or play.

Lash ceam *N* a coarse comb.

Lash cwom' *C, SW* A coarse comb.

Lash out *C* to use a comb; to spend money, almost without a second thought, *'T'oald lass has lash'd out on a new dress.'.*

Lash out *N* to hand forth; to kick.

Lassie See Laddie.

Lassie-lad a term of opprobrium (reproach, contem-pt or disdain) among boys, denoting effeminacy or undue preference for the society of girls. *'Oar lad's nivver a lassie-lad, he's just tak'n with t'lasses.'.*

Lasty of an enduring nature; lasting.

Lat lath or narrow piece of timber; Dutch lat. *'As thin as a lat.'.*

Latch *B* an occasional watercourse; a miry place.

Latch *C* a deep cart-rut; fastening on a door.

Latch lug't *C* ears hanging instead of being erect.

Lave *N* the rest or remainder.

Lavrick *N* the lark, *Alauda arvensis*.

Laws! *C* an expression of astonishment.

Laylac lilac.

Layt to seek. *'Gang an' layt t'kye heamm.'.*

Laytin' *C* the circuit invited to a funeral, etc.

Lazybed a bed of potatoes planted on the surface.

Lea arable land in grass.

Lea Sye *C, SW* a scythe.

Lead load; to convey by cart. *'Gang an' lead cwom to-day, it'll be dry.'.*

Leadd load, lade; to lift out water with a bucket or dish.

Leader *C* a tendon; a sinew.

Leady heavy, as in *'Cow't leady'*.

Leaf *B* the inner loin-fat of the pig.

(See Saim).

Leaf loaf.

Leaff loaf. *'T'mudders mead a leaff of bread iv'ry day this week.'.*

Leahstan' a stone used for whetting or sharpening scythes.

Leam lame.

Leamm lame.

Leand *C, E* a shelter from the wind.

Leann alone.

Leapp *C, SW* leapt.

Leas lace.

Leass *C* lace; to thrash or beat.

Leasst cup tea and spirits.

Leastways at least or leastwise. *'It niver was seah, leastways I niver knew 't.'.*

Leat late.

Leath loth.

Leatt *C* late.

Leatth a barn.

Leatth a loth. *'She was leatth to gang away.'.*

Leatth *N* a burn or small stream or rivulet.

Leav lug't *N* ears hanging instead of being erect. This spelling is very appropriate - the ears hang like leaves. (see Latch lug't).

Leave gang let go; do not hold.

Leave hod let go; do not hold.

Leaydy *C, N, E* lady.

Leayk *N* play.

Leck *C, E* leak; a hard subsoil of clay and gravel.

Leck to leak; a hard subsoil of clay and gravel. (see Pinnel).

Led farm *C* an additional farm on which the occupier does not reside.

Ledder to beat; leather.

Ledder heed *C* a blockhead or simpleton.

Ledder lungs a garrulous or very talkative person. *'Oald ledder lungs nivver shuts up.'.*

Ledder-te-spetch *C* a rustic method of heavy dancing.

Ledderer *C* a large one.

Leddy *N* lady.

Ledge allege. *'He 'ledges it was still seah.'.*

Lee a lie; tell a lie.

Lee co' *C* the ball thrown over the school-house. (see Hee bo'leep).

Lee-co' *C* look out - a term used in hand-ball play.

Leead *SW* lead (metal); to lead; to cart. (see Leed).

Leeak *SW* look.

Leear liar.

Leeas *SW* lease.

Leeath a barn.

Leeath *N* a burn or small stream or rivulet.

Leeav *SW* leave.

Leed *C* to lead; to cart. *'He's leedan' lime.'* In the seventeenth century work horses were conducted or led with halters; the term *'to lead'* still remains although the horses are now driven (1878).

Leed *C, N, E* lead (metal).

Leef teall *C* easy to sell or dispose of; easy to turn to account.

Leeght light; to slight.

Leem out *C* to drop out like ripe nuts. *'Ay lads! leukk yonder for brown leemers!'.*

Leemers hazel nuts, the fruit of the *Corylus avellana.*

Leesh *N* see List.

Leester *N* see Lister.

Leet *C* light; window.

Leet light; to slight; to enlighten or explain; to alight etc. (formerly pronounced *'leeght'* - 1878).

Leet on *C* to meet with. *'I leet on him at t'cross rwoads past Rowrah.'.*

Leeten lighten.

Leetly gitten leetly geann what is easily got is easily gone - relating to wages, etc.

Leetnin' lightning.

Leetnin' afoor deeth a lucid interval preceding death.

Leets *C, E, NW* lights, lungs.

Leetsom' *C* gay, cheerful agile, lightsome.

Leev to live.

Leeve live. *'Ah furst com ta leeve here ten year since.'.*

Leeve teall *C* easy to sell or dispose of; easy to turn to account.

Leever sooner; rather. *'I'd leever hev this nor that'n.'.*

Leevin living. *'He's gitten a reet geud leevin fray prentin.'.*

Leevs lives. *'He leevs someway out Cockermuth way.'.*

Legg it *C* run away. *'I telt the lad off and he legg'd it heamm.'.*

Leggan' away *C* walking quickly.

Len'me lend me. *'Wad ta len'me a shillin'?'.*

Lep *C* a bundle of straw; a lap.

Lert *C* to jerk; to pitch a light article out of the hand.

Let to alight, decend and settle, to get down. *'He leap off t'dike top an' let in a bog.'.*

Let leet on, or into to open up secrets or mysteries.

Let on speak; frequently used as *'Nivver let on'* - do not speak, keep it secret.

Let slap at to strike quickly at.

Let wit to pretend.

Let'n let. *'He sud ha'let'n that aleann.'.*

Leudge an entrance lodge; to lodge or deposit. *'He leudg't his goold in t'oald bank.'.*

Leuff *N* the palm of the hand.

Leugh *N* laugh or laughted.

Leuk *C, N, E* look.

Leukk *C, N* look.

Leukk tull him *C* attend to him; keep an eye on him; ask him.

Leukt *C* looked. *'Mattha was riddy fwor owt' at leukt like fun.'.*

Leumm loom; a tool; a term of reproach. *'He's an ill leumm.'.*

Leuv *C, N, E* love.

Leuvv the hollow of the hand. *'T'leuvv o't'hand.'.*

Leuvv *N* love.

Leve as soon prefer. *'I'd as lyve hev that as tudder.'.*

Ley arable land in grass.

Ley hay hay grown on old ley ground. The term is also applied to rye-grass and clover hay as well.

Leycence *N, NW* licence.

Leyfe *N, NW* life.

Leyghts *N* lights, lungs.

Leyke *N* in danger of; urgency; likely. *'He'll be like to come.'.*

Leyke *N, NW* like.

Leykin' *N, NW* fondness; liking. *'Mey leykin' for thee I can't smudder.';* a term of endear-ment to a child. *'Come hither, my leyl leykin'.'.*

Leykly *N* likely.

Leyl *B* small.

Leyle *N* little.

Leyme *N, NW* lime.

Leytel *N* the surname of Little.

Liable reliable; apt; having a propensity to. *'He's liable to get drunk if he's ought in his pocket.'.*

Lib *C* to castrate.

Lick to discover; to see.

Lick for smack *C* quick together.

Lick plate *C* a person who tries to gain favour by mean services.

Lick pot *C, B* the index or fore finger - in nursery play (see Fingers).

Lickin' a thrashing.

Licks a thrashing.

Lift *C* a term used at funerals. *'What time do ye lift'*- or start with the corpse?; the sky; a trick at cards.

Lift help or assistance. *'He'll give us a lift at a pinch.'.*

Lig to lie down.

Lig a leamm on to brutally injure a limb, etc.

Lig at lay to it; work at it vigorously. *'Lig at him, lad.'.*

Lig in *C* a mining term - to dig below the foundation.

Lig in tul him! *C* thrash him well.

Lig lick on to discover; to see. *'I could niver lig lick on him efter he went round t'corner.'.*

Lig ma lag *C* abundance; to much.

Liggan' upon very urgent. *'It's liggan' upon, and mun be done.'.*

Liggers *C* layers; growing wood notched and laid along a hedge.

Liggy *C* the loach fish, *Cobitis barbatula.*

Liggy bed *C* a person addicted to late rising.

Liggy boddam *C* the loach fish, *Cobitis barbatula.*

Light on *C* to rely on; trust; depend on. *'I'll light on thee to pay't.'.*

Like *C, SW* in danger of; urgency; likely. *'It's like to sno'.'.*

Like to disposed to. *'He was like to laugh.'.*

Liker *C, SW* more likely.

Likken *N, E* to compare; to match. *'Now, divvent liken me to hur.'.*

Likly *N* likely.

Lilly to flatter. *'She lilly 't t'cald man up till she gat him an' his money.'.*

Lilt a short and lively piece of music.

Lim a mischievous person; limb.

Limber *C* flexible; supple.

Limmers *SW* the shafts of a cart.

Limmish inclined to mischief.

Limp *C* flexible. *'As limp as an empty stocking.'.*

Lin linen.

Lin pin linch-pin

Line of eggs *C* the couse of laying eggs by a fowl.

Line wheel the wheel onto which linen thread is spun.

Lines *C* banns of marriage. *'T'*

lines have gone in to t'parson.'.

Ling heather, *Calluna vulgaris.*

Ling cowe *C, SW* a stem of heather

Lingbird *C* see Lingy.

Lingy *C* the ground lark, from the *Alaunda* genus of birds

Linn *N* a precipice or edge.

Linnert *C* the linnet or song bird, *Fringilla linato.*

Linsty wuinsty *C* cloth of a linen and wool mix.

Lipe *E* a large portion, usually applied to land. *'T' railways teann a girt lipe off our croft.'.*

Lire *C* oatmeal and water used to thicken broth or soup etc.

Lirk *E* a crease. *'Poo up thy stockings, theyre o'lirks.'.*

Lirt *E* to stick out the tongue.

Lish *C, SW* supple; active.

Lishlike well-made.

Lisk *C, SW* the flank or groin.

Lissen *C* listen. *'Oald Jack was lissenan to the birds singan.'.*

List enlist, *'Gweordy's gone an' listit for a soldier.'.*

Lister *C, SW* a pronged and barbed fish spear.

Listin *C* list; woollen selvages or edges of cloth.

Listy strong and active; ready-handed; numble.

Livver *C, E* deliver.

Lo' *C, E* law; low.

Loave! *C* exclaimation of suprise and delight

Loavin days! *C* see Loave!

Lob *C* to leap or run heavily; to throw in a quoit-like fashion.

Lobby lowe a nursery term for a flickering flame.

Lock an undefined quantity; to shuffle a pack of cards, some face up and some face down.

Lockin *C* a split iron pin for securing a window bolt; a drinking session in a pub after licensing hours, behind closed doors.

Lockin gowan *C* the globe flower, *Trollius Europoeus.*

Lofe *C* offer; chance or opportunity *'He'd nea lofe o'selling.'.*; in some cases - head. *'Use yer lofe.'.*

Loff *N* see Lofe.

Log still; quiet.

Lonnin narrow lane or track, usually leading to an isolated field or dwelling.

Lonter *C* loiter.

Looance *C, E* allowance.

Lood loud.

Look *C* to weed corn.

Loot lout.

Lopp't *C* chopped or cut. *'I's lopp't top off t' birk tree.'.*

Loppen leapt.

Lopper't milk turned sour and curdled.

Loss *N, E* to lose.

Lot allot.

Lot to allot.

Lough whol *C* a hole or cavity in rocks etc.

Lounder *C, N* to beat.

Lounderer *C, N* a large one.

Lowder *C* the foundations of a milestone.

Lowe flame, blaze; the touch used by fish poachers.

Lowmer the lowest; the one or part below.

Lowmest lowest.

Lown *N* calm, still.

Lownd *C* calm, still.

Lownd side the sheltered side

Lowp a leap or jump, either running or standing. The various kinds include Catskip, one hitch or hop and one jump. *'Yon lad's just lowp'd oor yer dyke.'.*

Lowpy dyke a cow etc., liable to leap hedges or fences; an unfaithful husband.

Lowse loose or loosen; out of service or apprenticeship.

Lowsely loosely.

Lowsish see Lowsely.

Lowt see Look.

Lowz'nin' *E* a party arranged when a young man completes his apprenticeship, the profits from which he uses to purchase his own set of tools.

Lowze out to unyoke.

Loze! *C* an expression of astonishment.

Lu-war lukewarm.

Lubbart *C, B* a lazy fellow.

Luckpenny a small amount of money returned to a buyer, said to bring luck to the purchaser.

Lucky big; easy; abundant.

Luff the hollow of the hand. (see Leuvv).

Lufter *C* abundance; a crowd, *'A heull lufter o' fwok co' frae Codebeck.'*.

Lug *C, B* the turned-up part of the paring spade.

Lug the ear; the handle of a pail or jug; to pull the hair etc; to carry often heavy or large items.

Lugs ears.

Lump a dim, dull, and stupid character. *'He's nobbett a gurt lump.'*.

Lurk lurch.

Lurry *C* hurry, *'Tak t'dog and lurry them sheep away.'*.

Lush to rush in the water fiercely; to splash.

Lush and lavey *E* wasteful extravagance.

Lutha! *C* look thou; listen thou.

Luv o' t'hand *C* the palm.

Lwoaf *C, N* loaf. *'T'mither beakk'd a lwoaf iv'ry day this week.'*.

Lwoase *C* to lose.

Lwof *N* see Lofe.

Lword *G, NW* lord. *'T'Curwins are lwords of t'manor at Workiton.*

Lwoze lose.

Ly 'a now! *C* listen ye!.

Ly ye! *N* listen ye!.

Lyer *C* layer; meal in the broth.

Lyery *C* bull-fleshed, coarse.

Lyle *SW* little.

Lype *C* the greater portion.

Lysta! *C* listen thou.

Lytel *C* the surname of Little.

Lythe *C* oatmeal and water used to thicken broth or soup etc.

Lythy *N* thick fluid.

Lyve as soon prefer. *'I'd as lyve hev that as tudder.'*; living. *'A lyve dog's better nor a deed lion.'*.

Ma me.

Maa *N, SW* to cut with a scythe; to mow.

Maak *N, SW* see Moke.

Maap *SW* mope.

Maapment *SW* blundering.

Maat *SW* malt.

Maatster *SW* maltster or a maker of malt.

Maddl't confused.

Maddle to talk incoherently; to doat or dote.

Maff *C* a simple person.

Maffan feast *E* When a married couple are dilatory in producing issue, a few sly neighbours assemble, unbidden, at the house of the barren pair and invite themselves to tea and make merry, and to wish better success.

Maffin *C* a simple person.

Maffle to blunder; to mislead.

Mailin' *N* a farm.

Mainer *N* manure.

Mair *C, N, E* more, *'Ey's plenty mair where 'at came fray.'*.

Mairt *NE* the fat cow killed at Martinmass.

Mairtenmas *N* Martinmas.

Maist *N* most.

Maister *C, N, E* master, mister. *'Maister Dickinsun was browte up at Kiprangill.'*; teacher, eg. skooalmaister.

Maister man a husband; master of a household.

Mak *C, E, SW* make.

Mak a poor mouth *C* to endeavour to excite compassion.

Mak at *C* to attack. *'Oor bull mead at him full smack.'*.

Mak count on *C* to reckon on; to take into account.

Mak on *C* hurry on; to treat kindly; to encourage. *'Mak on him and he'll dea better.'*.

Mak out to progress. *'How is he makkan out wi'ma lass?'*.

Mak up till to curry favour. *'Mak up till her man.'*.

Makkan *C* making.

Maks kinds or sorts. *'O'maks of fwok live rund here.'*.

Mallin *C* a dusting mop for the oven; an untidy woman.

Mam mother.

Man a rock or stone (see Mawn), a conical cairn, pillar or pike of stones erected on the top of a mountain. *'Such cones are on the tops of all our mountains, and they are called men.'*- Coleridge.

Man alive exclamations of wonder or surprise. *'Man alive! that's a grand clock!'*.

Man on encourage; to urge. *'They man't their digs on to feight.'*.

Man thy sel! act like a man.

Man trap *C* a green bog.

Man-grown *E* a stick or tree flattened in growing is oval, and of the form of the body of a man.

Man-keen a bull or cow given to attack people.

Mander *C, N, E* maunder, mutter or murmur; to grumble; to talk confusedly.

Mangrel mongrel.

Mank *E* to noddle with the head.

Manner *C, E* manure.

Mannish manage.

Mannishment manures applied to land.

Mannisht *C* managed.

Manny *C, SW* many.

Mans! exclamations of wonder or surprise. (see Man alive).

Mant *N* to stutter.

Map'm *C, E, SW* may happen; (See Mappen).

Mappen *C, SW* may happen; *'Mappem I may.'* - Gibson.

Marcy mercy.

Markin' iron *C* a branding-iron for marking tools, horns of cattle, etc.

Marra to match; a friend or partner *'H's me marra.'*; an equal; marrow.

Marra to bran much alike; a match for; equal to.

Marraless not alike; not having a friend or partner.

Marras two alike; friends.

Marry *C* verily. *'Marry dud ha'* - verily he did.

Marry come up! interjection sometimes used on the receipt of ridiculous news.

Mart'nmas *C, E, SW* Martinmas, the feast of St. Martin; the 11th November.

Martlemas *N* Martinmas. *(see Mart'nmas).*

Marvel marble.

Marypwort *NW* Maryport.

Mash *C, E* mess; to bruise; to crush.

Mash *W* to infuse. *'Mash t'tea, well lass.'*.

Mask *N* to infuse. (see Mass).

Mass *C* to infuse. *'Wilta mass t'tea well fray us, dowter.'*.

Masselton batch *C* a sack of mixed grain ready for being ground.

Massycree massacre.

Mastel *C* a patch or border of an arable field never ploughed.

Mastis mastiff.

Masty mastiff.

Matter *C* esteem.

Matter an undefined number. *'A matter o'twenty or mair.'*.

Matterable *C* of consequence; important. *'What he does is nivver matterable.'*.

Matterfangled *NW* in incipient dotage.

Matterless unimportant. *'Thee teals is matterless, I's still gitten wed.'*.

Matters nothing special; or to boast of. *'nea girt matters.'*.

Mattha *C* Matthew.

Matty *C* the mark to pitch to.

Mawk midge *N* the flesh-fly or blue-bottle, *Musca vomitoria*.

Mawld *SW* mould.

Mawld *SW* to cast in a mould.

Mawn a rock or stone.

Mawse *SW* mouse.

Mawse *SW* mouse.

Mawwstead *SW* see Mewstead.

Mayn't may not.

Mayzel *C, SW* to make stupid or stupify; deprive of sensesibility or understanding.

Mayzlin' a simpleton or fool.

Maze *N* see Mayzel.

Mead made.

Meadd made.

Meak *SW* make.

Meakk *C, SW* make. *'I's meakkin' yer a churry ceakk.'*; sort.

Meakk on to be kind to; make on; go on.

Meakk out to progress. *'How is he meakkan' out?'*.

Meal meal.

Meall a meal.

Meall o'milk the milk given by a cow at one milking.

Meally mouth't using soft words hypocritically; also applied to a soft spoken person; a bay or brown horse having a light-coloured muzzle.

Mean mane.

Mean-field *C* a field in which the several shares or ownerships are known by meer-stones or other boundary marks.

Mear *SW* more.

Mearr more.

Measson *C, E* mason.

Measst *C, E, SW* most.

Meat-heall *C, N* healthy; having a regular appetite.

Mebby may be. *'Mebby we'll see Jack agin on Setterday.'*.

Med *C, SW* might.

Med n't *C, SW* might not.

Meean *SW* mean.

Meeat-heall *SW* healthy; having a regular appetite.

Meeda *C, N, E* meadow.

Meeght *N* might.

Meeght n't *N* might not.

Meeghty *N* mighty.(this word is nearly obsolete - 1878).

Meen *C* to moan; bemoan or lament; to express sorrow.

Meent meant, did mean.

Meer mare.

Meer-stan a landmark of stone; a boundary highlighted with stone(s).

Meerish effeminate.

Meet *N* might.

Meety *N* mighty. *(*this word is nearly obsolete - 1878).

Meg-wi'-many-feet *C* the creeping crowfoot plant, *Ranunculus repens*.

Meg-wi-many-teazz *SW* see Meg-wi'-many-feet

Mek *N, E* make; sort or style.

Mekkin *C, SW* the yellow flat, *Iris Pseudacorus*.

Mel *C* a conical but not peaked hill standing alone, eg. *Melfell, Melbrek etc.*

Mel deers *B* the passage between the front and back doors of a farm house.

Mel scope *E* a confirmed dunce or stupid individual; a dullbert.

Mel supper See Kern supper.

Mel-heedit *C* large and square headed.

Melder the quantity of meal ground or milled at one time.

Meldeurs *E* the double doors enclosing the farm yard.

Meldoor *C* a door put together with knobbed wooden pegs.

Mell *C* meddle; to interest oneself

in the affairs or concerns of others. *'He'll nowder mell nor mak'* - he will not interfere.

Mell a mallet; the last cut of corn in the harvest field. This was once commonly platted around a large apple, and hung up in the kitchen till Christmas day, the corn is then given to the best cow, and the apple to the oldest servant.

Men *N* amend.

Mend *C, SW* amend.

Mends amends. *'He's at t'height of his 'mends '*- nothing more to be given or had.

Meng *N* to renew or refill.

Menna *N* must not.

Mennom *C, E* minnow, *Leuciscus phoxinus.*

Menny many. *'He's stopped at heamm menny a neet.'.*

Mense propriety; decency; decorum.

Menseful hospitable; generous; liberal. *'A menseful swort of a body.'.*

Menseless opposite to Menseful. *'A menseless greedy gut.'.*

Meooldy mouldy.

Meoor *N* moor.

Merrybegot a bastard.

Merryneet a rustic merry-making to benefit a public-house. (see Murryneet).

Mesher *NW* a messenger.

Mess confusion. *'He hez mead a mess on 't!'.*

Mess! oaths or affirmations.

Messet *E* a toy-dog; a term of reproach to an untidy child.

Mester *SW* master, mister; teacher. *'T'curate was t'skool mester too.'.*

Met a mete or measure. (formerly a measure of two Winchester bushels - 1878).

Metlam cworn *C* toll of corn paid by certain lands to the lord of the manor was measured in a *Metlam peck.*

Metlam peck *C* a dry measure equivalent to eight quarts (9.1 litres); a fourth part of a bushel.

Meud *C, E, SW* mood; mud.

Meudd *C, SW* mud,.

Meunn *C, N* the moon. Persons subject to great variations of temper are said to be *'owder at t'meunn, or t'middin'still.'.*

Meuthy weather *E* mild and damp weather.

Meutt ho' moot hall. A town hall, as formerly at Keswick, Cockermouth, etc.

Meuz *C, E* muse.

Meuzz to muse.

Mew mowed. *Jack mew'd t'meeda wid oald Bob.'*; a mow of corn or hay. (see Moo).

Mewbrunt *NE* overheated in the mow or stack.

Mewburnt *C* overheated in the mow or stack.

Mewstead *C, N* a place where a mow stands; a mow. (see Moo).

Mewtle *C* the call of a cow or ewe when yeaming over their new born-young, and uttering a low sound of fondness.

Mex! oaths or affirmations.

Mey *NW* my.

Meyle *N, NW* mile.

Meynd *NW* remember. (see Mind).

Meyne *NW* mine.

Meyre *NW* mire.

Meyse *NW* mice.

Meyser *NW* miser.

Mezzer *C, E, SW* measure; measurement.

Mezzles *C, E, SW* measles.

Mickle much.

Mickle what *C* much the same. *'She's mickle what, parlish feckless.'.*

Midd *SW* meadow.

Midda *SW* meadow.

Middin 'sum *N, SW* a sump; a pool for the drainage of a dung-heap etc.

Middin pant *N, SW see* Middin 'sum.

Middin suckam *C* the liquor that drains from a dung-heap.

Middlin' middling or in between; only middling. *'I's gaily weel to-day, but I was nobbet varra middlin' yisterday.'.*

Milk hannel *C* a larger pail into which the milk cans during milking.

Milkas milk-house, dairy, milking parlour.

Milker a cow that gives plenty of milk is a *'top milker.'.*

Milkin' hill *C* a dry and slightly elevated open place near the farmhouse, where the cows were milked formerly while standing loose. The name is still common in some of the central parishes.

Milkin' ring *C* a circle of over-hanging trees or bushes, usually of holly, within which the cows were milked in hot weather. There was a ring at Causeway Foot, near Keswick (1858).

Milkin' side the side on which the milker sits with the right elbow towards the cow's head.

Milkness *C* a dairy of cows and their produce. *'We've a girt milkness this year.'.*

Miller's thumb *C* the willow wren, *Sylvia trochilus.*

Millreet millwright.

Millsucken bound by tenure to carry corn to be ground at the manorial mill.

Milly thoom *C* the willow wren, *Sylvia trochilus.*

Mimps *C* to talk primly and mincingly.

Min man. - only really pronounced when speaking familiarly or with contempt, *'Thou's nea girt things, min.'.*

Mind inclination. *'I've a reet good mind to gang an' tell them.'.*

Mind *SW* remember. *'Mind and*

think on.'; he does not care *'He duz n't mind'.*

Minny *N* mother.

Minsh mince, *'Git yer minsh pies med for yuletide.'.*

Mirk dark.

Mis-co' *C* to mis-call or mis-name; to verbally abuse.

Mis-leer't *NW* led astray.

Mis-lest molest.

Mis-mave *N* This term is used negatively to express absence of fear. (see Mis-may).

Mis-may *C* This term is used negatively to express absence of fear. *'Our cowt met t'soldiers and nivver mismay't his sel.'.*

Miscanter *C* to miscarry; a defeat, mishap.

Mischief a beating. *'Hang leet o'tha for mischief!'.*

Mislikken *N* to compare disrespectfully; to neglect or forget. *'Divvent mislikken noo.'.*

Miss wythan *NW* the aromatic shrub, *Myrica gale.*

Mist *C* Missed.

Mistakken *C, N, SW* mistaken.

Mistal *C* cow-house.

Mistal heck *C* farm-houses were once built adjoining a cow-house or mistal, with a passage between them. The doorway opening from this passage into the cow-house was fitted with a half-door or mistal heck. (few buildings of this kind still remain, 1878).

Mistean mistaken.

Misteann mistaken.

Mitch *SW* much.

Miter to waste; to crumble away from age.

Mither *N* mother.

Mits see Mittens.

Mittens woollen gloves or bags for the hand. (see Pwok mittens).

Mizzer *N* measure; measure-ment.

Mizzle *C* small rain. (see Hadder).

Mizzle go away. *'It's gittan leatt an'I mun mizzle.'* .

Mizzles *N* measles.

Moam *C* mellow, soft.

Moat *C, E* malt.

Moatster *C, E* maltster or a maker of malt.

Moilin *C* a silly fellow.

Moithy *E* moist.

Moke *C* maggot. (see Whicks).

Molligrubs *C* bad temper; imaginary ailments; in the sulks. *'She's in t'molligrubs to-day.'.*

Monney *N* many.

Monnish *G, not E* money.

Monny *N* many.

Moo a mow - a heap or stack of corn or hay.

Mooan *SW* the moon. (see Meunn).

Mooas *SW* mouse.

Mooat *SW* must not.

Moold *C, E* a mould; to cast in a mould.

Mooldi't cannels *C* moulded candles.

Moon't *C* must not.

Moonge *N* to grumble in a low tone.

Moont *SW* moult.

Moortidy *C* see Lingy.

Moose *C, N* mouse *'I saw a speckel't la'al moose on yer drisser top.'.*

Moose *C, N, E* mouse.

Moot moult; meet

Moot *N* to mention.

Mooter *C, N* multure (a fee) or mill toll given to the miller for grinding grain.

Moppet a pet.

Moresby Ho' fwok *C* people of quality; court cards.

Morgidge mortgage.

Morrnin' *SW* morning.

Mort *C* a great quantity. *'A mort o'fine things.'.*

Mortal very - as *'Mortal lang.'* *'mortal short.'*; also used to give

force to an expression.

Moss-watter ceakk *E* a cake made of oatmeal with butter, lard, cream, or other shortening material. This inappropriate name would seem to have been given by way of abating the idea of extravagance.

Mossberries *C* cranberries, the fruit of the *Oxycoccus palustris.*

Mosscheeper *N* see Lingy.

Mosschilper *N* see Lingy.

Mosscrops *C* the flowers of *Eriophorum vaginatum.*

Mote *C* malt.

Mote heartit *C* timid, cowardly.

Moty sun *NE* sunbeams shining through an aperture and illuminating the dust floating in the air.

Mouth pwok a horse's nose-bag.

Mowd soil, mould.

Mowdy mouldy

Mowdywark *N* the mole, *Talpa europoea.*

Mowdywarp *C, SW* the mole, Talpa europoea.

Mowerkin *C* Mockerkin.

Moyder't *C, N* bewildered, confused. *'He gat moyder't in a snow storm and torfer't.'.*

Much sometimes used to express doubt. *'It's much if he gangs at o'now.'.*

Muck hack *C* a three-toothed drag or rake for drawing manure from the cart.

Muck hots panniers for conveying manure on horseback

Muck hots *NE* heaps of muck or lime in the field.

Muck wet very wet; perspiring copiously *'Dick's muck wet wi'sweat.'.*

Muckfork *SW* a dung-fork.

Muckle *N* much.

Muckment anything dirty. *'A heap o'muckment.'.*

Mucky *C* dirty; mean; cowardly.

Mud *C, SW* might.

Mud n't *C, SW* might not.

Mudder *C, E, SW* mother.

Mug *C* a small drinking-pot; the mouth.

Mug a drinking vessel; the face; a fool.

Mug sheep *C* the white-faced breed from which the improved Leicester breed originated.

Muggert *E* ragwort, *Senecio Jacoboea*.

Muggy weather *C* damp and misty.

Mull *C* to crumble; peat-dust; anything crumbled.

Mull confusion. *'He meadd a mull on 't.'*.

Mull't yal *C* ale mulled with eggs and spices to be drunk while hot.

Mummel to speak low and indistinct; to mumble.

Mump *C* to sulk. *'I ken yer meanin' by yer mumpin'.'*

Mun must.

Munge *C* to grumble in a low tone.

Munkister *SW* Muncaster, near Ravenglass.

Munnet *C* must not.

Mure moor.

Murk *C* see Mirk.

Murk dark. A farm in Bassenthwaite was called Murk-holme (1878).

Murl *C, NE* to crumble with the fingers. *'As murly as a short ceakk.'*.

Murryneet a rustic merry-making to benefit a public-house.

Mush *C* to crush; dry crumbling refuse.

Mushamer *C* mushroom or fungi.

Musty *C* sour-looking or gloomy; a smell of something damp and unaired.

Mwornin' *C, NE* morning.

Mwort *N* a great quantity. *'A mwort o'fine things.'*.

Mwotes *C, E* motes, dust; small particles.

My sartis! an exclamation of surprise.

My sarty! see My sartis!

Myld *C* mile.

Mysen myself.

Mysert *E, NW* miser.

Myter *C* to crumble or reduce to decay. Stone which decomposes by the action of the weather *'myters away'*.

Myzert *N* miser.

N't *C* not. *'I'll mebby n't see Jack agin.'*.

Na no.

Naa *N* no, nay.

Nab *C* arrest; to catch suddenly. *'Jwohnny nabb't t'theeaf afwore he legg'd it.'*.

Naebody *N* nobody.

Naff nave; the nave or central hub of a wheel.

Nag *C, SW* a horse.

Nag *N* always fault finding. *'Whats yer naggan at now?'*; a horse.

Nap *C* to strike gently and quickly.

Napery *C* the store of household linen.

Nar near. *'To kirk the nar, to God more far.'*

Nar gaan *N* near going, miserly.

Nar gangan' *C, SW* near going, miserly.

Nar-er nearer, nearest.

Narder nearer, nearest.

Narer *G, not E* nearer.

Narvish nervous. *'Iv'rybody's narvish when yer git wed.'*.

Nash *C, SW* fragile, brittle, tender.

Nashy *C, SW* fragile, brittle, tender.

Nastment *E* filth, nastiness.

Nater nature; human feeling or commiseration. *'He hes n't a bit o'nater for nowder dog nor man.'*.

Natterable *C, N* natural.

Nattle to make a light and quick knocking. *'He nattel't at t'window.'*.

Nattral *C* natural.

Natty *C* neat.

Naud *E* strange.

Nav see Naff.

Naww *SW* now.

Nawwt *SW* nothing.

Nay say refusal or denial.

Nay than! an exclamation of wonder, or doubt, or sympathy.

Nayber *C, SW, E* neighbour.

Nayber row *C, SW* neighbourhood; alike with neighbours or others.

Nayder neither.

Nayder dee nor dowe in a doubtful way of recovery.

Ne'er do weel a graceless person who never does well.

Nea no, nay (denial or refusal).

Nea body nobody. *'Nea body likes t'oald goat.'*.

Nea co'for't no reason for it.

Nea girt cracks *C, SW* nothing special or to boast of.

Nea girt things *C, SW* nothing special or to boast of.

Neaa *SW* no, nay.

Neabody *C, E* nobody.

Neah *C* no.

Neah *C, E, SW* no, nay.

Neak't naked.

Neakk't naked. *'Jack was stark neakk't in t'watter.'*.

Neam name.

Neamm name.

Nean *N* none.

Neann *N* none.

Near *SW* the kidney.

Near fat *C* the fat surrounding the kidneys.

Near hand near or close to. *'If you gang near hand you dog it'll bite.'*.

Nearder *G, not E* nearer, nearest.

Neavvel *C, E* navel.

Neb the bill of a bird; nose; peak of a cap; projecting hill; end, etc.

Neb-plate *N* the iron plate on the toe of a clog.

Nebber *C, SW* neighbour.

Nebby *N* a hook-headed stick.

Neck't *C* broken-necked.

Necklath neckcloth; handkerchief.

Nedder't *C* withered; not in a thriving state.

Nee *N* no, nay.

Neeadles *SW* needles.

Neeaf *SW* the clenched fist.

Neeak *SW* nook, corner.

Neean *SW* none; noon, lunchtime (dinner-time in 1878).

Neean *SW* noon.

Need-fire fire started by the friction of wood and carried quickly from house to house, for the purpose of passing cattle through the smoke as a preventive of epidemics. (still in use around 1841).

Needles *E, SW* needles.

Neef *C* the clenched fist.

Neegars *N* see Niggarts.

Neeght *N* night.

Neekkt *C* naked.

Neen *N* nine.

Neer ak *C* never mind.

Neers kidneys of beasts.

Neest *C, N* next.

Neest *N* nightest; next.

Neet *C, E, SW* night.

Neeve *N* the clenched fist.

Neevy nack a boyish rhyme of casting lots or picking players in games or sports. *'Neevy neevy nack, Whether hand will ta tack. 'T topmer or t'lowmer?'.*

Neeze sneeze.

Nep *C* to bite in play as horses do.

Ner *C* nor. *'Nowder mair ner less.'.*

Ner nor; than. *'My meer can trot faster ner thine.*

Ner *N* near.

Nerrer *N* nearer, nearest.

Nesh *N* fragile, brittle, tender.

Nessle nestle; as in a nest. *'Nes'lan' abed till past neunn.'.*

Nettle keall *C* a wholesome broth made with young nettles in place of vegetables.

Neuk *C, N, E* nook.

Neuk-window *B* In old farm houses there was generally a small square window in the corner nearest the fireplace of the house or sitting room, with two larger and mullioned windows on the same side.

Neukk *C, N* nook, corner.

Neun *C, N, E* noon.

Neunn *C, N* noon, lunch-time.

Nevvy *C, E* nephew.

Newdel 't bewildered; confused through excessive drinking. *'Jonty's newdel't wid yal an' fell't down t'cellar steps.'.*

Newdles a trifling or silly person.

Newdlin' see Newdles.

Newe *SW* new. (pronounced *'nay-oo'*, in some parts *'nu'*).

Newkel't newly calved..

Neyne *NW* nine.

Nib't stick *N* a hook-headed stick.

Nibbleties *N* novelties.

Nibbleties *N* novelties. *'Wi'nibbleties as guod as nyce.'* Stagg.

Nichol *C, N* Nicholas.

Nick't at heed rendered temporarily foolish or idiotic.

Nicka' *SW* Nicholas. *'Nicka Stib'nson.'.*

Nickel't newly calved.

Nicker *N* to neigh; to laugh loudly.

Nicker *SW* to laugh in an undertone.

Niebeheed *N* neighbourhood.

Nieber *N* neighbour.

Niggart plates *C* sheet-iron plates between the niggarts and the hobs.

Niggarts *C* upright cast-iron plates used for reducing the space in an openfire place.

Niggel't *C* bothered; annoyed.

Nigler *C* a busy, industrious person or animal.

Nim *C* to walk or run with short and quick steps.

Nin none. *'My mudder she thought nin like me.'* from Anderson's *Daft Watty*. A good example of a very common part of Cumbrian dialect, where both noun and pronoun are used in the same clause of a sentence.

Ningnang a silly person.

Ninnyhammer *C* a foolish person.

Nip to pinch with the fingers or nails; a minute quantity, *'a nip of snuff'*.

Nip up *C* to pilfer; to pick up quickly.

Nit *C, SW* not.

Nitch *N* gang, family, or set. *'They're a bad nitch, the heall lot o'them.'.*

Nither't *N* withered; not in a thriving state.

Niver never.

Nivver never.

Nivver let on keep it secret; take no notice.

Nivver let wit keep it secret; take no notice.

Nob *C* childish terms for the nose.

Nobbet nothing but, *'Mary's nobbet a slape clogs.';* only.

Nobby *C* childish term for the nose.

Nockles knuckles.

Noddle *C* the head; to nod.

Noddy *E* a game at cards similar to cribbage.

Noddy 't *B* to omit counting a point at the game of Noddy.

Nog *C, SW* a handle to fix on the shaft of a scythe.

Noggin the eighth of a quart measure.

Noggy *N* coarse thread.

Noggy-wife a maker of coarse thread.

Noo now. *'I hev' the noo.'-* I comprehend.

Nop *C* to crop; to nip the ends off gooseberries, etc.

Nope *C* to strike on the head.

Noppy *C* tidy, neat. *'Eye, a varra*

noppy laal body.'.

Noration a noisy conversation; great noise; oration.

Nottable clever at trifling manipulations.

Nought at dowe C not over good; nothing of importance. (see Dowe).

Nought at o' nothing at all.

Nought in a manner not much.

Nought o't'swort nothing of the sort or kind; not true.

Nought to crack on nothing to boast of.

Nowder neither.

Nows and thans at odd times; now and then.

Nowt C nothing; zero.

Nowt N cattle. *'Tam, gan'an 'fodder the nowt, my man.'.*

Nowt n'summat nothing or anything, *'T'oald hag knaa's nowt n'summat.'.*

Nowte nothing. *'I lost nowte when I selt t'oald horse.'.*

Nowtfit oil oil obtained from the feet of cattle by boiling.

Nowther N neither.

Nub to nudge; to jog or push secretly or to awaken attention; to butt with elbow or knee.

Nudge to butt or prode with elbow or knee.

Num numb; clumsy.

Num chance luck and not skill. *'He dud varra weel, bit it was o'num chance.'.*

Num luck by chance and not by ability.

Num thooms clumsy person; an indifferent workman.

Nunty E formal, old-fashioned, shabby (applied to female dress only).

Nut not.

Nut i'shaft for C, SW unable to accomplish it.

Nut o'theer not all there - silly, foolish or idiotic.

Nut reet not right; idiotic, *'Yer Mary's nut reet in t'heed.'.*

Nut to ride a watter on C not to be depended upon; Some saddle-horses have a propensity to lie down in crossing water of a ford.

Nut varra reet see Nut reet.

Nutcrack feass B the nose and chin approaching.

Nwos C nose. *'His nwos is brock, but yer sud see t'tudder lad.'.*

Nwose nose.

Nwote the period when a cow is due to calve. *'She'll be up at her nwote at April day.'.*

Nwotice C notice.

Nwotion notion; idea. *'Our lad hes a nwotion o'gangan' to sea.'.*

Nwotis notice.

Nwotish notice.

Nwoze nose.

Nyber row N neighbourhood; alike with neighbours or others.

Nyfel to pilfer or take.

O' all, of.

O'as yan all the same.

O'geats N always.

O'riddy C, E already. *'I's seen him o'riddy fishing in t'beck.'.*

O'ruddy N already.

O't of the. *'This yal hes a tack o't'cask.'.*

O'tha of thee; on thee.

O'that C all that; more of the same. *'She fand it varra sweet an' good an o'that.'.*

Oa C owe, own.

Oaf C a blockhead; an idiot. *'I telt yer he's a reet oaf.'.*

Oal N old.

Oalas always.

Oald C, E old. *'T'oald church needs a new bell.'.*

Oald bat C, N the usual state or condition; an aged person, often a little forgetful.

Oald fashin't sly; sagacious; precocious; old-fashioned.

Oald fashint NE old fashioned.

Oald lass C an older lady, usually a mother, *'T'oald lass has meadd churry ceakk.*

Oald man E a game among schoolboys.

Oald man father (or occassionally the head of household).

Oald she The old custom of wishing good luck by throwing an old shoe after a person or wedding-party (still occasionally in use 1878).

Oald standards old residents.

Oaldfwok's neet C In the country married people assemble one evening, soon after Christmas, at the principal inn in the parish, for a roast beef and sweet pie supper, and dancing etc. (1878)

Oalfarrant N see Oald fashin't.

Oalus C always.

Oan G owe, own. *'Who oans this?'*; to visit. *'Ye nivver oan us.'.*

Oblege oblige.

Obstropolus C unruly; turbulent; obstreperous *'He's reet obstropolus.'.*

Occashun C occasion.

Od C God.

Odments C scraps; odds and ends; things worthless, etc.

Ods what difference does it make, what does it matter. *'What ods.'.*

Of'ner N more often.

Off an'on G uncertain; vacillating; thereabouts. *'When's oald Jwon to come heamm?'.... 'Off an'on about May day.'.*

Off his bat out of health.

Offal a butcher's term for wealth. *'Hes he offal't weel?'.*

Offcome C result.

Offen often.

Offis C office.

Offish office.

Offskeum the refuse; the worst; the offscourings.

Ofner N oftener.

Oft *C* off or farther side.

Oft *C, E, SW* often.

Ofter *C, E, SW* more often.

Ogre ochre; a fine clay used as a pigment.

Oil o'hezzel *C* a sound drubbing or beating.

Okart *C, E, N* awkward. *'Divvern't be sea okart.'.*

Olas *C, E* always.

Omas *C* alms. a payment given to relieve the poor.

Ome *C* the elm-tree, *Ulmus compestris.*

On upon.

On lig an oppressive and continuous charge. *'A morgidge is a sair on-lig on a house.'.*

Onder under.

Onder set *C* to underpin or support a wall by building below its foundation.

Onderhand *C* undersized. *'A laal onderhand creter.'.*

Ondermer the one under the other.

Onny *C, N* any.

Ons *C* puts on. *'I ons wi'my cwoat and off to wark.'.*

Onsett *NE* farmhouse and outbuildings; homestead.

Onstead *C, N* see Onsett.

Onta on to; upon; unto.

Oo' wool.

Ooa wool.

Ooerder *SW* order.

Oomer *C* shade; to shade.

Oor *C, N, E* our; hour.

Oor *SW* over; too much.

Oor lass *C* my wife, *'Oor lass is still at heamm wid t'barns.'*; our daughter.

Oor side *C, N* our part of the country.

Oor wife *C, N* my wife. (seldom heard by 1878).

Oors *B* ours; also a curious excision or abbreviation spoken by a wife - instead of saying *'my*

husband', she calls him 'oors'. (see Oor wife and Oor lass).

Oot out. *'Git oot of yer bed and gaa to wark.'.*

Oot at t'elbas in declining circumstances.

Oot bye *N* not far off.

Oot liggers cattle not housed during winter.

Oot o'cue *C, N* of health; not in good humour.

Oot o'geatt *C, N* out of the way; stand by.

Oot o't'way *C, N* uncommon, exorbitant.

Oot o'teunn partly offended; dispirited.

Oot ower *NE* across the country.

Oot powl't *C* beat, defeated.

Oot ray *C, N* to exceed propriety; incorrect behaviour or morals, not fit or right.

Oot shot a projection of an upper story or window in an old house, or of a wall or fence.

Oot! exclamations of unbelief. *'Oot! it was nea sek things.'.*

Oot-rake *NE* a freeway, route or rake for sheep from the enclosures to the common.

Ootener *C, N, E* a stranger or new-comer.

Ootfield land *C* land enclosed at a later period than the infield land, and generally inferior.

Ootgang a narrow strip of land connecting the common with the farm-yard or village.

Ootin' *C, N* an outing, a pleasure jaunt or trip.

Ootside outside; at the most. *'He's nobbet six feutt hee et t'oot side.'.*

Ootwart dissipated, ill-conducted.

Ootweel *C, N* to discharge

Ootweels *C, N* outcasts; refuse.

Op'n open. *'Is t'winda op'n ?'.*

Opengilt *C, SW* a young sow intended for breeding purposes.

Oppen open.

Oppengowan *C* the marsh marigold, Caltha palustris.

Or are. *'Or ye finely?'*; ere, before. *'Cuckoo 'll nut come or April.'.*

Orchat *C, SW* orchard.

Orndinner *N* a lunch. (not in use of late years 1878).

Orts *C* the refuse of fodder left by cattle.

Other-guess *N* another kind.

Other-some *C, SW* other, some other. *'Some flowers is blue, and other-some yellow.'.*

Ought-like *C* appropriate; anything like.

Ours *B* see Oors.

Out houses farm buildings and not dwellings.

Ov *C* of. *'Safe as the Bank ov Ingland.'.*

Owee c come on. *'Owee lets gah to t'Wild Duck at Branthet.'.*

Owder either.

Ower *C, E, N* over; to much.

Ower over.

Ower by *N* over the way.

Ower lap *C* overlap; an encroachment by the sheep of a flock or parish on the common of another.

Ower word *C* words repeated at the end of a verse; a habitual saying.

Ower year *C* belonging to a second year. *'You have a fine pig there, Betty.'....'Eye, it's a ower year swine.'.*

Owerance guidance; governance; superintendence.

Owercassen *N* overcast.

Owergit *C, SW* overcast.

Owertak *C, SW* overcast.

Owner teunn *B* words repeated at the end of a verse; a habitual saying.

Ows *N* owns. *'Who ows tis?'.*

Owsen oxen.

Owt anything. *'Mattha was riddy fwor owt' at leukt like fun.'*; aught.

Owther *N* either.

Owts *C, N* anything; this word is commonly used as an interrogatory. *'Hez ta gitten owts o'fish to-day?'*.

Oxters armpits.

Paap *SW* see Pope.

Paat *SW* see Pote.

Pack be off; go away. *'If thou does n't mind thy wark I'll send thee a-packin', an'seunn teah.'*.

Pack *N* tame - spoken of animals.

Pack threed coarse thread; nonsense.

Packs heavy clouds; thunderclouds. *'T'sky's packy to-day, and like thunner.'*.

Pacquet *C* the *Cumberland Pacquet* newspaper.

Pad a kind of saddle for carrying two on horseback. Now (1878) superseded by light vehicles.

Pad the hoof to go on foot.

Pad-saddle *C* a composite article between pad and saddle (now out of use 1878).

Paddick *N* the frog or toad.

Paddick rid *N* the spawn of frogs or toads.

Paddick rud *N* see Pandick rid.

Paddock *N* the frog or toad.

Paddock fish *C* the toadfish, *Batrachoididac*.

Paddock peyp *NW* the *Equisetum arvense* plant.

Paddock steull *C, N* toadstool or mushroom, all non-edible fungi.

Pag't *C* laden; full. *'Pag't wi'dirt.'*.

Paiks a boyish term for a thrashing.

Pain *B* that part of the common which was forbidden under penalty to be dug for turf.

Pain beukk *E* a register of pains (punishments) and penalties hand out in manorial courts.

Palterly *C* paltry.

Pan an' speunn *C* When a child or young animal is brought up without being suckled, it is reared by the aid of a pan to warm the milk, and a spoon to be fed with.

Pan on togidder to associate; to pair (see Pan on wid).

Pan on wid to associate; to pair - from cooking in or eating from the same pan.

Panceakk *C* pancake.

Pang't *C* quite full.

Pankeakk Tuesday *C* Shrove Tuesday; on which day pancakes are provided for dinner.

Pant a sump.

Par *C, SW* pair. *I want a par o'new shun.'*.

Pardsah *C* Pardshaw village, near Cockermouth.

Pare *C* to diminish; a cow pares in milk when the quantity yielded grows daily less.

Parfet perfect.

Parfit perfect.

Parin' speadd a breast-plough.

Parjery perjury.

Parlish *C, SW* wonderful; extraordinary; parlous.

Parral *G, not E* peril. *'It's at te parral to strike.'*.

Parridge *N* porridge.

Parritch *N* porridge.

Parrock a small enclosure near the house a little larger than a garth and smaller than a croft.

Parshal *G, not E* parcel.

Partles *C* the globular droppings of sheep.

Pash *C, N* very wet, *'wet as pash.'*; heavy and sudden *'A pashan'shower.'*; entirely *'Rotten as pash.'*.

Past beyond. *'A bad teuthwark's past o'bidin'.'*.

Paster *C* pasture. *'Sum o't' paster land is as bare as a barn flooar.'*.

Pat *C* small mass of butter, which is beat into shape using pats;

Pat fit; correct; suitable.

Pat *N* has put; did put.

Pats *C* the broad wooden blades or paddles used to beat butter into shape before wrapping.

Patten a wooden shoe with an iron ring, worn to keep the shoes from the dirt or mud.

Patter to beat quickly, *'It patters and rains.'*; to talk convincingly with confidence. *'H's a greet patter, he'd sell any yan ought.'*.

Patterin hole *C* a deep fissure in the rock at St. Bees head, where a stone thrown in can be heard pattering as it descends.

Pattle *C* A scraper for the wooden mould board of a plough.

Paw *C* the hand - and especially if dirty. *'Keep yer dirty paws off.'*.

Paw heeds *NE* tadpoles.

Pawky *N* too familiar; sly.

Pawt *N* to walk heavily.

Paww *C* to kick when in the last extremity. *'It'll nivver paww mair.'*.

Pawwder *SW* powder.

Pawwnd *SW* pound.

Pay to beat.

Pays *C, N, E* peas.

Paze to prize, or force, or lift with a lever.

Peace appease.

Peakle *C* to tread or walk silently.

Peal *C, N, E* appeal.

Peaper *C* paper.

Pearch pierce. *'It's a pearchan' cold wind, this! '*; penetrate.

Peart pert.

Peass *C* pace; a raised approach for horses to an upper floor of a farm building.

Peass eggs dyed and boiled eggs handed out at Easter time.

Peasst paste.

Peast paste.

Peat coom *N* the dust and débris of peats.

Peat dote *C* see Dote.

Peat hee *C* the height of a peat; about knee height.

Peat mull *C* the dust and débris of peats.

Peat pot the hole out of which peats have been dug.

Peat skeall *SW* a house on the

fell to store peats in.

Peav pave.

Peazz *C* see Peass.

Pedder a pedlar; to attempt to dispose an inferior article on a buyer. *'Don't pedder that rubbish on me.'.*

Pee *C, SW* to shut one eye on taking aim.

Pee in yer oan pok neukk *C* mind your own business; see how it applies to yourself.

Pee't having only one eye.

Peeak *SW* to peek or pry into secret matters. *'He com gloppan' and peeakan' into ivry corner.'.*

Peeal *SW* appeal.

Peeas *SW* peace; peas.

Peeat *SW* peat.

Peeaz *SW* peace; peas.

Peekle *E* to peek or pry. (see Peeak).

Peel *C, N* appeal. *'I rackan its 'rang to 'peel to court.'.*

Peel a baker's dough or bread-spade.

Peel house *N* a peel tower or house of defence in the time of the border wars.

Peelgarlic *N* a tall, slender, and starved girl.

Peenjan' *N* starving with cold.

Peer *C* poor.

Peer appear; pear; pair *'McAleer at Workiton selt him a peer o'beutts for three bob.'.*

Peer *N* poor.

Peercock *B* peacock.

Peesweep *N* the lapwing, *Vanellus cristatus.*

Peg a thump; a child's tooth.

Peg away go along; hurry on.

Peggy nut *C* a boyish game played with nuts.

Peggy white throat *C* one of the willow wrens.

Pegh *C, N* to pant with a stifled groan.

Pelk *C* to beat.

Pelt *C* to throw, separately or in a great number or amount. *'T'lads pelt'd the lasses with sno'balls.'.*

Pelter *C, N* a large one.

Pen'lam pendulum.

Pen'orth *C* a pennys worth of, or as much as you can buy for a penny. *'I want a pen'orth of treeacle taffy.'.*

Penjy *N* of a complaining habit.

Pennerth pennyworth.

Penny doctor *B* a small red bodied beetle.

Penny pie *N* a fall on the ice.

Pennysom' profitable by small items.

Pennystans *C, N* stones used in playing pitch, instead of pennies.

Pensy *C, N* sticky; of weak or poor appetite.

Pent paint.

Pentas *C, SW* penthouse; a roof fixed to the side of a house. (common in the 18th century in farm-yards; scarce in the 19th).

Perfit *N* perfect.

Perlang belong. *'Whee perlangs this?'.*

Pestle tail *C* a horse's tail without any hair.

Pether *N* pedlar.

Pettle to occupy time over trifles.

Petty *C* a privy or lavatory; a necessary; small

Peull *N* a pool or dub.

Peur *N, E* poor.

Pewder *C* pewter. Large dishes and dinner-plates of pewter succeeded wooden trenchers about the beginning of the 18th century.

Pewther *N* see Pewder.

Peye *N* pie; pye.

Peype *N, NW* pipe.

Pez *C, N, E* peas.

Pez scodin' Grey peas when young are boiled in the pod. A cup of butter is added in the midst, in which each person dips

the end of the pod, and strips out the peas between the teeth, and the pods are then pelted at each other.

Piannet *C* the peony plant.

Pichnichety *N* exact in small matters; neat in dress.

Pick *C, N* to lift with a pitchfork; to push. *'Ned pick't Joe ower the dyke.'.*

Pick a coal hewer's work tool; entirely dark; pitch.

Pick at to invite a quarrel. *'They're always pickin' at yan another.'.*

Pick t'cofe abortion in cows.

Pickle *C, E* a grain of corn; a pinch; a small quantity; a quandary or uncertain state.

Pickless *C* incompetent, feckless.

Picks *C* an old name for the diamond suit of cards.

Picky *E* of weak appetite; fussy.

Pig in *C* to nestle close as pigs do. *'Come, barns, pig in to bed wi'ya.'.*

Piggin *C* a small wooden pail to hold about a quart, hooped like a barrel and having a stave handle.

Pik-thank *C* a slanderous mischief-maker.

Pike pick; the conical top of a mountain or hill; the peak; a pillar or high cairn erected on the top or point of a mountain; a large-sized haycock.

Pike-thank *C* see Pik-thank.

Pikelins *C* half-sized haycocks.

Pile a blade or flat part of a leaf, *'a pile o'girse'* - a blade of grass.

Pilgarlic *C* a simpleton or fool.

Pillion seat a seat to fix behind the saddle for a female to ride on. (out of use since about 1830).

Pin *C* When the ewe gives much milk the excrement of the young lamb glues the tail down upon the anus and prevents all discharge. The lamb is then said to be *'pin't'* or pinned.

Pin pointin' *B* too exact in trifles or without seriousness (1878); determine an accurate location, problem or reason.

Pin't into t'hard yerth *C* the grass eaten off to the bare ground.

Pinch't *C* falling short. *'He'll be pinch't to git it done.'.*

Pinchgut a miserly person.

Pinion tied strong in opinion; obstinate. *'Oor Mary's varra 'pinnion tied.'.*

Pinjy *C* of a complaining habit.

Pinnel *C* a hard subsoil of clay and gravel.

Pinner't *C* shrivelled, lean, starved.

Pinnin'in t'belly *C* a depressing sensation in the bowels. *'It isn't t'grips, it's a pinin'.'.*

Pipe stoppel *C* a fragment of the tube of a tobacco-pipe - probably a corruption of pip-stopper.

Pippin pips or seeds of the apple etc.

Pishmidder *N* see Pissimer.

Pissamoor *C* see Pissimer.

Pissibeds *C* the flowers of the dandelion plant, *Leontodon taraxacum* or *Taraxacum densleonis.*

Pissimer *C* insects such as the ant, emmet or pismire.

Pissmudder *C* see Pissimer.

Pitch Dark entirely dark.

Plack *N* a very small sum.

Plad plaid, a stripped cloth.

Plain as pike staff very distinct, clear and evident.

Plantin' plantation.

Plash *C* to cut or trim the sides of a hedge.

Plat *C, N* plot; a line of hay ready for cocking; a broad ridge of land.

Plat *NE* to walk heavily.

Plate *C* to clinch; to rivet; iron or steel plate.

Play't *C* played.

Pleague *NE* plague.

Pleas place.

Pleass place.

Pleass *C* please.

Pled pleaded. *'He pled hard for his life.'.*

Pleean *SW* to complain.

Pleeasant *N* pleasant.

Pleeaz *SW* please.

Pleen *C, N* to complain.

Pleesant *N* pleasant.

Pleeshur *N* pleasure.

Pleezer *N* pleasure.

Pleezter more pleased.

Plennets *NW* abundance.

Plennish to furnish a house or stock a farm; replenish, to stock.

Plet *C* plain or flat; a small piece of flat ground; to plait, weave or to twist. *'He gangs plettan his legs, and wammels like an eel.'.*

Pleugh *N* plough.

Pleukk *N* a pimple on the face.

Pleutery *NE* useless things; refuse. *'Rid away that pleutery, Maggy.'.*

Pleyn *C, N* to complain.

Plezzer *C, SW* pleasure.

Plies *C* apply or employ diligence; ply - the foldings of garments. *'We put on three plies o'flannin for a sare throat.'.*

Plimlan' *C* the parish and village of Plumbland.

Plivver *N* the plover bird, *Charadrius* - once eaten as food.

Plizzant pleasant.

Plizzer *E, NW* pleasure.

Plode *C* to wade through thick and thin; work relentlessly.

Plodge *N* to plunge; to wade in water.

Plook see Pleukk.

Ploom *C* a plum. (no longer common in 1878).

Plote *C* see Plode.

Plowmb *SW* plumb.

Plu' *C, E, SW* plough.

Plu' bote *C* timber to make a plough of, which the lord of the manor was bound to allow to his customary tenant.

Plu'co'er *C, SW* the driver of each pair of plough oxen or horses in the last century, usually a lad or stout girl, whose duty it was to steer the animals and keep them moving steadilyl.

Plu'pattle *C* an instrument used to clear the soil from the plough-share.

Plug *C* to pull.

Plump *C* to sink or fall quickly. *'He went plum down like a steann.'.*

Pluttery *NE* see Pleutery.

Plyace *C* place.

Poach to trample land in wet weather; when a cow is said to have seven mouths destroying the grass, viz. four feet, one mouth, and two droppers of excrement.

Poc *C* pox or any virus disease producing pus-filled pimples, that leave scars or pockmarks on healing. eg. chickenpox. (see Watter jags).

Pock arr't *N* marked by small-pox.

Pock fret *C* see Pock arr't.

Pockerr't *N* see Pock arr't.

Pod *C* to poke.

Poddinger *C* a porringer or coarse earthenware pot with a handle on one side.

Poddish *C, SW* porridge - the usual breakfast and supper, with bread and cheese and milk, of the farm-servants over the greatest part of the county; and till lately, of farmers and their families.

Poddish kite *C* a gluttonous child or youth. *'It's nut t'skin of a clap ceakk 'at'll sarra that paddish kite.'.*

Poddish stick *SW* a stick used for stirring a boiling pot.

Pode *C* uphold. *'Aa'l 'pode ta it's*

true.'.

Podgy *C* a short and fat person.

Polk *C* to steal when playing a game of marbles.

Poll the head of a person; a register or list of 'heads', that is of persons. eg. at election time.

Polly *SW* a cow without horns.

Pomes *C* the blossoms of the willow tribe.

Pon very commonly used for upon. *'Pon my word.'.*

Poo pull, pluck, pulling.

Poo *SW* a pool or dub; a wide and watery ditch.

Poo't pulled; pull it.

Pooan pull, pulling.

Pooar *SW* poor.

Pooder *C* hurry, *'Off he went in sec a pooder!'.*

Pooder *C, E* powder.

Pool *C* a pool or dub.

Poor lean; out of condition - usually applied to live stock.

Poother *N* powder.

Pop *C* a dot.

Pope *C* to walk as in the dark - 'popan' and stopan'.'.

Poppinoddles *C* a boyish term for a summersault or som- ersault.

Por poker.

Porpas *SW* purpose.

Portcher poacher.

Portinskeal Portinscale village, near Keswick.

Poss *C* saturated with liquid, *'O'in a poss.';* to tread and clean wet clothes etc. *'She was possan' blankets in a tub.'.*

Posset *C* to vomit - an infant possets when it is sick and upcasts part of its food.

Posset milk curdled with wine or other liquor.

Possinger *SW* porringer.

Pot *C, E, SW* has put; did put.

Pot boilin' day the day on which broth is made in the *'keall pot'* - commonly Sunday in country

places.

Pot luck a friendly welcome to a share of what may happen to have been provided for the family.

Pot metal *C* cast-iron. (see Kessen metal).

Pot't *SW* put it.

Pote *C* to paw with the foot; pawed.

Pote to walk clumsily.

Pots crockery, dishes and cooking utensils. *'Oor lass has wesh'd the pots.'.*

Pottek *C* pocket. (almost out of use - 1878).

Potter to trifle; to work without any real effect.

Pottle see Potter.

Pow-cat *C* the foumart or polecat; a fungus which grows in hedges and has a very offensive smell, the *Phallus impudicus* or Stinkhorn.

Powe *C* sump.

Powe the head. *'Daionty Davy, curly powe.'* from an old song; poll or a register or list of *'heads'*, that is of persons.

Powe *SW* a pole; to clip the hair off the head or poll.

Powe head *NW* tadpoles.

Power a great deal. *'It's done him a power o'good.'.*

Powl *C, N, E* a pole; to clip the hair off the head or poll.

Powny pony.

Powsowdy an ale-posset.

Praytha *C* pray thee or prithee.

Preen *C* to comb and dress the hair.

Preen *N* a pin.

Preese *C* to press; to importune or request with urgency. *'Aa's preezin' her for an answer.'.*

Preest *C* priest.

Prent print, *'T'weddin nwotish war prent'd in the Pacquet.'.*

Prentas apprentice.

Prentin printing. *'T'prentin in this beukk's varra la'al.'.*

Presarve *C* preserve.

Pretha *C* pray thee.

Preuf proof.

Preuve prove, try.

Preuvv prove.

Preyce *NW* price.

Preyd *NW* pride.

Preyde *NW* pride.

Preym *NW* prime.

Preyme *NW* prime.

Prial *C* three of a sort.

Prick *B* for fastening clout, and string for tying; a skewer.

Prick-me-dainty *E* a pert (forward, saucy or bold) and showily dressed girl or young man.

Prickers iron prongs to fix on the front of on open fire grate to make toast or cook sausages, etc., upon.

Prickin' *C* short thorn branches stuck on the top of an earthen fence.

Pricky back the stickleback or thornback fish, *Gasterosteus.*

Pricky board *N* When a person's means of living are exhausted.

Prig to beat down in bargaining; to pilfer.

Prin *N* a pin.

Priss *C, SW* to press.

Prithee pray thee.

Prize *C* to raise by lever power.

Prizzent present.

Prizzently presently.

Proag *C* provender or meal to be eaten in the field.

Prod a thorn or splinter; to poke with the end of a stick, etc.; to stir up.

Proddle to poke with the end of a stick, etc.; *to stir up.*

Proffer offer; a tender of services. *'He proffer't to help us.'.*

Prog *C* see Proag.

Proud vigorous or luxuriant, as applied to rank vegetation; set forward or proud.

Providance *C* a providing of victuals or food, etc.

Prowk see Proddle.

Prush *C, SW* to press.

Pruss *C, SW* to press.

Prut! Prut! a call to a horse to come. This word or sound cannot be expressed in writing. It is a jarring expulsion of the breath and voice through the lips with some force.

Pruzzent *G, not E* present.

Pruzzently presently.

Pry *C* a very short bluish grass, difficult to cut with a scythe; the carex or sedge plant, *Cyperaceae.*

Pubble *C* plump. Grain well fed is *'pubble as a partridge.'.*

Pucker *C* alarm, flutter. *'In a sad pucker.'.*

Pucker't drawn together like the mouth of a purse.

Puddin' clout linen cover for dumplings, etc., whilst being cooked.

Puddin' pwoke a bag containing herb pudding, potatoes, etc., during boiling.

Pulopt pulpit in a church or chapel.

Pulpot pulpit.

Pult *C* a fat and lazy cat or woman. *'Mary's nobbet a girt fat pult.'.*

Pum *C* to pummel or beat.

Pummer anything large.

Pun *C* pin.

Pun *C, N* pound, *'Fwoortin puns to yan steann.'.*

Pun'o'mair weight *B, C* a game where one boy lies on the ground and several others climb upon him, one at a time.

Punchis *C* purchase; the mechanical advantage of a lift or pull. *'He"nivver git it up, because he can't git a purchis at it.'.*

Pund *C, E* a pound in money; a pound, the former measure containing 16 ounces. (equates to approx 454 grams).

Pund butter *C, SW* butter made up in pounds as opposed to being sold in bulk (see Pund).

Pund o'mair weight *C* a rough game among boys, adding their weight one upon another, and all upon the one at the bottom.

Punder *C* to crowd.

Punfaal *N* See Punfoald.

Punfoald *C, E, SW* pin-fold, cattle pound.

Punsh to kick with the foot.

Purdy *C* a short and thickest person.

Purls *B* dried cowdung used for lighting fires.

Purmit *C* permit.

Pursy broken-winded; asthmatic, *'Oor lass is reet pursy at present.'.*

Put *C* to butt with the head.

Put on hurry on; go quick; to tease; to take advantage of.

Put out ashamed, troubled, extinguished. *'Nelly was sair put out about it.'.*

Put tee reets *N* to keep orderly or in a tidy correct manner.

Put tul't obliged to use expedients. *'He's gaily sare putten tul't to git a leevin.'.*

Putten put. *'Yon steann wall badly putten togidder.'.*

Puttin' through severe examination; a righting up.

Putty cow *C, N* a cow given to attack people.

Puzzen poison.

Pwok *C* poke or probe.

Pwok mittens *C* gloves knit without the fingers being divided.

Pwok't *C* Sheep tainted with rot or consumption often exhibit the symptom of a poke or bag under the jaws.

Pwoke a poke; a bag. *'Nivver buy a pig in a pwoke'* - examine first; take nothing on trust.

Pwoke shakklin's the youngest child.

Pworch porch.

Pwort *E, NW* port. *'Ey, Marypwort.'.*

Pwosy a nosegay - a bunch of flower used to regale the sense of smell; a posy; a flower.

Pwsowdy *C* see Lamplugh puddin'.

Pyannet *C, N* the peony plant, *Paeonia.*

Pyat the magpie, *Corvus pica.*

Qho' quoth.

Quart an old measure of capacity, equates to 2 pints or 1.13 litres.

Quartern a quarter of a pound of flax ready for being spun.

Queen cat *E* a female cat.

Queerly *C* odd. *'A rayder queerly swort o'chap.'.*

Quentance acquaintance.

Quern an ancient hand-mill of stone; the shout of rejoicing or thankfulness raised in the field when the last of the crop is cut.

Quest *C* the early morning search for a hare by the scent of the hounds. *'Jwon Peel questit a hae up Skiddaw side and pot her off beside t'man.'.*

Quey heifer or young cow

Queyt *N* quite.

Quilt *C* to beat.

Quishin cushion.

Quit rid of; the act of leaving. *'He's quit t'farm and gaan to sea.'; acquit.*

Quits *C* the share of the bill, *'Lets gaa quits.'.* (see Shot).

Quits even, both clear, *'It's deunn, an'let's be quits.'.* (see Double or quits).

Quittance receipt or acquittance. *'Aa'll nit pay yer a penny without a 'quittance.'.*

Raa row. *'Workinton's nobbet raa upo raa of laal hooses.'.*

Raa *N, SW* raw.

Raaish *N, SW* rather raw.

Raak *SW* to scratch glass, etc., with a point.

Rabbets *C* rabbits.

Rabblement *C* the dregs of the

people; rabble.

Rack an' manger *C* on plenty, *'He's at rack and manger now.'.*

Rack'nin reckoning.

Rackan reckon; calculate.

Rackle *C* rash, unruly, incau-tious.

Rackon reckon; calculate; disapprove. *'I rackon nought o'sek wark.'.*

Raff *C* an idle fellow.

Raffish *C* of idle habits.

Raft *C* a large concourse, meeting or assembly. *'A raft o'fwok.'.*

Rag *C* hoar-frost or frozen dew.

Rag to rate; to scold; to reproach.

Rageous *C, N, E* outrageous.

Raggabrash lower class people; vagabonds.

Raggelt *C* an active young person of bad conduct. *'An ill raggelt of a thing.'.*

Raggy nwos'd *C* a sheep having a grey face and a lighter shade of muzzle resembling hoar-frost. The common marks of the Herdwick breed.

Rain knots *C* a scurf which collects in lumps among the hair on the skin of a lean, outlying horse.

Raiser *C* an addition to a beehive put in beneath.

Raiser an additional ring put under a bee hive to increase its size.

Rak *SW* rake.

Rake *C* a mountain track up a steep slope; to follow in line as sheep do.

Rake a journey. *'He's teann a rake ower to Kendal.'.*

Rake shank *N* the handle of a rake. *'But that tale is not worth a rake-stele.'.*

Rake steel *C, SW* see Rake shank.

Rakes *C* lines of white foam on lakes often noticed previous to a storm.

Rakkeps *C* a game among boys.

Rakkle heedless or careless; rash.

Rall *SW* rowel, seton.

Ram *C, SW* a strong fetid or offensive smell. *'As ram as a fox.'.*

Ram to rush; to use force. *'Ram at it!'* - to butt.

Ramman a special example of something, usually large or big; *'A ramman girt an'.'* - a very large one.

Rammel ramble.

Rammel sleatt *C* a very coarse kind of slate.

Rammer see Ramman.

Ramp *C* a sprain or twist; to sprain. *'He ramp't his ankle at t'feutt bo'laik.'.*

Ramps *C* wild broad-leaved garlic, *Allium ursinum*. Cows occasionally eat of this plant and their milk acquires an onion flavour.

Ramshackle *N* rude and vulgar.

Randi't *C* streaked. This form is applied to butter when of two colours.

Randy *B* an outrageous and disorderly person (1878) - then not necessarily associated with sexual or lecherous behaviour.

Randy *C* a termagant - a boisterous, brawling turbulent woman.

Randy whang *B* a randy lump.

Rang wrong. *'Yer fadder thinks yer nivver rang.'.*

Range *C, B* ring; to exercise a young horse in a ring.

Rank close together; numerous. *'As rank as mice in a meal kist.'.*

Rannel boke *N* the beam on which the chimney-crook hangs.

Rannel tree *C* see Rannel boke.

Rannigal *C, N* a masterful child or animal.

Rantipow *NW* a termagant; boisterous, brawling, turbulent woman, *'Mary's a rantipow if ivver I saw yan.'.*

Rantle tree *B* See Rannel tree.

Ranty *C* riotous; in high spirits; in a towering passion.

Rap ho'penny *C* a halfpenny worn smooth; a counterfeit.

Rap on t'knuckles to snub; to control sharply.

Rap out *C* to speak with rapidity. *'He rap't and his ugly woaths as fast as a hen could pick.'.*

Rap't *C* a ragged sheep is rap't; unwrapped.

Rapacallion a worthless, ill-mannered fellow.

Rappack *C* a pet name for an unruly child.

Rash *C* brisk.

Rashleet *C, SW* rushlight or rush candle.

Rat *N* to scratch glass, etc., with a point.

Ratch to ramble; to ransack vigorously. *'Ratchan' about like a hungry hound.'*; a white streak down the face of a horse.

Rate to whiten by bleaching on the grass; an appraisal of cirumstances or a situation. *'At this rate yer nivver gangan to git t'house riddy.'.*

Rattan rat.

Rattan tails *C* the seed stems of the broad-leaved plantain, *Plantago major*.

Raw *N, E* row of booths, stalls.

Rawwl *C* to grumble; to be quarrelsome.

Rawwnd *SW* round.

Rawwnd *SW* round; a circuit.

Rayder *C, SW* rather; ironically very, *'Rayder o't'wettest.'* - very wet.

Rayther *N* see Rayder.

Reace race.

Reach *E* The natural divisions into open parts of lakes, such as Ullswater.

Reach teah a common expression of welcome at the table, signifying 'help yourself' or reach to and take.

Read *C, E, SW* rode.

Readd *C, SW* rode; a spawn bed.

Reader Scripture reader or unordained clerical substitute, whose office ceased c.1740.

Reak rake.

Reakk rake.

Reakk t'fire to cover up or damp down an open fire for the night.

Reamm *C* to roam; to talk wildly; to covet or desire. *'He's olas reamman efter mair land.'*.

Reann *C* a balk left for a boundary line in a common field.

Reap rope.

Reapp rope.

Rear *C* rise, raise; rally; bring up; underdone; nearly raw.

Reass race.

Reasses *N* races.

Reatt wrote. *'Thomas Farrell reatt Betty Wilson's Cumm-erland Teals.'*.

Reav *C, E* rove, tore.

Reav to rave.

Reaven raven.

Reavv *C* tore; rove; rave.

Reavvel *C* to use loose talk in a quick manner; to utter untruths; to entangle; to unravel the loops or knitting.

Reavven raven.

Reaz arose, arisen.

Reazz arise, arisen.

Rebbat rivet; rebate - to form or join by rebates. eg. in joinery.

Recklin' the smallest of a litter.

Reckon reckon.

Redchester register.

Redshanks *C* the plant *Polygonum Persicaria*.

Ree to riddle corn in a 'ree-an sieve' so the chaff collects to the centre of the sieve, and the dust and small seeds of weeds fall through. Superceeded by the winnowing machine.

Ree-a-zan *SW* reason.

Reeat *SW* root.

Reed red; to read; to strip.

Butchers reed the entrails of slaughtered animals to obtain the fat.

Reed row When barley approaches ripeness the grains are streaked with red, and are said to be reed row, not yet ripe enough to be cut.

Reed rowe *B* red raw, applied to a sore before it begins to heal.

Reeden redden.

Reedent *C* irritable; red-faced.

Reeght *C* right, (out of use 1878).

Reeght *N* wright.

Reek smoke. *'Flicks of hams were reeked on t'chimla boke.'*.

Reek't smoked; hams and other meats cured in smoke.

Reel a frame onto which yarn, thread or lines are wound.

Reeler *B* a slender iron pin (often with a brass head) on which the bobbin was placed when the spun thread was wound off.

Reep o'cworn a handful of corn in the straw, used as a bait to catch a horse with in the field.

Reep up to refer often to some unpleasant subject.

Reest *C, SW* to be obstinate; to arrest. (see Tetch).

Reestit *C, SW* rancid; rusty.

Reesty *N* rancid; rusty.

Reesty *NE* see Reest.

Reet right; a cartwright, wheelright, shipwright etc.

Reet wright.

Reet up to put things right; to give scolding advice.

Reg'lar regular.

Reggalate regulate.

Reggylar regular.

Reglar *N* regular.

Reivers *N* robbers on the borders lands between England and Scotland.

Reklas *C* a speices of Primrose, the *Auricula* plant.

Remembert *C* remembered.

Render to melt tallow, etc.

Renky *C* lengthy.

Repwort report.

Resait a corruption of receipt.

Resh *N* the rush, the *Juncaceae*.

Reshleet *N* see Rashleet.

Reshleet *N, E* rushlight.

Resk *G, not E* risk.

Restles *C* the stakes to which cattle are fastened in the stalls.

Resto *C* to change position during a game of marbles.

Reststaks *C* see Restles.

Reud *G, not E* see Reudd.

Reudd *C* rode; rood, rod or perch - a former measure of land etc.

Reudd *N* rode; a spawn bed.

Reuf *G, not E* roof.

Reuff roof.

Reull *C* an unruly boy, colt, or ox, etc.

Reunge *C, E* to plunge as the unruly colt does.

Reust *E* praised, commended.

Reut *C, E* root.

Reutle *C* to work underneath or in the ground, as a pig does.

Reutt *C, N* root; to uproot; grub up. *'Reuttan like an unrung swine.'*.

Reuuzz arose; raised.

Reuvv *C, N* to uproof. *'T'wind reuvvt our haystack.'* (see Tirit).

Reuz arose, arisen.

Reuzz arise, arisen.

Reyce *NW* see Cockgard.

Reyde *NW* ride.

Reyle *N* to vex; to annoy.

Reyme *NW* rhyme.

Ribbin ribbon.

Rice *C* see Cockgard.

Rid to uproot trees or hedges, etc.

Rid *G, not E* red.

Riddy ready.

Ride an'tie riding by turns - the horseman dismounting so the footman can take his turn in the saddle.

Ridsom' *C* ready; expert.

Ridsteakks *C* the stakes to which cattle are fastened in the stalls.

Rife *C* plentiful.

Riff-raff *C* disorderly people. *'They're nought bit riff-raff.'.*

Rift *C* to belch; to win a trick with a trump card.

Rig ridge.

Rig an' fur ridge and furrow, as stockings were formerly knit.

Rig an' reann an arable field held in shares which are divided by narrow green lines (ranes) and the intervals usually cultivated.

Rig reapp the chain or rope resting on the cart-saddle; the back-band.

Riggelt an animal with one testicle in the loins.

Riggin' ridging, the ridge of roof; ropes of a sailing ship.

Rim *B* the rim of a spinning wheel included all that part of a wheel which turn, eg. the rim proper, the spokes, and the nave.

Rime *C* hoar-frost or frozen dew.

Rin *N* run.

Ring man *C, B* the ring finger - in nursery play (see Fingers).

Ringe *C, E* rinse.

Rinje rinse.

Rip to swear; a reprobate; a horse of the worst description. *'An oald rip of a horse.'.*

Rip and tear *C, N* to swear and vociferate violently.

Ripe to search by force.

Ripple *B* to ripple flax is to pull off the seeds.

Ripple *C* a slight scratch.

Ris'ms straws left on the stubbles.

Rissel *G, not E* wrestle.

Rist rest; repose. *'Rist ye a bit.'.*

Rit *C, N* to cut the first line of a trench or drain, etc; a cart-rut etc.

Rive to tear; to vomit; to eat voraciously.

Rive-rage *C* a careless and headstrong person or child.

Rivy rags *B* one given to waste.

Riz *G, not E* arose, arisen.

Roan the roe of fish.

Roantree the mountain ash, *Pyrus Aucuparia*.

Roap rape seed.

Rock the distaff.

Roke *C* to scratch glass, etc., with a point.

Ron *C* did run.

Roo *SW* row with oars.

Rooad *SW* road.

Rooar *SW* roar.

Room *C* instead of. *'He com in t'rooms of his fadder.'.*

Roon' *N* round.

Roon' *N* round; a circuit. *'Aa've been a lang roon' to-day.'.*

Roond *C, E* round; a circuit.

Roop't *E* hoarse with bawling.

Roostit *C, E* rusted.

Roosty *C* rough in manner.

Rost *C, N, SW* roast.

Rosy a rose.

Rote *N* to scratch glass, etc., with a point.

Rough reet *E* a carpenter who works rough jobs; an unskilled one.

Roughness *C, SW* grass left for winterage.

Round *C* large. *'Fetch a trugful o'round cwols, lass.'.*

Rouser a large one. *'It's a roosan lee at is 't.'.*

Rove *C* did rive.

Rovven rivven, torn.

Rowe *C, E* raw.

Rowe *C, N* roll. *'He's rowan' amang plenty.'.*

Rowe *E, NW* row with oars.

Rowish *C* rather raw.

Rowk the mist of the valley; to search. *'Aa rowk't o'my pockets and could n't find ya plack.'.*

Rowl roll.

Rowm *SW* room.

Rowt *C, N* the prolonged roar of the cow. *'Rowtan' at t'yat.'.*

Rowth *C, N* abundance. *'Rowth o'gear.'.*

Royster *C, N* to vociferate; to bully. *'He's a girt roysteran'foul.'.*

Rozzel *C* to beat. *'Aa'l rozzel thy back wid an esh stick.'.*

Rozzel *C, SW* resin; to heat strongly before a fire. *'Come in an' rozzel thy shins a bit.'.*

Rozzet *N* see Rozzel.

Rub *C* tore; rove; rave.

Rub *C, N* rib.

Rub on *C* to continue as usual. *'How's o'at heamm?' 'Rub-ban'on at t'cald bat.'.*

Rub t'wrang way o't'hair *C* figuratively to irritate. When the hair of cats or dogs is rubbed upwards it can causes angry feelings in them.

Ruck *C* the chief part; the majority.

Ruckle *C* a crowd; a great number.

Ruckshin *C* riot or disturbance. *'There was a reet ruckshin when he came heam last neet.'.*

Rud *C* soapy hematite iron ore used for marking sheep.

Rud *G, not E* red. *(see Rid).*

Rudden ridden.

Ruddle *C* see Rud.

Ruddle *SW* the coloured ownership marks upon sheep.

Ruddy *C, E* ready.

Rudsom' *E* ready; expert.

Rudsteakks *E* see Rudstowers.

Rudstowers *E* the stakes to which cattle are fastened in the stalls.

Rue-bargain an agreement cancelled by something given.

Ruff *C, SW* ruff at cards.

Ruff *SW* see Rift.

Ruffel't-sark *C* a frilled shirt. (see Cranky-sark).

Ruffs *B* defective parts of the ears of corn; light grain and chaff boiled for cattle food.

Ruft *B, E* to play a card of a different suit. (see Rift).

Ruft *E* see Rift.

Ruft *E* the plot of ley ground to be

ploughed in the year.

Ruft *E, B, NW* ruff at cards.

Rug *C* to pull rudely. *'Rug at it, lad.'*.

Ruinate *C* to reduce to ruin.

Rule o'thoom guess-work.

Rum droll; queer. *'He's a rum an'.'*.

Rumbustical *C* rude; over-bearing.

Rumbutter *C* butter and sugar mixed with spices and flavoured with rum. Traditionally eaten by wives during their confinement; and offered to, and expected to be partaken of, by visitors.

Rummel rumble.

Rummel buck *C* a riotous boy.

Rummel't 'taties *B* boiled and mashed potatoes and mixed with milk and butter.

Rummish rummage or ransack; rather droll.

Rump an' stump entirely, completely.

Rump-neet *E* a night set apart for romping or rude, boisterous play.

Rumpas disturbance. *'They kick't up a rumpas.'*.

Rumplement *C* coarse materials; disorder.

Rumps a game with marbles.

Rumpshin an affray; disturbance.

Run *C* rum.

Run a rig on to banter; to ridicule.

Run bull-neck *B* to proceed rashly.

Runbutter *C* see Rumbutter.

Runch *C* a hardy and thickset person or animal.

Rung *C* the round step of a ladder or gate.

Runnan' bur *C* a short run to gain impetus for a leap or jump.

Runner a small stream.

Runnin ceavvel *N* see Turn deall.

Runrig see Turndale.

Runt an aged ox; a strong and low-set man; the smallest of a litter, the *'Recklin'*.

Rus *N* see Resh.

Rus *N* the rush.

Rusk *N* see Resh.

Russel to wrestle.

Rust *G, not E* rest; repose.

Rute *N* root.

Ruttle a difficult breathing. *'T'ruttle's in his throat and he's deean.'*.

Ruv *C, E* rove, tore.

Ruvven *C, N* rivven, torn.

Ruz *N* arose, arisen.

Rwoad *C, N, E* road.

Rwoan *N* roan.

Rwoar *C, N, E* roar.

Rwode *N* rode; a spawn bed.

Rwong *N* rogue.

Rwor *C* roar. *'He com rworan like a girt bull.'*.

Rwost *C, N, E* roast.

Rwosy rosy; ruddy; a rose.

Ryle *N* see Reavvel.

Ryle *SW* to vex; to annoy.

Ryne rein; to fasten the horse by the rein.

Ryner *C* a tapering augur.

Rype to search by force; to examine under a search-warrant; to rape.

Ryse brushwood used in hedging.

Rysel *C* a rollicking child.

Ryve *C* to devour voraciously; to tear.

Sa so, *'It was sa nasty, it was fit to set a dog.'*.

Saa *N, SW* to sow corn, etc.

Saan't *SW* shall not.

Saas *N* sauce; impertinence.

Saasiter *N, SW* sausage, *'Cummerlan saasiter fra Wabberthet.'*.

Saat *N, SW* salt.

Sackless feeble, weak-minded, simple; a former meaning was guiltless.

Sad sodden; pasty; bad. *'She's in a sad way.'*.

Saddan a sad or bad one.

Sae *N* so.

Safftree *N* a willow.

Sag See Swag.

Saggy *C* a game with marbles.

Saim lard.

Saim't overcome with heat.

Sal shall.

Sal n't *C* shall not.

Salladin *C* the celandine plant, *Chelidonium majus.*

Sallant *C, E* shall not.

Sallar cellar.

Sally sober *B* game among girls.

Sam-cast two or more ridges ploughed into one.

Sampleth a sampler.

San' *N* sand.

Sang song.

Sank *C* having sunk.

Sanna *N, E* shall not.

Sannat *N, E* shall not.

Santer saunter.

Santerment trifling employment.

Sap wet, rainy.

Sap heed a simpleton or fool; soft-headed.

Sap whissle a boy's whistle made from a green branch of sycamore or willow.

Sappy wet, rainy.

Sapskull a silly person.

Sare sore; very much. *'He's sare wom.'*.

Sarious *SW* remarkable. *'It's a sarious fine day.'*

Sark a shirt.

Sarman *C, E, SW* sermon.

Sarmant *E* sermon.

Sarr *SW* to bestow or give alms to relieve the poor; serve.

Sarra *C* see Sarr.

Sarten certain.

Sartenty certainly. *'Nay, I could n't say for a sartenty.'*.

Sarv't *C* served, *'Furst come furst sarv't.'*.

Sarvant servant.

Sarve *N* see Sarr.

Sarvice service.

Sary *N* poor; pitiable. *'He's down i't'warl noo, sary man.'.*

Satisfys't *N* satisfied.

Sattle a wooden sofa; a settle or swab.

Saucer een *N* large and full eyes.

Saugh *N* the willow.

Saughtree *N* the willow, of the genus *Salix*.

Savver taste or smell; savour. *'It teasts oald savvor't.'.*

Sawwer *SW* sour.

Sawwer milk *SW* butter-milk.

Sawwnd *SW* sound.

Saxon *SW* sexton.

Say *C, N* authority, influence. *'He hes full say ower o'.'.*

Say to check; to restrain. *'I could n't say him, for he wad n't be said.'.*

Sayen *N* saying.

Scaad *N, SW* scald.

Scaal *N* scold.

Scaald *SW* scold.

Scab't esh *C* an ash-tree having cancerous bark.

Scabble *C* to rough dress building stones.

Scabskew *C, N* a boyish game or the crook-ended stick used in the game.

Scale dish *E* a skimming-dish.

Scallion a thick-necked onion.

Scantish *C* deficient; scarce. *'It's amak of scantish or scantly.'.*

Scap *N* the scalp.

Scar *C* shy; wild. *'Your cowt's parlish scar.'.*

Scar *C, N* to frighten; scare; the rough gravel and stone beds on the shore of the Solway are called scars; screes.

Scar scare.

Scart *N* scratch; the itch; a saving industrious person; a female hermaphrodite sheep.

Scave salve.

Scaw natural copse of wood.

Scawer *SW* scour, cleanse.

Scoald *C, E* scold.

Scode *C, E* scald.

Scold a rude, clamorous (noisy and vociferous), foul mouthed woman.

Sconce *C* the head.

Sconce *C, B* stone shelf commonly near the kitchen door, and if inside sometimes with a hole through it as a sink. Used to keep food cool and fresh.

Scooar *C, N, E* score.

Scool *C, N, E* scowl.

Scoor *C, N, E* scour, cleanse.

Scop *C, SW* the chaffinch, *Fringilla coelebs*.

Scop to hit; to throw.

Scope *C, E, SW* scalp.

Scopperel in veterinary surgery a seton or large needle.

Scopy thin of soil - as usual on the edge of a brow.

Scorrick *C* the smallest value. *'I'll nut give a scorrick mair.'.*

Scotty kye Scotch cattle or cows.

Scour a violent purging.

Scover *N* discover; a look, *'Let's tak a 'scover through the fair.'.* - Stagg.

Scovver *N* discover.

Scowp *B* to empty out or throw away; throw.

Scowp *C* a tin or iron dish; scope.

Scowp scoop; scope.

Scra-mally *N* scramble.

Scrabble *B* to scrawl or write poorly with a pen on paper.

Scram *C, SW* the hard rid of bacon or cheese.

Scrammel scramble.

Scrapple *C* iron scraper.

Scrat *C, SW* see Scart.

Screap scrape.

Screapp scrape.

Scree *B* to separate small seeds from corn.

Scree *C, SW* the running loose debris on the side of a mountain.

Screuf *C, E* scurf.

Scribble *C* to scrawl or write poorly with a pen on paper.

Scrimmish *C, N, E* scrimmage, skirmish.

Scrimpy *C* pinched, mean; of pinched pattern.

Scroby *C* mean, niggardly.

Scrogs stunted bushes.

Scroo *C* a slide; the act of sliding. (see Skurl).

Scrow-mally *N* scramble.

Scrowe *B* a great many. *'A scrowe o'fwok were at t'berryin.'.*

Scrowe *C* disorder, confusion, untidiness. *'Her hoose was in sec a scrowe as thou nivver saw.'.*

Scrub *C* a small bundle of stiff birch twigs once used for cleaning the inside of the porridge-pan.

Scrub-grass *E* the *Equisetum* or horse-tail plant, once used for scrubbing or polishing fire-irons, etc.

Scruffle scuffle.

Scrummage *N, E* scrimmage, skirmish.

Scug *B* to shelter under a hedge; to hide. (see Skug).

Scug *E* an old word meaning the shade.

Scumfish *C* to defeat a person or party; discomfit.

Scunner *E* to disdain.

Scush! *C* exclamation of wonder; a kind of oath.

Scut *C* scud, flee or fly with haste; to make short runs. *'He can scut and run gaily fast til his dinner.'.*

Scut the tail of a hare or rabbit.

Scutter *C* a bustling run without much speed.

Scutty *C, W* short.

Scworn scorn.

Sea so.

Sea purse *C, B* the egg of the dogfish.

Seaff safe; sure; certain.

Seag *N* the *Iris pseudocorus* plant.

Seah so.

Seah *SW* sea.

Seak sake.

Seakk sake.

Seal sale.

Seale *C* sale.

Seame *C* same.

Seamm same.

Seapp soap.

Searent *C, B* seared; cauterized.

Searr sore; very much. *'He's sare wom.'.*

Seaskeall *C* Seascale.

Seavv save, 'A tack i'time seavvs nine.'.

Seavv his bacon to escape. *'Tell yer fadder I seavv'd his bacon, yer oald lass will nivver finnd out.'.*

Seavv thy bacon see Seavv his bacon.

Seavv yer bacon see Seavv his bacon.

Seb'm *C, E, SW* seven.

Sebben *C, E, SW* seven.

Sec such.

Sec a ta-dea *C* Such a too do, a suprising and eventful happening, often with an unhappy result. *'Yer fadder's furst weddin' was sec a ta-dea.'.*

Secint *N* second.

Seck sack; sackcloth.

Seck-like such-like.

Seckin' sacking or hemp cloth.

Secklin' see Seckin'

Sed said.

See to visit. *'You mun co' to see us when you come our way.'.*

See-how't *B* pursued.

Seeah! *C* see you!; attend.

Seeal *SW* seal.

Seean *SW* soon.

Seeat *SW* seat.

Seeat *SW* seat.

Seeave *SW* the rush, the *Juncaceae*.

Seed *C, N* saw; did see. *'I seed him hoddin her han' in church.'.*

Seed *SW* saw.

Seed hopper *C* the basket from which corn is sown.

Seed sheet *C* the sheet from which corn is sown.

Seed-fire the fire under the drying kiln, usually made with the husks of dried oats.

Seegh *N* sigh.

Seeght sight (see Seet).

Seeght *N* sight; sigh.

Seeghty *N* sighty; far-seeing; prudent.

Seein' glass *N* a mirror.

Seek sick.

Seek *N* to bring.

Seek wife an pregnant woman confined and about to give birth.

Seel *E* the willow.

Seem become or beseem. *'She does n't 'seem her new cap.'.*

Seer *N* sure.

Seesta see there or look!

Seet sight, *'It was a grand seet to see.'* (older people pro-nounced it *'seeght'* in 1878).

Seeter *C, SW* a worn or frayed place in a garment.

Seety *C, SW* sighty; far-seeing; prudent.

Seeve *C* see Seeave.

Seeven *N* seven.

See Yers *C* goodbye.

Seg *C, SW* a callosity on the hand or foot; a castrated bull.

Seggin *C, N* see Mechin.

Seggin *C, SW* the yellow flat, *Iris Pseudacorus*.

Sek sack.

Sel self, *'Behave yer sels.'.*

Selt sold. *'He's selt t'oald picture to a dealer fra Cockermuth.'.*

Semple *C* the contrary of gentle. *'Gentle and semple' in station and degree, are the people of quality and the commonalty.*

Sen *C, E, SW* since.

Sen' *N* send. *'Sen' the cat out, hizzy.'.*

Sennat *C* seven nights; a week.

Serious remarkable. *'Ey, it's serious het an'all.'.*

Serra *N* see Sarr.

Set to appoint; to fix, *'He's set a day for the weddin'.'*; to plant; to equal; to escort, to accompany; to suffer or allow. *'She fell asleep and set t'fire out.'*; nauseous. *'It was sa nasty, it was fit to set a dog.'.*

Set a feass *C* to gurn or distort the human face. At rustic sports such as Egremont Crab fair, a prize is given to the person who sets the most unseemly face framed through the opening of a horse-collar.

Set by held in esteem, *'He's girtly set by hereaway.'.*

Set down *C* a rebuke. *'She gave him a good set down.'.*

Set on to employ. *'He set me on to work in t'garden.'.*

Set pot a boiler set or fixed - not movable on the fire; the next to the largest vessel once commonly found in the Cumbrian farm kitchen, bigger than a *keall pot*, but smaller than a *brass pan*.

Set tail't horse The fashion was (upto about 1800) to divide the under ligaments of the horse's tail, and to suspend the tail by pulleys and weights till the wounds healed and the tail had acquired an elevated and permanent set.

Set'lins sediment.

Setchelt satchel.

Setfast a hardened substance in a sore.

Seton *C* a foreign substance inserted in the dewlap of a cow to cause a discharge of matter.

Setten *C* appointed; com-menced. *'Mary's setten up shopkeepin' in Workinton.'.*

Setten set, did set.

Setterday Saturday.

Settle a wooden sofa having a box below the seat.

Settle-steanns *C, N* the curb-stones in a cow-house.

Seugh *N* a wide and watery ditch.

Seun *C, E, N* soon.

Seunn *C* soon. *'We'll seunn be wed lass.'*.

Seunn and syne soon and late.

Seur *N, SW* sure.

Seurr *N* sure.

Seut soot.

Seutt soot.

Sewe *SW* a sow or female swine.

Seyde *NW* side.

Seyk *N* a small wet hollow.

Seyn *N* since.

Seyne *N* since.

Shab off to sneak away; to leave in disgrace.

Shackle *C* the iron (formerly a willow) ring which slides upon the cow's restle.

Shaf! *C* an expression denoting contempt. *'Shaf o'tha!'*.

Shaff *C* a sheaf; to bind a sheaf.

Shaffles a weak-legged creature.

Shagrag *C* a mean person; a vagabond.

Shairn *N* fresh cow-dung.

Shak *C, N, E, SW* shake, a shaking, shook or shaken.

Shak't *C, N, E* see Shak.

Shakes *W* nothing special; or to boast of. *'H's nea girt shakes.'*.

Shakky down *C* a makeshift bed on the floor.

Shaks *C* see Shakes.

Shaktly *C* shaken; of loose construction.

Shally wally! *C, SW* an expression of contempt.

Sham shame; be ashamed.

Shammel *N* to walk in a shuffling manner. *'He's a shammellan ill-geattit thing!'*.

Shangle *C* To shangle a dog is to fasten a tin can to its tail and let him go.

Shank pan a small pan having a long handle; The next to the smallest pan once commonly found in the Cumbrian farm kitchen, bigger than the *la'al pan*, but smaller than the *bule pan*. Used to boil ham shanks etc. from which it probably took its name.

Shankum naggum the legs; on foot. *'He rides on shankum naggum.'*.

Shanky naggy see Shankum naggum.

Shap *C* offer; to set about. *'How does he shap?'*.

Shap *C, E* shape.

Shaply *C* well-proportioned; of good appearance.

Shaps very light grain; grain only in shape.

Sharn *SW* fresh cow-dung.

Sharp quick, active. *'Be sharp, lads!'*.

Sharp set'n *C* very hungry.

Sharpin' corn *NE* corn once given as payment to the blacksmith for sharping the plough-irons.

Sharps coarse flour containing bran.

Shaugh *NW* an expression denoting contempt. *'Shaugh o'tha!* '.

Shavs sheaves.

Shavvins *C* shavings.

Shaw natural copse of wood.

Shawle *C* to walk in a shuffling manner.

Shawwer *SW* shower.

Shawwt *SW* shout; to cry out; to call.

Sheaff *C* a sheaf; to bind a sheaf.

Sheak *C, N* shook, shaken.

Sheakk *C, N* shook; shaken; shake it.

Sheam shame; be ashamed.

Sheamm shame.

Sheap *E, SW* shape.

Sheapp *SW* shape.

Shear to reap or cut with the sickle.

Shearr *C, SW* reaped.

Sheavins *N* shavings.

Sheavs sheaves.

Sheavvins *N* shavings.

Sheavvs sheaves.

Sheckle *N* see Shackle.

Sheeaff *SW* a sheaf; to bind a sheaf of corn etc..

Sheear *SW* share.

Sheeers *N* scissors.

Sheen *C* machine.

Sheep furm a seat on which a sheep is laid to be shorn or salved.

Sheep steell see Sheep furm.

Sheers *N* scissors.

Shek *N, E* shake, a shaking; to dance.

Shellcock *C* the missel thrust, *Tordus viscivorus*.

Shellies *N* shore-gravel.

Shelly *C* any animal thinly formed.

Shelvins *C, SW* board or frames to raise the cart-sides.

Shem *N* shame; be ashamed of.

Shemmel't *NE* twisted; bent out of truth.

Shep *N* shape.

Shepherd's book *C, E, SW* a book illustrating the marks of each owner's flock for identifying strays at the annual Shepherd's feasts.

Sheuk *C, E* shook.

Sheukk shook.

Shevvins *N, E* shavings.

Sheyn *NW* shine.

Shiar *N* to skim; to pour off from the settings.

Shift *C, N* to remove.

Shifty apt at contrivance.

Shill to shell out; to unshell; cold, chill.

Shill out pay. *'Yer fadder will nivver shill out for t'weddin.'*.

Shill-apple *N* the missel thrust,

Tordus viscivorus.

Shilla *SW* shore-gravel.

Shillies *C* shore-gravel.

Shilly shally *C* hesitating, trifling.

Shilvins *N* see Shelvins

Shindy disturbance. *'Kick up a shindy.'*.

Shinny *C, N* see Scabskew.

Shippen *SW* a cow-house.

Shippert shepherd.

Shippert *C, E* shepherd.

Shirk a slippery character; to avoid. *'He'll shirk iv'ry hard job if he can.'*.

Shive a slice; a cut.

Shivver *C* slaty debris.

Shivver *N* to disperse by force; to punish; debris.

Shodders *C* shoulders.

Shoe cappin a patch of leather on a shoe.

Shoe-buckles large silver or other buckles worn on the shoes upto about 1800.

Shoeless horse *C* the *Botrychium Lunaria* plant.

Shog to shake. *'He's shoggan' wi'fat.'*.

Shog bog a shaking bog.

Shoo *C* shoe.

Shoo swol *C* shoe sole.

Shoo! terms used forcibly to drive away fowls.

Shooal *SW* shovel.

Shooar *C, N, E* shower.

Shooar *SW* shore. *'Let's ga dawwn to t'shooar an'hev a dook.'*.

Shooder shoulder.

Shooder spaw *N* the shoulder-blade.

Shooder spole *C* a shoulder-slip.

Shool *C, N, E* shovel.

Shool web *N* the blade of a shovel or spade.

Shoon *C, N, SW* steps in old-fashioned dancing.

Shoon *N* shoes.

Shoop *C* the fruit of the wild rose.

Shoor *C, E* sure.

Shoot *C, N, E* shout; to cry out; to call.

Shorpen *E* to shrivel or contract leather or other substances by heat.

Short *C, SW* crumbly like a rich fruit cake; peevish.

Short ceakk rich fruit cake.

Short tongue't said of one who lisps.

Short'nin' *E* butter, fat, or dripping used in pastry.

Shorten to put a child into a short dress for the first time.

Shot did shut; a half-grown swine; the share of the bill eg. at an inn etc; quit; rid of. *'Yer should git shot of t'oald yowe.'*; broken, damaged, in need of repair. *'That oald cart is well shot.'*; the worst.

Shot ice *C* ice frozen on a road or on the surface of the ground.

Shot lambs *N, E* lambs, the worst of the flock.

Shots the refuse; the leavings; the worst. eg. Shot sheep or cattle.

Shots *N, E* see Shot lambs.

Shottel *N* schedule.

Shottelt *N* warped; out of truth.

Shrosies *B* white sweet cakes. eg. Shrewsbury cakes.

Shrumps *C* shrimps.

Shudder *C* to shiver; a sudden decline in markets.

Shuffle *C, SW* steps in old-fashioned dancing.

Shuffle and cut *C, SW* steps in old-fashioned dancing.

Shuggy *N* to sway; swing.

Shuk *C* shook.

Shun *C, E* shoes.

Shup'm *SW* a cow-house.

Shurdavine *B* a short and fat person.

Shurt *E* a shirt.

Shut to shoot; to discard the worst of sheep or cattle from a drove; a violent purging.

Shutten *C* shot. *'You fellow's shutten a hare.'*.

Shwor *N* reaped.

Shwort *N* crumbly like a rich cake; peevish.

Shwort *NW* short.

Shyve *C, N* a slice. *'Cut thy sel a shyve o'cheese an' breed.'*.

Sib *N* akin. (not often used 1878).

Siccan *C* see Seccan.

Sicker *N* careful safe; reliable. *'He's varra sicker body.'*.

Sidders *C, E, SW* scissors.

Side *C* to decide; the slope of a hill.

Side up to put things to their places.

Side-bank sloping land.

Side-boards movable boards to set up on the sides of carts.

Sidement a putting of things to their places. *'We nobbet skiftit here this week an'hes n't gitten a sidement yet.'*.

Sidlins *N* in the neighbourhood. *'He's geann to t'sidins o'Caarel.'*.

Sight a great number or quantity. *'Theer was a sight o'fwok at Rosley fair.'*.

Sile trees *N* the timber roof-blades of a thatched clay house. The lower ends were placed on a dwarf wall The curved oak the upper ends met at the ridge reassembling a pair of whale's jaws.

Sill silt. *(see Cwol sill)*.

Sillaly *C, SW* sillily, foolishly.

Siller *N* silver.

Sillican a simpleton or fool.

Silly *N* a term of sympathy. *'He's nobbet hed peer luck, silly man.'*.

Simmer *N* summer.

Simmon't cemented.

Sin *N* since.

Sin-syne *N* since.

Sind down *C* to drink after eating. *'An sind it down wi'good strang yal.'*.

Sing-el *C, E* single.

Singan hinny *B, E* a rich girdle cake common associated with the Alston area.

Sinsyne *N* since.

Siplin *N, E* sapling or seedling.

Sista *C, SW* look; see thou; seest thou.

Sista see Seesta.

Sitfast a hardened substance in a sore.

Sitten sat. *'She'd sitten o't'efterneunn.'.*

Sitten in *C* set in; long unwashed. *'Fairly sitten in wi dirt.'.*

Sitten land *C* grass land where the soil is stiff and unproductive through lack of cultivation.

Sitten to t'bottom burnt in the pan.

Sizel *C* to saunter or wander about idly; to loiter or linger.

Sizes assizes.

Skaad *N, SW* to scald.

Skaal *N* scold.

Skaald *SW* scold.

Skabscew *C* See Shinny.

Skairn *N* fresh cow-dung.

Skaitch *C* to beat or thrash with a stick or rod.

Skale to spread about.

Skarn *C* fresh cow-dung.

Skary *N* wild, feary.

Skawer *SW* scour, cleanse.

Skeall a scale; a shed or building on the fell.

Skeap *C, E* escape.

Skeapp escape.

Skeapp greass *C* a graceless fellow.

Skearce scarce.

Skeat *C, E, N* the skate-fish; to skate.

Skeatt *C, N* see Skeat.

Skeel *N* large water-kite.

Skeery wild, feary.

Skeet *C, SW* see Skeat.

Skeevs *B* broken pieces of the stems of flax not sufficiently

dressed. *'A skeevy rockful.'.*

Skelf *E* shelf.

Skell *C* shell. *'Borrowdale nuts hes thin skells.'.*

Skell *C, E* shell.

Skelly *C* fish found in Ullswater, often called the freshwater herring, *Corregonus fera* of Cuvier.

Skelp *C, N* to whip or beat; to leap or run. *'He skelp't ower t'dykes and sowes like a mad greyhound.'.*

Skelper a large one.

Skemmel a long seat used in a farmer's kitchen.

Sken *SW* to squint.

Skep *N* a basket made of straw or rushes; a beehive.

Sker *N* a scar, the mark of a healed wound; a cicatrix.

Skerr *N* a precipice.

Skeul *C, E N* school.

Skeybel *N* a good-for-nothing person.

Skiander *C* to reproach severely; to scold; to blow up.

Skiar *C, SW* to skim; to pour off from the settings.

Skidy *C* thin, slender.

Skift *C, N, SW* to shift; to remove.

Skilbins *C, N, SW* see Shelvins.

Skilly *B* thin broth or soup.

Skilly *N* skilful; having skill. *'He's gay an' skilly at his trade.'.*

Skilvins *C, N, SW* see Shelvins.

Skint short of money; skinned.

Skipjack *B* a beetle (elator) which if laid on its back recovers its feet by a sudden spring.

Skipjack *C, N* the breast-bone of the goose; a dandified fellow.

Skire *C* to skim.

Skirl to screech.

Skit to asperse, slander vilify by innuendo; to cast reflections upon.

Skite *C* diarrhœa in calves etc.

Skitters diarrhoea.

Skivver *C* to disperse by force;

to punish; debris.

Skleat *N, E* slate.

Skleatt *N* slate.

Skoald *C* scold.

Skode *C* to scald.

Skoder *C* a scalder or scald; the skin frayed with heat and friction during violent exercise.

Skoggers *C* footless stockings wore for sleeves.

Skole *N* scold.

Skollick *C* see Skuddick.

Skonky *C* very slender and bare, especially about the head and neck - chiefly applied to short-woolled sheep.

Skons *N* scones, barley cakes.

Skooal *SW* school.

Skooar score.

Skooder *C* to take great effect upon; to bring down quickly. *'Ned went a shuttin' an' he skooder't them down.'.*

Skooder *N* to burn a girdle cake in baking.

Skool *N* scowl.

Skoor *C, N* scour, cleanse.

Skowder *C* disorder.

Skowe *B* a severe beating.

Skraffle *C* to scramble; dispute; struggle. *'He's hed a sare skraffle for a leevin', an' he skraffles an' disputes wid ivry body.*

Skrapple *C* a tool to scrape with; a coal-rake.

Skreapp scrape.

Skreed *C* a narrow strip of cloth or land, etc.

Skreed *N* a long and monotonous harangue or speech.

Skreek screech, scream.

Skreen *C* a wooden sofa.

Skreuf scurf.

Skribe to write; to subscribe. *'I niver hed t'skribe of a pen sent he went.'.*

Skrike *C, N* to screech or scream.

Skrike o'day *E* break of day.

Skrimmish *C, N* skirmish, scuffle

or scrimmage.

Skrimpy scanty; mean; pinched hospitality.

Skrowe *C* disturbance, riot.

Skrowmally *N* see Skrowe.

Skrudge *N* to squeeze; to rub hard as in scouring.

Skuf see Skruff.

Skruf o' t'neck the nape or back of the neck *'Jack grabbed him by t'skruf o' t'neck.'*.

Skruffins *N* scrapings from a pan in which sowens have been boiled.

Skrummidge *N* skirmish, scuffle or scrimmage.

Skrunty dwarfish or small; worn, *'A skrunty besom'* - one far worn.

Skrush *C* a rubble quoin.

Skry *C* descry; to discover; find out. *'Jemmy skry't 'am makkan off wid his plunder.'*.

Skuddick *C* used to denote something of the very lowest value. *'Nay, I'll nut give a skuddick mair.'*.

Skuff *C, N* the back or nape of the neck.

Skufter hurry. *'He com in sek a skufter he fell't ower the dog.'*.

Skumfish to disable; put down; suffocate; discomfit.

Skunner *N* to loathe.

Skurl to slide on the ice in clogs.

Skurrick *C* see Skuddick.

Skurry *C* bustling hurry.

Skutter *B* to run without drawing attention.

Skybel *N* a lazy fellow; an oak twig.

Skyfa *C* of pinched pattern.

Slaa *N, SW* slow.

Slab *C* smooth, soft; the outside plank.

Slack a shallow dell or hollow; slow; loose; not filled. *'Slack at a pinch.'* - giving way when most needed.

Sladder *C* mud, filth, mire.

Sladderment *C* mud, filth, mire.

Slafter *C, SW* slaughter; the hides and skins from a slaughter, *'Tanner Tom's bought Butcher Bob slafter for a heall year.'*.

Slagger *C, SW* to loiter; to be untidy; .

Slagger *N* to scatter.

Slagger *SW* a soft sandy place or other soft substance.

Slaghter *N* see Slafter.

Slain *C, SW* blighted.

Slaister *C* to cut up; to disfigure. *'He gat a slaisterin' when he fought wi' Jock.'*.

Slak Slack, small pieces of coal under the size of an egg.

Slake *C* a slight rubbing.

Slam *C* to win the rubber at whist before the adversaries make a score; to win all the tricks.

Slank *N* to walk away abjectly.

Slant to tell untruths.

Slap to beat with the open hand.

Slape slippery.

Slape finger't guilty of pilfering; apt to let things fall out of hand.

Slape guttit subject to attacks of diarroea.

Slape shod used to describe poor or inferior work, *'T'pent'ins varra slape shod.'*; a horse is slape shod when his shoes are worn smooth.

Slape-clogs one whose word is not to be relied on. *'Mary's nobbet a slape clogs.'*.

Slapper something large. *'A girt slapper.'*.

Slare *C* to saunter.

Slare *N* to be careless.

Slashy wet and dirty.

Slat slit, split.

Slatch *E* a lazy vagabond; a term of reproach.

Slaters *N* see Winnick.

Slatter See Out.

Slatter to spill.

Slatter can *B* an untidy person.

Slattery raining or showery weather.

Slavver slobber, saliva.

Slea *C* sloe.

Slea tree *C* the sloe-tree, *Prunus spinosa*.

Slea worm *C, N* the so-called blind worm, slo-worm.

Sleaa *E, SW* sloe.

Sleaa tree *SW* see Sleaa tree.

Sleaa worm *SW* the so-called blind worm, slo-worm.

Sleak *N* slake, quench.

Sleakk *N* to quench; to abate.

Sleat slate.

Sleatt slate. *'Yer git green sleatt fray Borrowdale.'*.

Sleatt off somewhat lunatic.

Sleattit *C, B* spoken of female attire when an upper garment is too short for covering an under one.

Sleck small coal; to slack lime, etc.

Sleck trough a blacksmith's cooling trough.

Sled a sledge.

Sledder *B* to walk about in shoes much too large.

Sledder *C, NE* to saunter; to walk lazily.

Sledder geggin *C* a sauntering slovenly person.

Sledge *C, NE* see Sledder.

Slee *N* sloe.

Slee *N* sly.

Sleep't *C, E* slept.

Slem *C, SW* to slight; to perform carelessly.

Slenk slink.

Slent *N* to tell untruths.

Sleugh *B* a white grub found in watery places, and used as a bait for trout.

Slevver *N* slobber, saliva.

Slew *C* to turn partly round. *'Slew that kist round a bit.'*.

Slew't *C* partly intoxicated.

Sleype *NW* to sweep off hastily.

Sliar *N* to slide on the ice in clogs.

Slidder *C* to slip down to some distance; the sliding of wet earth.

Sling to move by long and steady strides. *'He slings ower t'grund at a girt rate.'*.

Slinge *C* to walk away abjectly.

Slink *N* see Slank.

Slink cofe *C* a cast or rejected calf.

Slip to slide; to go quickly and quietly. *'Slip away for some watter, lass.'*; a child's pinafore.

Slipe *C* to sweep off hastily; to convey away; to steal. *'Cush! if they hev n't slipe't my geese ageann!'*.

Slipe *C, N* to unroof a building; to abscond; an old-fashioned desk having a sloping lid.

Slippy slippery.

Slit whol *SW* a vent hole in the wall of a barn, etc.

Slitch *SW* the mud on the shores of an estuary; silt.

Slither *N* to slip or slide on wet ground.

Slobber *C* to weep with many tears. *'He slobber't an' yool't like a barn.'*.

Slocken to quench thirst; or to slack lime.

Slodder *C* mud, filth, mire.

Slop *B* See Slorp.

Slopper *B* bespatter or soil by splattering with water and or mud or dirty.

Slops *C, B* fragments left. *'Yer pigs hev got the kitchen slops.'*.

Slopstan sinkstone, an old form of sink carved out of a block of stone.

Slorp *N* the noise made in drinking from a spoon or in drinking from a glass and drawing in air at the same time.

Slot *C* a door-bold or a wooden cross-bar; a quarryman's term for a wedge-shaped block of stone in situ; a drainer's term for a fall of earth from the side of his drain.

Slotch *C* to walk heavily as a cart-horse does.

Slowdy *C* untidy.

Slowmy soft and weak straw which has been laid or lodged while growing.

Slowp *C, E* slope.

Slowpy *C* sloppy; muddy or soft as mud.

Slummer slumber.

Slur to do things ineffectively - to 'slur them ower.'.

Slush slops; thin mud; snow broth (melting snow); a dirty person.

Slysh *SW* a slice. *'Cut thy sel a slysh o'keeak.'*.

Smaa *N, SW* small.

Smack *C, N* to whip; the sound of a hearty kiss. *'Wi' kisses et soundit like t'sneck of a yat.'* - Robert Anderson.

Smack quick. *'He ran down like smack.'*.

Smash to break. *'He smash't it to atoms.'*.

Smasher *B* a larger one - a small child who had never seen a baby larger than a doll, when shown his newborn sister, exclaimed - *'It is a smasher!;* a fine or good example of something.

Smasher anything large and powerful; a good example of something.

Smatch a smattering. *'He'd a smatch of o'things and was clever at nin.'*.

Smee *N* smooth.

Smeeak *N, SW* smoke.

Smeer *N* to anoint or apply; besmear; smother.

Smeeth *C* smooth.

Smell a rat to suspect.

Smeuk *C, N, E* smoke.

Smeuk't smoked; hams and other meats cured in smoke.

Smeukk *C, SW* smoke.

Smeur *N* see Smeer.

Smiddy smithy.

Smit *C* the coloured ownership marks upon sheep.

Smith corn *NE* see Sharpin' corn.

Smithers *C* small fragments. *'It was o'broken to smithers.'*.

Smittle infectious, *'It's as smittle as t'scab.'*; sure.

Smo *C, E* small.

Smo' *C* small.

Smoot *C* a hole to creep through; the act of creeping through a hole. *'A hare smoot.'*.

Smoot hole *N* see Smoot.

Smudder *C* smother

Smudge *B* to spot.

Smute *SW* see Smoot.

Sna *C, N, SW* snow.

Snaa-broth *SW* half-dissolved thawing snow.

Snaat *SW* snowed.

Snaf'lan' trifling; petty pilfering. *'T'Wallace lads are saf'lan' oald Jonty's apples.'*.

Snaffle *C* to steal.

Snags *C* projecting ends where branches have been cut off trees.

Snap a gingerbread cake about the size of a crown piece (a crown was a former British coin equal to 5 shillings or 25p).

Snap't up to eagerly acquire everything on offer. *'Dick snap't up all t'oald beukks at t'sale.'*.

Snape to curb; restrain; snub. *'Our taty tops gat a snapin' wi'frost.'*.

Snapper *C* to hit the ground with the toe in walking.

Snappy *C* short-tempered. *'Yer Marys a reet snappy lass at present.'*.

Snar *E* cross-tempered; unsociable; currish, snarling or quarrelsome.

Snar snare.

Snarl a snare.

Snarl knot a knot that cannot be drawn loose.

Snarl't caught in a snare; tightened, contracted.

Sneck the latch or catch on a door

Sneck or gate; a hitch or stop.

Sneck drawer *C* a covetous or desirous person; formerly one who pulls the snecket, lifting the latch of a door and enters without ceremony.

Sneck hay *C* hunger.

Sneck posset a disappointment - commonly applied to suitors who are not admitted.

Snecket *N* the string attached to a latch of a door.

Sneel snail.

Sneels *C* see Kneuls.

Sneer snort. *'If a horse sneers efter he coughs he's nut broken windit.'.*

Sneevel *N* to speak through the nose.

Snell *N* sharp or severe, a biting wind is a snell blast. *'Here a sharp mwornin', John.'....'Ey, as snell as a stepmother's breath.'.*

Snerls *C* nostrils.

Snerp *C* a snare.

Snerp up *C* to draw together like the mouth of a purse.

Snerp't *C* caught in a snare; tightened, contracted.

Snertan' laughter suppressed with difficulty.

Snew *C, N, E* snowed.

Snews *N* snooze, half-sleeping.

Sneyp *NW* snipe. *(see Hammerbleat).*

Snick *C* a minor clip or cut; to clip a sheep, etc., in uneven ridges.

Snife *C* knife (see Strikin' Snife).

Snifter *C* to inhale sharply through the nostrils; quickly done, 'In a snifter.'.

Snig to drag timber by horse and chain; to lop the branches off fallen timber.

Snip feasst having a white streak down the face.

Snip't a weak but healthy person.

Snite *E* to blow the nose, *'He snitit his nwose wid his finger and thoom.'.*

Sno'an snowing. *'It's been sno'an hard sen Setterday.'.*

Sno-broth *C, N* see Sno-broth.

Snod smooth; velvety. *'As snod as a mowdy-warp.'.*

Snoor *SW* snore.

Snoot band *C* the iron plate on the toe of a clog.

Snoozle *C* snooze, half-sleeping.

Snork *C* to noisily inhale through the nose.

Snot *B* the unconsumed part of the wick of a candle.

Snotter *C, N* to blubber. *'Snotter an' yool.'.*

Snotty mean, disagreeable. *'He's a laal snotty cur of a fellow.'.*

Snow pattens *B* snowballs on feet of men or horses.

Snowk *B* to inhale through the nose - *'Tak girter snowks, lads, an'it 'll seunner gang away,'* said he who had broken wind and produced an evil smell among his fellow workmen.

Snowk *C* to work with the snout as a pig or a mole does; to act in an underhand way.

Snuffle *C, SW* to speak through the nose.

Snuffles a cold affecting the nasal organs.

Snurl't *C* drawn together; shrunk.

Snwoar *C, N, E* snore.

So to sow corn, etc.

Soam psalm.

Sobby *C* bulky and heavy as a sod.

Sock ploughshare.

Soddy *N, SW* to sow corn, etc.

Soder *E* solder.

Soft soder flattery.

Softish soft, not hard or solid.

Softly see Softish.

Soggy *N, SW* see Soddy.

Soght *N* sought, brought. *'Jimmy's soght the keye heamm.'.*

Soil to feed cattle, etc., on green food in the houses in summer.

Solid an occasional substitute for solemn.

Somewhoars somewhere.

Sonks *N* turves - once used instead of saddles, and girthed with hay-bands.

Sonsy stout and heavy; plump.

Sonsy *N* lucky; full; generous.

Soo *C* the distant sighing or surging of the wind or sea.

Soo *C, E* sough of wind.

Soo *N* a sow or female swine.

Sooa *C, SW* so; be quiet; let alone. Often doubled as *'sooa sooa!'.*

Sooal *N, SW* sole of the foot, shoe, etc.

Sooals *C* a swivel joint in a chain, commonly termed a pair of sooals.

Sooins sowens; pottage of oatmeal dust.

Sook *C, E* suck.

Soom *N* swim. *'Can ta soom any?'.*

Soon *N* sound.

Soond *C, E* sound.

Soop *C* to sweep.

Soop't *N* swept.

Soople *C, N, E* supple flexible; the second half of a flail used in threshing corn etc.

Soor *C, N, E* sour.

Soor dockin' wild sorrel, Rumex asctosa.

Soor milk *C, N* butter-milk.

Sooren *C* to become sour; leaven.

Sooth south.

Sop *C* a milkmaid's cushion for the head.

Sop *C, SW* a tuft of weeds or grass, etc; a piece of blacklead.

Sose *N* sauce; impertinence.

Sositer *C* sausage, *'Woodall's mak reet teasty Cummerlan sositer.'.*

Soss *C, N* to plunge into water; to fall heavily. *'He fell wid a soss like a wet seck.'.*

Sote *C, E* salt.

Sotter the noise or sound of boiling pottage etc.

Sough *N* the distant sighing or surging of the wind or sea.

Soup *N* to sweep.

Sour milk butter milk.

Souse *C* something very sour; brine, *'Sour as souse.'.*

Souse to wet a person copiously.

Sove salve.

Sowder *C* a mixture by a bungling cook. *'See a sowder Betty meadd.'* - Old Song.

Sowder *E* solder.

Sowderment *C* see Sowder.

Sowe *C* a wide and watery ditch.

Sowe to sew.

Sowens *N* a flummery made from the husk of oats.

Sowjer *N* soldier.

Sowpy *C, N* soft; spongy or watery.

Sowt the joint-ill in lambs and calves.

Sowt *N* sought, brought. (see Soght).

Spak *C, E, SW* spoke, spake.

Span new *C* brand new, never having been used.

Spang *C, N* to leap; to spring; to span.

Spang't *C* blotched. *'A spang't cow.'.*

Spang-fire new, never having been used.

Spanghue *C* to pitch up violently.

Spangles *C* the spade suit of cards.

Spangwhew *N* see Spanghue.

Spanker a tall and active young person; a fast-going horse.

Spankin' *C* a beating.

Spar spare, save.

Sparables short nails for shoe heels, resembling the shape of sparrows' bills.

Spare rib the vertebae and ribs of pork.

Sparragrass asparagus, Liliaceae.

Spats *C* gaiters.

Spatterdashes *C* gaiters.

Spead spade.

Speadd spade.

Speaddin' *C* a trench of one spade in depth.

Speak *C, E, SW* spoke, spake.

Speall a chip; a splinter.

Speann to wean.

Speatt *C* a sudden and heavy fall of rain; a water-spout. *'A speatt o'rain.'.*

Speavv *C* to castrate a female animal.

Speckets spectacles.

Specks spectacles.

Speeak speak.

Speeak *SW* spoke of wheel.

Speeaks *SW* wheel-spokes.

Speer *N* enquire. *'Speer at him.'* - ask him.

Speke *C, N, E* spoke of wheel.

Spekes *C, N* wheel-spokes.

Spelk *C, N* a splint; rib of a basket; a rod to fasten down thatch.

Spelk hen the hen once paid annually to lord of the manor for liberty to cut spelks in the lord's woods.

Spell a chip; a splinter.

Spell a turn of work, etc. *'Let's tak a spell at kernin'.'.*

Spenticles spectacles.

Speshul *C* special.

Spetch a patch on a shoe etc.

Spete *N* see Speatt.

Speun *C, N, E* spoon.

Speunn *C, NE* spoon.

Speyder Wob *N* spider's web.

Speyse *NW* spice.

Speyther wob *N* a spider's web.

Spice wife a hawker or seller of gingerbread etc.

Spick-and-span new, never having been used; tidy and clean.

Spiddick spigot.

Spider shanks *C* one having very slender legs.

Spile *C* the vent peg of a cask; a stake.

Spinjy *C* greedy, stingy.

Spink See Scop.

Spink *C, SW* the chaffinch, Fringilla coelebs.

Spinnel spindle. *'Our wheat's spinnellan' up and gaan to shut.'.*

Spirin' *E* piercing, penetrating, applied to a cold, rainless wind; droughty.

Spirit to eject a small quantity of saliva.

Spirits *C* slender and weakly-grown rushes.

Spirt a short-lived energy. *'Put a spirt on lad or we'll nivver git heamm.'.*

Spit When the warning drops of a shower fall. *'It rayder spits.'.*

Spite defiance. *'It sal be done in spite of his teeth.'* - or in defiance of him.

Spitten picter *C* a strong likeness. *'You barn's his varra spitten picter.'.*

Spittle saliva or spit.

Splat had or did split.

Splatter to bespatter (see Slopper).

Splatter-dashes *C* gaiters.

Splinter new, never having been used.

Splitten being split.

Spluffan *N* a bag or pouch.

Splutter to speak too quick for distinct utterance.

Spoalder *C* to partially separate the shoulder-blade of an animal from the chest.

Spoalder *N* to stagger; awkward in gait or walk. *'He spoalder't like a new drop't fwol.'.*

Spok *N* spoke, spake.

Spok'n spoken.

Spokkan spoken.

Spole *C* see Spoaler.

Sponsible responsible, *'It's nivver*

her 'sponsilblity.'; sub-stantial.

Spooan *SW* spoon.

Spoots *N* dry stems of the kesh or cow-parsnip, or of hemp, once used to light candles.

Spot *C* a position or place; a place of service. *'I gang to my spot at Martinmas hirins.'.*

Sprag a clubby lump of wood to put in a wheel to act as a brake.

Spreckel't *C, E, SW* speckled.

Spreckelt spotted, speckled.

Spreead *SW* to spread.

Spreed *C, N, E* to spread.

Sprent *C* to sprinkle. A pen sprents when it scatters the ink over the paper; a snare for game birds.

Sprickel't *C, SW* speckled.

Spring *C, B* the cleft of a quill pen (an old style pen usually made from a goose feather).

Sprinj't *E* half-starved; miserable-looking.

Sprint *C* see Sprent.

Sproag *C* a jaunt. *'Let's gang for a sproag.'.*

Sprung *C, B* when the cleft of a quill pen is too long.

Spunk animation; spirit.

Spunky lively.

Spurt to eject a mouthful. *'He spurtit bacca slaver o' t'fleer ower.'.*

Spurtle *N* a thin piece of wood used for turning cakes on a girdle; an implement used in thatching; to kick with the feet as a often child does.

Spwort sport.

Spy'd *C* saw. *'I spy'd them hand in hand down t'beck.'.*

Squab *C* an inferior sort wooden bench or sofa not having the seat-box of the settle.

Square true, correct, a good fit. *'That breks nea squares'* - it does not disarrange the precision.

Squary short and broad.

Squash quash.

Squinshes quinsy.

Squirtle see Swirtle.

Staa *N, SW* stall; surfeit or overfeed. *'Plenty o'butter wad staa a dog.'.*

Staap *SW* to walk as in the dark. (see Pope).

Stack stuck. *'He stack in a t'mud.'.*

Staddam *C* a dam or weir across a stream.

Stadlin' *SW* straw or brushwood etc., laid under a corn or hay stack to prevent damp rising. (formerly dry turves were most used 1878).

Staff herdin' *N* herding cattle etc., by stealth in another man's pasture.

Stag a colt; a young game cock.

Stagger to confound; to confuse.

Stait *C, E, SW* estate.

Stakker stagger. *'He stakker't a bit an' than he fell't ower efter all that yal.'.*

Stakkery *G* staggering from drink.

Stan stand.

Stand *C, SW* a cattle grass.

Stand cost. *'Them lambs 'll stand me in laal short of a pund a piece.'*; the large washing-tub in which the dolly is worked.

Stand for *C* to become a sponsor for.

Standert *C* standard; a post or upright, eg. against which the double barn-doors shut.

Stang to sting, stung, did sting; a pole; a cart-shaft.

Stanger *C* the wasp or any hymenopterous insects.

Stangin' men guilty of beating their wives have been forcibly hoisted astride of a pole or stang, and borne through the village in derision; unwary travellers were once entrapped on Christmas and New Year's days and threatened with the stang until they contri

Stank *C* stink or bad smell. *'T'hoose stank to high heaven.'*;

to groan short. *'Stankan' and greannan' as if he ail't summat.'.*

Stank the pain accompanying the short groan.

Stank *N* an artificial pond; water dammed; a midden.

Stap stave of a tub; step of a ladder or gate; become insolvent, *'Tom's gone o'to staps.'.*

Stape up *C* to upset or overturn.

Stappel *SW* staple.

Stapple *SW* staple.

Star bent *C* the *Juncus squarrosus* plant.

Star sleet *C* frog spawn dropped on the ground.

Stark *C, SW* hide-bound; unnaturally stiff.

Stark mad in a towering or high passion.

Stark neakk't entirely naked; raw spirit.

Stark weather *SW* continued dry and cold north and east winds.

Starken *C* to stiffen; coagulate or curdle.

Starken *SW* to stiffen.

Starn stern.

Start *C* the long handle of a wooden pail.

Startle Cattle startle when they erect their heads and tails, and gallop madly in hot weather through fear of the stinging flies.

Starty *C, SW* nervous; subject to jump or start on alarm.

Stashin *C* station.

Statesman *C, SW* the owner of an estate, *'Curwin is t'statesman of Stoneyheugh.'*; a yeoman.

Stay't *C* stayed, staid, sedate.

Stayk *C, N* to wander listlessly; to blunder. *'A girt staykan' feull!'.*

Stayvel *C* see Stevvel.

Steabble stable.

Steable *C, N, E* stable.

Stead *C* an unenclosed plot on a mountain or common on which certain parties have defined rights, as on Borrowdale, Wythbum, and other fells.

Stead *SW* stood.

Steadd stood.

Steaddlin' *B* a stand for bees.

Steaddlin' *C* see Stadlin'.

Steak stake, steak.

Steakk stake; steak.

Steakk an' reyse *N* a mode of hedging. (see Cockgard).

Steakk an' ryse see Steakk an' reyse.

Steal *C, E, SW* stole.

Steall *C, SW* stole.

Stean stone.

Steann stone.

Steann't horse *C, N* stallion; an entire horse.

Steanny *C, N* see Steann't horse.

Steapel *C, E* staple.

Steappel *C* staple.

Steat *N* estate.

Steatt *N* estate.

Steck *E* to resist; to be obstinate or tetchy.

Stee a ladder.

Steeak *SW* stuck.

Steeal *SW* steel; steal; stool; to tiller; to spread in growing.

Steeam *SW* steam.

Steedit supplied.

Steek *N* to shut, close, fasten.

Steel *C, E, SW* stile.

Steep cheese rennet.

Steepin' rain heavy pen-etrating rain.

Steeple *N* staple.

Steg gander or male goose.

Stencher *C* a stanchion, post or upright support.

Steng *N* to sting, stung.

Stenk *N* an artificial pond; water dammed; a midden. (see Stank).

Stensh *C* strong, staunch. *'Hes ta gitten stensh ageann?'.*

Stent *N* to limit; to send out to grass or graze; a cattle-grass.

Stepmother bit a scanty allowance.

Sterk neakk't *N* see Stark neakk't.

Steud *C, E, N* stood.

Steudd stood, did stand.

Steukk *C* to shut, close, fasten. *'Steukk that deur, lad.'.*

Steukk *N* a silly fellow.

Steul *C, N, E* stool.

Steul *N* stole.

Steull *C, N* stool; to tiller; to spread in growing.

Steull *N* stole.

Stevvel *N* to saunter like a person without employment.

Stew *C* dust.

Stew *C, N* excitement; haste. *'In a girt stew.'.*

Stey *N* a ladder.

Steyl *NW* style; stile.

Steyle *NW* style; stile.

Steyme *NW* very dark, used to express perfect darkness. *'Can n't see a steyme.'.*

Steyne *NW* stye on eyelid.

Stibble *N* stubble.

Stick up for to advocate. *'He stack up weel for Tom.'.*

Stickle *C* fright; alarm. *'In a parlish stickle.'.*

Sticky adhesive; clammy; tenacious.

Stiddy steady; an anvil; stithy or blacksmith's shop; a disease in oxen.

Stife *E* foul air in a mine or quarry after blasting.

Stife *N* strong; sturdy; obstinate.

Stiff an' *C* a manifest falsehood. *'That is a stiffener!'.*

Stiffener *B* see Stiffan'.

Stigh! a note used to alarm pigs and drive them into the sty.

Still always. *'He still does that way.'.*

Still an' on *C* yet, etc. *'Still an' on, tudder was better.'.*

Stilt the arm and handle of a plough; to walk in a stiff manner.

Stinjy *C* miserly; unlikely to freely to part with anything.

Stinjy aal carl *N* cross-tempered old man.

Stinkin' Roger *C* the knotted figwort, *Scrophularia nodosa*.

Stint *C* a measure of work; in coalmines an area 2 yards long by 1 yard broad, which each miner clears removing to another place (equates to approx 1.67 square metres).

Stir *C* bestir, exert or rouse. *'Stir thy feet, Bob.'*; excitement.

Stirk a yearling heifer or bullock.

Stirran' *C, SW* stirring, active. *'He's a stirran' lad, yon.'.*

Stirrup cup the parting glass drank at the door.

Stirrup oil *C* a beating with a strap.

Sto *C* see Staa.

Stob *B* a splinter entering the flesh.

Stob stab; a post or stake.

Stomach unbelief. *'I can't stomach that teal.'.*

Stomachful *C* having a good appetite.

Stooary *SW* story, an untruth.

Stoon *N* astound; to benumb; the pain resulting from a blow.

Stoond *C* see Stoon.

Stoop *N, SW* a gate-post; the turning-post in a race.

Stoor *C, N, Sw* dust blown about.

Stoot stout.

Stoov't *C* the mark cut into the ear of a sheep.

Stop to stay; to stow or pack. *'Stop them things into t'drawer.'.*

Stope *C* to walk as in the dark. (see Pope).

Stoppan' spot the limit. *'Iv'ry thing hes a stoppan' spot bit time.'.*

Storken *C* see Starken.

Storken *N* to stiffen.

Stormcock see Shellcock.

Stormcock *C* the missel thrush, *Tordus viscivorus*.

Storten *C* see Starken.

Stot a young ox.

Stott to jump with all feet together as a sheep or deer does.

Stotter *C* to walk clumsily.

Stove to stifle or suffocate bees with brimstone.

Stowe *C, N* to place; to cram.

Stower estover - in law a reasonable return; a stake.

Stower an' yedder *C, SW* a mode of hedging. (see Cockgard).

Stown stolen.

Stowp *B* a place where slate pencils are obtained from the clay slate overlying the coal measures.

Stowter *B* to stagger or stumble. 'Oald Jonty stowtert ower, and down he went.'.

Stowter *N* to walk clumsily.

Strack struck, did strike.

Straik to stretch; lay out a corpse. A 'streekin' was once commonly followed by a tea-drinking and afternoon's gossip in a low tone.

Straive *N* strove, did strive.

Straker *SW* a straight-edged ruler used to sweep off the extra quantity from a measure of grain; a strike.

Strakes lengths of iron in former use for wheel tire.

Strang strong. 'Jennings mak varra strang yal at Cockermuth.'; fetid, strong or rancid scent. 'Strang as rotten cheese.'.

Strangely strongly.

Strapp't short of money. 'Dicks a laal bit strapp't efter t'weddin.'.

Strea *C* straw.

Streaa *E, SW* straw.

Streak *C* see Straker

Streak struck, did strike.

Streaker *C* see Straker.

Streav *C, E* strove, did strive.

Stree *N* straw.

Streeamers *SW* northern lights, *Aurora borealis*.

Streek see Straik.

Streemers *C, N* northern lights, *Aurora borealis*.

Streen to strain, press or make great effort; sprain; distrain.

Street straight.

Streetan straight; straighten.

Streight straight.

Strenth strength.

Strenth o'men an' pitchforks *C* power; influence.

Streuv strove.

Streuvv strove.

Streyk *NW* strike.

Streyn see Streen.

Streyve *NW* strive.

Strickle a sanded piece of wood used for sharpening scythes.

Striddle stride, straddle.

Strike street *C* to balance the matter even hands.

Strikin' Snife *C* a butcher's cleaver.

Strinkle sprinkle.

Strinklin' sprinkling.

Strint *C* a term for the milk drawn from the teat by the hand; the smallest quantity. 'A strint o'milk.'.

Strinty *C* dwarfish or small.

Strip to draw the after-milkings of cows.

Strippins the last of the milking.

Stritch *C* to strut haughtily.

Stritcher stretcher; a softened term for an untruth.

Stroke *C* a comparative term of augmentation. 'A good stroke o'biz'ness.'; step, measure. 'He hes a lang stroke o't'grund '- he takes long strides.

Strone see Strint.

Strop *C, N, E* strap.

Stroppan' strapping; tall; active, 'Yer Jack's a reet stroppan lad.'.

Strowl stroll.

Strucken stricken; fly blown.

Struddle *N* see Striddle.

Strunt *N* pet, a fit of peevishness; to sulk.

Strunty *C* see Strunty.

Strwoan *E* to milk laboriously.

Stub *C* to grub up.

Stubs *C* the old nails from a horse's shoe, reused for clog-nails.

Stud *N* see Stott.

Studden *C, E* stood, 'Thou sud ha'studden up for us.'.

Studdy *N* see Stiddy.

Stuffment *C, SW* something worthless; doubtful information.

Stulp *C* see Stoop.

Stummer stumble.

Stump an' rump the entirety. 'He snap't it up stump an'rump.'.

Stumps legs, 'Stir yer stumps.'.

Stumps *N* see Stubs.

Stunchy short and stout. 'It's a good laal stunch of a powny.'.

Stunner *C, N* something extraordinary.

Stur stir; agitation.

Sturk see Stirk.

Sturran' *N* see Stirran.

Sturrups stirrups.

Stutt *N* see Stott.

Stutter stammer.

Stuv't *C* see Stoov't.

Stwory story. 'Varra weel than, to mak a lang stwory short.'; an untruth.

Styan *C* sty or stye, an inflamed swelling on the eye-lid.

Styme *C* see Steyme.

Styne *C* see Styan.

Styth *C* foul air in a mine or quarry after blasting; a suffocating vapour.

Su a sow or female swine; did sow; did sew; to sew. 'He su his cworn yisterday.'.

Suck! *C, SW* a call-note for calves.

Suckam *C* liquor or fluid. (see Middin suckam).

Sucken see Bond sucken.

Suckeny land *E* moist land of good quality.

Sud should, 'Thou sud ha'studden

up for us.'.

Sud ta should thou. *'Sud ta not gaa an' find her.'.*

Suddent sudden; should not.

Suer *C, E* sure.

Sugger sugar.

Suller't *C* stuffed or choked up with a cold.

Sum *C* some.

Summat something; somewhat.

Summat-like something like or adequate for the purpose; pretty or becoming. *'Theer, that's summat-like!'.*

Summer geatt *C* summer pasturage. *'Our why was summer't on t'fell.'.*

Summerset somersault or summersault.

Sump *C* a puddle; a hole at the bottom of a pit to collect water.

Sumph *N* a blockhead or fool.

Sunday best the best outfit in your wardrobe, generally worn to attend church on a Sunday.

Sunkets *NW* query something.

Sunnyside south side.

Sup to sip; to take liquid food from a spoon; an indefinite measure of liquids. *'A girt sup.', 'A laal sup.', 'A sup o'tea.'.*

Supping *C* drinking.

Suppwose suppose.

Swab *N* a wooden sofa, settle or sattle.

Swad a pod.

Swadder *C* to dabble or play in water. *'Swadderan' like a duck in a puddle.'.*

Swadderment *C* drink.

Swadler *C* a methodist.

Swag to sag.

Swag belly't corpulent around the stomach, the lower part of the abdomen enlarged.

Swag't bent downwards in the centre.

Swageatt the cut of a saw.

Swally to swallow.

Swally whols *C* large funnel-shaped holes in the ground which swallow and sink the water. Usually seen at the outcrop of the cavernous limestone.

Swamish *C* squeamish.

Swang *C, N* a wet hollow; did swing.

Swang *C, N, E* did swing.

Swanky *C* loosely put together; inferior; showy or conceited actions or speech.

Swanky *N* a strapping young man; posh.

Swap swop or exchange; barter.

Swape *C* a lever; pump-handle.

Swarf *C* to swoon.

Swarm *B* an overpowering host or army of lice; a great number or multitude.

Swarmel *SW* to creep along a pole or up a tree; to scramble.

Swarth *C* the skin of hams and bacon; sward, the grassy surface of land etc.; the ghost of a dying person.

Swash *C* wet stuff.

Swat *C* a heavy fall. *'He fell wid a swat like a wet seck.'*; sit. *'Come in, and swat ye a bit.'.* (see Coo swat).

Swat *N, NW* did sweat.

Swatch *C* a bill-book.

Swatter *C* to indulge in drink; drink.

Swattle *B* to use by little and little, according to the song of the swallow.

Swattle *C, N* to waste; to sip intoxicating beverages.

Swayth boke the visible line of higher grass between the swayths or sweeths of a mown field.

Swayve *E* to pass backwards and forwards.

Swayvel *C* see Stevvel.

Swayvel to walk unsteadily.

Swayvlin' a weak and unsteady walking person.

Swear *C, E* swore.

Swearr swore.

Sweel *C, N* to burn swiftly with flame; the melting of a lighted candle in a draught.

Sweels o'laughin' *C* peals of laughter.

Sweemish *N* squeamish.

Sweep't swept.

Sweepless *E* ignorant.

Sweer swear.

Sweet perspiration or sweat.

Sweet mart *C, SW* the marten-cat. (this animal still existed sparingly in the Cumberland mountains 1876).

Sweeth *N* the line of grass thrown off the scythe.

Swelly whols *E* see Swally whols.

Swelt *C* to swoon.

Sweltan *C* to die.

Swelter *C, N* to perspire copiously. *'O'in a swelter.'.*

Swenn't *C* twisted; bent out of truth.

Swet *C, E, SW* did sweat.

Swey *C, N, E* swing, sway.

Sweyn *NW* swine.

Swidder *C* to shiver with cold. *'O'in a swidder.'.*

Swifts a wooden cross from which yarn is wound off. Swifts stood upright six or seven feet high; winnels moved hori-zontally. (see Garn winnels).

Swifts see Garn winnels.

Swig *C* a long drink. *'Oald Dick could swig a quart at a wind.'* (see Wind).

Swig swag *C* a pendulum.

Swill a rough basket.

Swiller *SW* a swill or basket-maker.

Swilly *NE* to swallow.

Swin'ler swindler.

Swine bow *C* a bow hung around the swine's neck to prevent it creeping through hedges etc.

Swine creuh *N* a pig-sty; a dirty hull or house. *'Her hoose is na better ner a swine creuh.'*.

Swine feast *B* an entertainment or party after killing a pig.

Swine hull a pig-sty.

Swine ring an iron ring in a swine's snout to prevent its routing up the ground.

Swine ringer *C* an officer appointed by the lord of the manor's court to ring swine. (see Swine ring).

Swine stuff *C* a collection of scraps etc., kept in the swine-tub for pigs' food.

Swine thistle *C* sow-thistle, *Sonchus oleraceus.*

Swinge *C, E* singe.

Swingle tail *C* a smart dress-coat.

Swingle tree *C* the wooden bar each plough-horse draws by.

Swinglin *C* see Swingle tree.

Swinje *C* to singe with fire.

Swinjer *C* a great, an astounding assertion.

Swinn't *C* see Swènn't.

Swinnle tree *N* see Swingle tree.

Swint squint.

Swipe *C* to sweep off or remove hastily; to drink hurriedly; to drink or sup the whole.

Swiper *C* a hard drinker.

Swirl *SW* to whirl round.

Swirrel *C* squirrel.

Swirt squirt; a syringe.

Swirtle *C* to move quickly and tortuously as a small fish does in a shallow stream.

Switch *C* a flexible twig used as a rod; to whip.

Switcher any fast-going animal or thing.

Switchin' *B* one of the processes of dressing flax by hand.

Switchin' *C* a beating with a switch or rod.

Swoak soak.

Swober sober.

Swodger *C* soldier.

Swok soak.

Swol *C* sole of the foot, shoe, etc.

Swolly to swallow.

Swom *C* did swim.

Swops *N* sups; messes.

Sworry sorry.

Swort sort; to select; to arrange.

Swory sorry.

Swuft swift, rapid.

Swuk *N* suck.

Swum *C* swim. *'Can ta swum ower t'Derwent?'*.

Swun *N* swoon.

Swurd sword.

Swurl *N* see Swirl.

Swurt *C, N* see Swirt.

Swurtle *C* see Swirtle.

Swyke *C, SW* a thin-made animal; a worthless fellow.

Swyth *C, SW* see Sweeth.

Sydle *C, N* to saunter; to approach sideways or obliquely in a fawning or coaxing manner.

Sydlins *N* in the neighbourhood.

Sye *C, N* a very small quantity. *'Robin sank a well, and ther was n't a sye o'watter in 't.'*.

Sye a scythe.

Sye heel the crooked part of the scythe blade let into the shaft.

Sye nail *B* a small iron hook connecting the scythe blade with the shaft.

Sye nog *C* the handle fixed on the scythe shaft.

Syke *C* a small wet hollow.

Syle a copious drip; a straining sieve; to strain through a sieve. *'It syl't and bled'* - after the manner of a syle.

Syle brig a frame for supporting a syle or sieve etc.

Syle clout *C* economical housewives do not always incur the cost of wire gauze, but substitute a linen cloth as a filter.

Syme a straw rope.

Syne *C* to decant; drain off; to give up drawing milk from a cow.

Syne *N* since.

Syne ways *C* sundry ways. *'They ran ivry yan syne ways.'*.

Sype to drain off.

Syper a toper.

Sypins the last drops.

Syre *N* a gutter or vennel; sewer.

Syte a great deal. *'A syte o'fwok.'*.

Syzel to saunter; to trifle.

T *C, SW* the.

T'laal an *C* the little one; the child. *'Emilly's t'laal an in ma hoose.'*.

T's it *C* it is it; that is it.

T'year this year; the year.

Ta thee, thou; thanks; to or too.

Ta *SW, NW* tall.

Ta year this year. *'She's deun lile wark ta year.'* - Anderson.

Ta-dea *C, SW* to do.

Ta-mworn'o mwornin *C* to-morrow morning.

Taa thanks.

Taak *N, SW* talk.

Taarble *N* see Tarrable.

Tab *C* the narrow end of a field, etc., *'Tab end.'*.

Tack *C* a peculiar flavour or taste; a taint. *'This yal hes a tack o't'cask.'*.

Tack *C, E* thatch.

Tack *N* a stitch, *'A tack i'time seavvs nine.'*.

Tacks *C* tacket-nails or small pins; stitches in dressmaking.

Taffle *C* to throw into disorder; to perplex. *'It's a tafflan wind to-day.'*.

Taffy *C* toffy or toffee, treacle hardened by boiling. *'Margaret Marsh's laal shop in Powe Street selt taffy and mint marbles.'*.

Taffy a weak-minded person; a derisive term.

Taffy joinin' *C* toffee club. Young people in the country sometimes assembled on a winter evening and subscribe a few pence each to buy treacle for making *'taffy'*.

Tag the end; the metalled end of a boot-lace. *(see Aglet)*.

Taggelt *C* a vagabond or tramp.

Tagidder *C* together.

Taglet *E* the end. *(see Aglet)*.

Taistrel a person of vagabond life.

Tak *C, SW* take; a trick or lift in card-playing.

Tak efter to resemble. *'Jack hes rid hair and taks efter t'fadder fworsuer.'*.

Tak neyberheed *B* accept assistance. When a poor person dies the neighbours subscribe to bury him.

Tak off to mimic; to ridicule; to abscond; a satirist. *'Nea body likes him for he's a fair tak off, and he taks ivry body off.'*.

Tak on to be much affected by a melancholy event. *'He taks on sair'* - is much distressed.

Tak t'shine off *C* to spoil the appearance of; spoil what was a happy or successful event; to excel. *'He teuk t'shine off o't'rest.'*.

Tak up wid to associate with. *'He's tak'n up wid her fray Eggermouth.'*.

Tak't tul his sel *C* to apply an innuendo.

Takkan *C, SW* taking; infection.

Takkin' *C, SW* hurried perplexity. *'In a sad takkin'.'*.

Tan to beat. *'Yer fadder will tan his hide for him.'*.

Tang tine, grain or spikes of a fork; a prong.

Tangle dote *C* specified area or share of the sea shore. *(see Dote)*.

Tangs *C, SW* tongs, prongs.

Tanner six old pence coin (equates to 2½ new pence).

Tansy *N* a public-house ball.

Tansy *NE* see Merryneet.

Tantrums fits of passion.

Tap lash *B* the weakest part of a brewing of ale; generally three kinds - yel or yal; smo' beer, and tap lash.

Taptire *N, E* waiting with great impatience.

Targe *C* to thrash. *'He'll gi'thee a targin, my lad.'*.

Tarm *N* term.

Tarn a small lake.

Tarnt *N* ill-natured.

Tarrable *N* terrible; This word is also often used to indicate something extraordinary eg. *'tarrable nice', 'tarrable hee', "tarrable low'* etc.

Tarrier terrier, a book detailing land ownership; a dog; a wood working tool.

Tart sour, acidic.

Tassy *N* pleasant, nice.

Tat *C* that, *'Is tat t'reet way t'Workinton?'*.

Tat *C, SW* that. (a fell-dale word exclusively, and nearly obsolete. 1860)

Tath heaps *E* tufts of grass where cattle have dripped dung.

Tathy grass *N* soft grass growing under trees.

Tatter hurry. *'In a tatter.'*; to scold. *'She gev him a rare tatteran.'*.

Tatter can a termagant; a kicking cow.

Tattit matted. *See Cottit*.

Tatty *N* matted, uncombed.

Taty potato.

Taty ceakk *C* a frying-pan cake made of barley flour and potatoes.

Taty crab the fruit of the potato. (abundant before 1836, but scarce since)

Taty gun a pop gun made from a goose quill or feather. The quill punches the bullets out of a slice of potato.

Taty hash potato soup.

Taty pickin' *C* the time when whole families were employed to pick potatoes.

Taty puddin' potatoes and groats boiled in a bag among broth.

Taty scoose *B* See Taty hash.

Taw *C* a boy's favourite marble.

Tawpy *N* a silly person.

Tawwn *SW* town.

Tawwzle *SW* to ruffle; to pull about rudely; tussle.

Taylear tailor.

Te *C, N, SW* to.

Te sel *C, SW* thyself. (this form was nearly obsolete by 1878).

Te-draw *C, N* a place of resort; a newsmonger's house; a place of shelter.

Te-enn *N* taken.

Te-lick te-smack *C* as fast as possible. Generally applied to persons in the act of running.

Te-sel thyself.

Tea board *C* a wooden tea-tray, usually of mahogany or walnut and formerly accounted a mark of gentility.

Teaa *C, E, SW* toe.

Teaa the one.

Teaa hegh! on one side. *'It's o'o'teaa hegh like granfadder wig.'*.

Teabbel *C, N, E* table.

Tead toad.

Teadd toad.

Teadd pipe *C* the *Equisetum arvense* plant..

Teadd spit *C* see Cuckoo spit.

Teah *C* to. *'Put t'deer teah'* - close the door.

Teah *SW* tea.

Teak *C, N* take, took.

Teak *SW* take.

Teakk took.

Teakk efter went after. *'He teakk efter t'hare.'*.

Teal tale.

Teall tale.

Teally pyet a tell-tale; a betrayer of secrets.

Team tame.

Teamm *C* tame.

Tean *C, SW, E* taken.

Teangs *N* see Tangs.

Teann *C, SW* taken.

Teann the one.

Tear to rally or bully.

Tearan' tearing, careering. *'Tearan' like a crazy thing.'.*

Tearin' *SW* the rendering of a roof.

Tearm *N, E* term.

Teasst taste.

Teast taste.

Teatt a very small quantity. *'A teatt o'woo'.'.*

Teattit matted, uncombed.

Teaun *C* taken, *'T'squire's teaun the farm back fray yer fadder.'.*

Teavv *C* to pick the bed-clothes.

Teavv *N* see Keavv.

Teaylear *N, NW, E* tailor.

Teazz toes.

Teck *C* see Tack.

Tedder tether or tie.

Tee *C* thee, thou. *'Is tat tee, Bobby?'.*

Tee to fetter a cow's hind legs during milking.

Tee *G, not E* too.

Tee *N* to tie; toe.

Tee-tak-up-o' teetotum, a childs toy resembling a top and twirled by the fingers.

Teea *C, SW* toe.

Teeam *SW* to pour out; empty.

Teeas toes.

Teeght *N* tight.

Teem to empty; to pour out. *'Bob Elliott teems t'rid hot stile at Workiton's Moss Bay warks.'.*

Teemfull *E* full to running over.

Teen *N* taken.

Teen leatth *C, SW* a tithe barn to store the tenths in.

Teer *N* there, there is.

Teeram *C, SW* term.

Teethan' teething; getting teeth. *'La'al Jack's not yet teethan'.'.*

Tek *N, E* take.

Tell able to remember and able to tell of. *'He niver h'ard tell on't.'.*

Telt told.

Tem *C, SW* them.

Tems a hair sieve.

Tengs *N* see Tangs.

Tent' tenth.

Tep *C* a smart blow; a tap on the head.

Teppy teazz *C* tips of the toes.

Ter a contraction of there.

Terriers *N* tubers on the stems of potatoes.

Tersy versy *N* topsy turvy; in confusion or disorder.

Tetch *C* to be restive or obstinate.

Teu too.

Teu-draw see Te-draw.

Teu-fo' *C* too-fall; a lean-to shed.

Teuf *C, E* tough.

Teufet *C* the lapwing, *Vanellus cristatus.*

Teuff *C* tough.

Teufish *C* rather tough.

Teufly *C* rather tough.

Teugh *N* tough.

Teuh *C* to.

Teuk *C, E* took. *'His teuk himsel' off back t'London.'.*

Teukk took.

Teull tool.

Teulment *C* good-humoured mischief.

Teumm *C, N* to pour out; empty.

Teun tune.

Teunable having a musical ear.

Teunn tune.

Teup *N* a tup or ram.

Teurd *C, N* turd, excrement.

Teuth tooth.

Teuthwark *C, SW* tooth-ache.

Teuthyik *N* tooth-ache.

Teutle *C* to trifle. *'He teutles an' daddles about o't'day and gits laal or nought done.'.*

Teutt Hill *C* an elevated place where watch was kept in times of danger.

Tewet *SW* see Teufet.

Tey se *N* thyself. (this form was nearly obsolete by 1878).

Teydins *NW* tidings; news.

Teydy *NW* tidy.

Teyke *NW* an unruly fellow; a dog.

Teym *NW* time.

Teyny *NW* tiny.

Teyper *N, NW* toper.

Teyt *NW* tight.

Teytel *NW* title.

Teyth *NW* tithe.

Thaa *SW* thaw.

Thack thatch; to thatch.

Thack bottle a bundle of thatch.

Thack spelks *C* rods for securing thatch with.

Thack spittle *C, N* a tool used in thatching.

Thack stopple a handful of straw prepared for thatching.

Thaim *N* them.

Thairty *N* thirty.

Than then.

Than-abouts about that time.

Thank *C* obligation. *'He com i'my thank an'I mun pay him weel.'.*

Thar' ceakks *E, C* thick cakes of barley or oatmeal and water, and baked on the hearth among the embers.

Tharm *C* the material of which fiddle-strings are made.

Tharth *E* reluctant, unwilling.

Tharth ceakks *E, C* thick cakes of barley or oatmeal and water, and baked on the hearth among the embers.

That so. *'I was that vex't I could ha'bitten t'side out of a butter-bowl.'.*

That at' donnet *C* that evil one.

That'n that one.

That'un that one.

Thaw *SW* thou.

Thaww *SW* thee, thou; thaw.

Thaww'l *SW* thou wilt or will.

Thawws *SW* thou shall. *'Wait and thawws hear o'about it.'.*

Thawwsan' *SW* thousand.

Thawwz *SW* thou art.

Thay *C* They.

The *C* Thee, thou or you. *'I know the noo.'*.

The dickens! *C* an exclamation of surprise; and also a kind of oath.

Thea *B* these.

Theak thatch; to thatch.

Thear *SW* there; there is.

Thearr *SW* there, there is.

Thee *C, SW* thigh.

Thee thine, thy.

Theeaf *SW* thief.

Theeas *SW* these, those.

Theek thatch; to thatch.

Theer *C, N, E* their; there is, there. *'Yer lad's ower theer wid oor lass ageann.'*.

Theesal *C* yourself. *'Hev a thrippenny bit ta treat theesal wid.'*.

Thenk thank.

Thersells *C* themselves.

Theye *N* thigh.

Theyn thine, belonging to thee etc. *'I'll tak nowt of theyne, when am geann.'*.

Thick *N* familiar, friendly; unintelligent. *'Thick as pig shit.'*.

Thick as inkle weavers *C* very intimate.

Thick o'hearin' partially deaf.

Thick o't'thrang middle of the crowd; busiest part or time.

Thick on 't the major part. *'She brought a heap o'kilter an' t'thick on 't o'hard gold.'*.

Thick set low and strongly built.

Thick skin't not sensitive; unfeeling.

Thimmel thimble.

Thing used to refer to an event or happening, eg. *'It's a good thing.'* or *'It's no bad thing.'* etc.

Thing o'nought a trifle; not really worth taking into account.

Thingamy *C, N* a contemptuous appellation. *'What is yon daft thingamy about?'*.

Things any necessary materials, eg. tea things, dinner things, etc.

Thingumbob *C, N* a useless and trifling ornament; an item or person whose name has slipped your memory or you have forgotten.

Think me on remind me.

Think on to remember; to keep in mind.

Thinly rather thin.

Thinnish rather thin.

Thir *N* these, those.

Third man an umpire between two arbitrators.

Thirl *N* to bore through.

Thirt-teen thirteen.

This'n this one; this thing. *'This'n better than that'n.'*.

Thissel thistle.

Thole to endure; to suffer. *'He'll nivver thole the oaldfowk alone.'*.

Thonky *C, E* mist and small rain.

Thoo *C, E, N* thee, thou.

Thoo bad'n, thoo! Thou bad one, thou. this form of speech was in frequent use, and especially for reproach 1878.

Thoo's *C, E, N* thou shalt, thou art. *'Too's nivver gangan to see her ageann at this rate.'*.

Thoo's like *C, N* thou must *'Thoo's like to come in.'*.

Thoom thumb.

Thoom shag *C, N* bread and butter spread by the thumb.

Thoosan' *C, N* thousand.

Thou'l *N, E* thou wilt or will.

Thou'll git it a threat of punishment etc.

Thought a trifle or unserious act or talk. *'Skift on a thought, will ta?'*.

Thought on esteemed. *'He's girtly thought on about heamm.'*.

Thousans *C* thousands.

Thowe *C, N, E* thaw.

Thowt thought.

Thowte thought.

Thraa *SW* throw.

Thrang throng; busy. *'Thrang as Botchergeatt ivry Setterday neet.'*.

Thrast thrust, did thrust.

Thraw throw.

Threav *C, E* throve.

Threavv throve.

Threead *SW* thread.

Threeav *SW* a measure of twenty-four sheaves of corn.

Threed *C, N, E* thread.

Threep doon *C, N* to persist in an assertion. *'He threeps me doon 'at aa dud say seah.'*.

Threeplands *N* lands in dispute or debateable lands, generally on the borders of parishes.

Threeptree the wooden bar the two plough-horses are yoked to.

Threesam' reel *N* a three reel.

Threeten threaten.

Threshurt *N* threshold.

Threshwurt *C* threshold.

Threve *C* see Threeav.

Threy *N* three.

Thribble treble; three times.

Thrimmel tremble.

Thrins *C* triplets or three at a birth.

Thrinter *C, SW* a sheep of the third winter.

Thrippence Three pence.

Thrippenny bit a former coin worth three old pence.

Thrist *G, not E* thrust, did thrust.

Thro' *C* a flourish in writing thrown by a free hand; a turning lathe; to turn in a lathe.

Throddy *C* plump; well grown; throughly.

Throo through; threw or throw.

Throo ither *N* mixed, confusion.

Throo leet light all night; full moon.

Throo other *C* mixed, confusion.

Throo steanns long piece of stone passing through a rubble

wall to bind it or tie the front and rear faces or leaves together.

Throoly portly.

Throos see Throo steanns.

Thropple the windpipe.

Throssan *C, E, SW* thrust, did thrust; thrusting.

Throssan up *C* thick set; conceited. *'He's nobbet a throssan up thing.'.*

Throssel the thrush.

Through *N* a flat tombstone; or through stone. (see Throo steanns)

Thruff *C* see Through.

Thrufstan *C* see Thruff.

Thrummel't *N* crowded; confused.

Thrunter *C, SW* a sheep of the third winter.

Thrussan *N* thrust, did thrust; thrusting.

Thrwoat *N* throat.

Thud a heavy stroke with a dull sound.

Thumb shag *C* see Butter shag.

Thumkin *C, B* the thumb, in nursery play (see Fingers).

Thummel thimble.

Thummel pwok *C* a cap for protecting a sore finger.

Thumper a great one.

Thunner thunder.

Thur *C* these; those.

Thurd *C, N, E* third.

Thurl *N* to bore through.

Thurrans *C* these ones.

Thurt-teen thirteen.

Thurty *C, E* thirty.

Thwaite a cleared space in a wood or wilderness. A very common termination to placenames.

Thwol *C, E* to suffer.

Thworn *N* thorn.

Thwort *C* thought.

Thy adjective of thou; belonging to thee or you; your *'Yer fadder paid t'rent and seavv'd thy farm.'.*

Thyvel *C* a stick used for stirring a boiling pot.

Thúmmel pwok *E* see Huvvel.

Ti't *C* tied, bound, obliged. *'He was ti't gang an' ti't to work when he dud gang.'.*

Ti't by t'teeth cattle etc., tend to stray from a bad pasture, but linger in a good one.

Tic-tac *C* tick of a clock; a short period. *'Aa'll hev 't done in a tic-tac.'.*

Tice entire.

Tiddious tedious.

Tiddysom *N* tedious.

Tidy man *C, B* the little finger - in nursery play (see Fingers).

Tiff angry words passing. *'It was nivver a fratch. It was nobbet a bit of a tiff.'.*

Tift *C* condition as regards health or spirits. *'He's i'girt tift to-day.'.*

Tift to pant.

Tig *C, B* a childrens game where the touching of wood gives freedom; a game where the last-touched child is loser, often referred to as 'it'. They must then chase the other players and attempt to touch them.

Tig to touch gently; a childs game.

Tiglet *N* the metalled end of a boot-lace.

Til't *N* to it.

Till *C, N* to, too. *'Put that dooer till.' 'Is ta gaan till t'market?'.*

Tiller *C, SW* to spread; to send out side shoots.

Tilt quickly. *'He went full tilt doon bank an'fell an' brak his nwose.'.*

Timmer timber.

Timmer raisin' *N* a festivity held on occasion of putting the roof timbers on a new building.

Timmer rearin *C* see Timmer raisin'.

Timmersom' *C, N* timorous or timid.

Tine *N* to close off a pasture field till the grass grows again.

Tip a tup or ram.

Tipe *C* to drink. *'Tipe 't up, man,*

we've plenty mair.'.*

Tiper *C, E* a toper, drunkard or sot.

Tirl't *N* unroofed; the thatch blown off. *See Reuvv.*

Tiry *C* tired, fatigued.

Tis this.

Tis'n this one; this thing.

Tit *N* soon. *'I'd as tite dea 't as nut.'.*

Tit for tat giving as much as you get.

Tite see Tit.

Titter sooner. *'Titter up co' tudder up.'* - The first who rises to call on the other; rather. *'I'd titter hav't young 'an.'.*

Tittermest *C* nearest; soonest. (see Bain).

Titty *N* sister. *'Mary's yer titty, nut yer mam.'.*

Tittyvate to put into order; decorate; fit out.

Tiv *N* to. *'He wad gang tiv o't'merryneets this winter.'.*

Tizzik *C* a slight illness prevailing generally. *'It's a tizzik 'at's gangan' amang oald fwok.'.*

Tizzy *N* an old sixpence coin (equates to 2½p); a worked up state. *'Divvern't git yersel in a tizzy ower nought.'.*

To *C* a boy's favourite marble.

To *C* tall.

To t'fwore *C* living; alive. *'Is t'oald man to t'fwore?'.*

To year this year (almost out of use 1878).

To'rtly *SW* kindly.

To'rts *SW* towards.

To-mworn o'mwomin to-morrow morning.

To-neet tonight.

Tocken *G, not E* taken.

Tod a fox.

Toddle to walk unsteadily and child-like; to go. *'It's time to be toddlan' heamm.'.*

Toft a homestead.

Togidder together.

Tokker *N* dowry; portion. *'He tokker't his dowter wi'twenty pund.'*.

Toks *C* talk.

Toller *C* to holler or speak loudly and roughly. *'Tolleran' like a mad bull.'*.

Tom beagle *C* the cockchafer, a may-bug or dorr-beetle.

Tom speadd *C* a heavy spade for cutting sods only.

Tom tayleor *B* a water insect.

Tome *C* a hair fishing-line.

Tommaty taa *C* the titmouse bird or tom tit as it is commonly known.

Tommy Tee *C* see Tommaty taa.

Too *C* thee, thou.

Too'l *C* thou wilt.

Tooa *C, SW* two.

Tooar tower.

Toom *B* to tease wool.

Toom *N* a cord or string partly untwisted; a hair fishing-line.

Toon town.

Toon bull *C* a bull kept by turn in an farming village. *'He com rworan like a toon bull.'*. (a custom now extinct 1878).

Toon geatt the roadway through a village.

Tooz *C, N* thou art.

Toozle *C, N* see Tawwzle.

Top full full to the top. *'That fellow's top full o'mischief.'*.

Top lad! *C* good boy! an interjection of encouragement to a young man.

Top sark *C* a loose overcoat of coarse grey wool, much in use by farm servants in the first quarter of the 19th century.

Top speadd *C* see Tom speadd.

Top' taties *C* tubers on the stems of potatoes.

Topmer the one above the other; uppermost.

Topper one who excels.

Toppin the hair of the forehead; the crest of a fowl.

Toppin peats *C* turf cut with the herbage on. The edges resemble a man's unkempt *'toppin'* or head of hair.

Tops *C, N, SW* the best; a selection of the best annually.

Topsman the man in charge of a drove of cattle etc.

Topsy turvy in great disorder; overturned.

Toptire *C* towering passion; great disturbance.

Torfel *N* to die; to fail; to be defeated.

Torfer *C, SW* see Torfel.

Torfet *E* see Torfel.

Torious *N* notorious.

Torn *SW* turn. *'Ga' rawwnd t'hawwse an' torn that aa'd caww back into t'faald.'*.

Torna *SW* attorney.

Torrs *SW* turfs.

Torts *SW* towards.

Tosh *SW* tusk.

Tossicatit *N* intoxicated.

Totter bog *C* a shaking bog.

Tottle *E* toddle.

Toucher *C* a near approach. *'It's as near as a toucher.'*.

Touchious see Touchy.

Touchy easily offended.

Tov't *N* the mark cut into the ear of a sheep.

Towel *C* to beat. *'Rub him down with a yak towel.'*.

Towertly *C* kindly.

Towerts *C, N, E* towards.

Towgh *SW* tough.

Towp *C* see Towple.

Towple *C* to upset; overturn or topple over.

Towry lowry all in disorder.

Toytle ower *C* to topple over; to upset.

Trab *C* a long narrow field.

Traffic *C* lumber; useless things.

Traily slovenly, lazily.

Traips a saunterer; to saunter; an untidy female.

Traipsy *C* a saunterer; to saunter; an untidy female.

Tram *C* see Trab.

Tramp *C* a beggar; a vagabond.

Tramper *N* a beggar; a vagabond.

Trantlements *C* useless trifles. *'Laal trantlan' jobs and things.'*.

Trape *C* to drag the dress in the dirt; to walk in a slovenly manner.

Trash *C* rubbish; to walk quickly over wet ground. *'Trashan' through thick and thin for a heall day togidder.'*.

Trash't fatigued.

Travvish *C, E* traverse.

Trawwnce *SW* see Troonce.

Trawwt *SW* trout.

Tread *C, E, SW* trode.

Treadd *C, SW* trode.

Treak *N* an idle fellow.

Treas trace.

Treeacle *SW* treacle.

Treed tread. *'Treed o'my teazz an' yer fwor it'*.

Tret treat or treated. *'She's been reet badly trettan by him.'*.

Treud *N* trode.

Treudd *N* trode.

Treuth truth.

Trevally *N* disturbance, quarelling.

Trice moment, *'In a trice.'*.

Trig *C* tight; well filled, *'trig as an apple.'*.

Trim *C* to beat or whip; order; condition. *'What trim is t'oald horse in t'year?'*.

Trimmel tremble.

Trimmer a neat one.

Trinkams trinkets; useless finery.

Trinkle trickle. *'Bleudd com trinklan' down his feass like drops o'rain.'*.

Tripe *C* utter nonsense.

Trippet *C* a piece of wood used in a boy's game. *'Deed as a trippet.'*.

Trivet *C* a threefooted iron frame for supporting pans, etc., on an open fire. *'As reet as a trivet'*- perfectly right.

Trod a footpath.

Troff *C, E* a trough.

Trolly bags *C, N* tripes or the entrails of an animal; a jeering name for a fatman

Trones *E* steelyards.

Trooan *C, E* truant.

Trooin *C, E* trowel.

Troonce *C, N* trounce; to whip; to punish; to travel fast and far. *'Sec a trounce we've hed ower t'fells!'.*

Troot *C, E, N* trout.

Trowan *N* trowel.

Trowan *N* truant.

Trowf *SW* a trough.

Trowh *N* a trough.

Trudgin *B* a little boy following some one is *'lyel trudging'*.

Trug *C, N* a wooden coal-box.

Trumlins *C* coals about the size of apples.

Trummel trundle.

Truncher *B* An old game requiring dexterity. A young man lies face down, resting only on his toes and on two trenchers (wooden plates) held vertically in either hand. He then tries to move the trenchers apart as far as possible without falling.

Truncher *C* trencher; a wooden plate or platter. (long out of use by 1878).

Trunnel *C, SW* trundle or roll; the wooden wheel of a barrow.

Trunnel pie *N* a pie made of the small entrails of a calf.

Tu *C* to teasc; annoy; struggle. *'He's been a tusom barn.'.*

Tu *SW* too. *'I's frae Oofa tu.'.*

Tu-deuh extra work; excitment; confusion; wrangling.

Tudder the other.

Tuk *C, N* took. *'Ah tuk it oot o'his hand.'.*

Tukkan *C, SW* taken. *'She's tukkan tul'it varra well.'.*

Tul to.

Tul't *C, SW* to it. *'She's tukkan tul'it varra well.'.*

Tull *C, SW* to.

Tully *N* a wooden toy. *'Tee tak o', daily an'o'.'.*

Tum *B* to tease wool.

Tum'lan' *C, SW* tumbling. *'A tum'lan steann gedders nea moss.'.*

Tummel tumble.

Tummel car *C, N* the clumsy cart of old times, the axle of which revolved along with the wheels.

Tummel tails *B* apt to fall.

Tummellan kist *E* a post-chaise, a coach and horses.

Tummins *C* rough cardings of wool.

Tun'ler an ale glass. Originally a round bottomed glass which could not be made to stand, and was obliged to be emptied at once, or held in the hand.

Turmap see Turmat.

Turmat *C, N, not E* turnip.

Turn habit. *'He's of a nargangan' (greedy) turn.'.*

Turn deall *C* in some undivided common fields the ownership of the parcels changed annually in succession.

Turna *C* attorney.

Turney *N, E* attorney.

Turras *C* turfs.

Turrs *N* turfs.

Turves *B* turfs; peats used as fuel on an open fire.

Tush *C, N, E* tusk.

Tussle a struggle; contest.

Twaddle unmeaning talk.

Twang a pang of toothache; the sound of a stringed instrument; an accent.

Tweea *N, E* two.

Tweesom' *N* two in company.

Tweezle *B* to shake or ruffle violently.

Tweyn *NW* to whine; complain. *'She tweyns an' twists on, peer laal body!'.*

Twig *B* to lay hold of; to catch the meaning; to twig or pull his hair. *'It's a twiggan neet o'frost'- as if it grasped land and water keenly.*

Twig to see, recognise, perceive or understand. *'She's twigg't yer gangan to leave us.'.*

Twill *C* quill; a quill pen, the long strong feathers of a goose or other large bird.

Twilt quilt.

Twine twist; a course string or rope.

Twing *C* a small scarlet-coloured insect, said by the superstitious to occasion fatal illness to cattle.

Twinter a sheep of two wintes.

Twiny complaining; poorly. *'She's nobbet varra twiny to-day.*

Twist appetite. *'That fellow hes a famish twist.'.*

Twit *C* to sneer at.

Twitch a cord twisted round the upper lip of an unruly horse as a holdfast.

Twitchbell *E* the earwig, *Forficula auricularis.*

Twitter *B* very near.

Twitter *C* edge. *'Just in a twitter'* - on the very edge.

Twonty *N* twenty.

Twult *N* a quilt; to beat.

Tyke *C* an unruly fellow; a dog.

Tyl'd *SW* toiled; wearied; annoyed.

Tyl't *SW* see Tyl'd.

Tymerly *C* defective. *'It's a varra tymerly an' badly putten togidder.'.*

Udder *C, E, SW* other.

Um *C* him.

Um a common note of assent or agreement.

Un one (as in 'baddun' - bad one).

Unbiddable obstinate; untractable.

Uncanny *N* suspected of evil doings; unruly; difficult to deal with; suspicious; unbelievable.

Unco *N* strange or a stranger; wonder; very.

Unfewsom' awkward; unbecoming.

Unket *N* see Unco.

Unkos *N* wonders; news.

Unlick't cub *C* a rude and ignorant young person.

Unlucky *C* mischievous. *'Yon's an unlucky brat of a lad.'.*

Unpossible impossible.

Unreg'lar irregular.

Unsarra't *C, N, E* not served or unserved.

Unsayable wilful; uncontrollable.

Unserra't *N* not served.

Unshoe the horse *C* the *Botrychium Lunaria* plant.

Up abeunn above.

Up an' down perfect. *'He's eb'm up an' down honest.'.*

Up bringin' *C* rearing, training.

Up ov end upright; going about. *'Is 't wife up ov end yet?'.*

Up wid *C* to be even with; to raise or lift. *'He up wid his neef and doon't him, and he was up wid him than!'.*

Up-hod *C* maintenance. *'He's of a parlish girt up-hod an' can swallow two basonfulls o'poddish to t'brekfast.*

Up-hod uphold. *'Aa'll uphod ta'it's true.'.*

Up-kest a reproach.

Upbank uphill; upwards.

Upboil water springing in the bottom of a well or drain, resembling the appearance of boiling water.

Upo' *C, N* upon. *'Out upo' tha for a good-to-nought!'.*

Uppermer *C, B* the higher.

Uppish *C* conceited; holding a high head.

Uppoad uphold.

Ups *C* fatigues. *'This het weather an' hard wark fairly ups a body.'.*

Upsides wid *C* to retaliate; to be revenged on.

Uptak lifting; finding. *'Aa fand his watch on t'rwoad and he ga'me summat for t'uptak.'.*

Ur *C, N* are. *'Ho ur ye to-day, oor Jack?'.*

Url't *E* ill-thriven; stunted in growth.

Urlin *C* a dwarf; a small or dwarfish thing.

Urph *N* a dirty and diminutive person or child; one of dwarfish growth.

Urrant are not. *'You urrant to gang to-day.*

Us me. *'Please give us a lift.'.*

Usable *C* fit for use.

Use brass interest on money lent.

Use money see Use money.

Use n't used not. *'He use n't to be so queer when he was a lad.'.*

Usefuller more useful. *'Tom's mearr usefuller than t'udders.'.*

Vallidom *C, SW* the value. *'I wad n't give t'vallidom of an oald sang for o't'set o'them.'.*

Var'ly *C* verily; truly.

Varjis *C, E* verjuice, *'It's as sour as varjis.'.*

Varment *C, E* vermin.

Varra *C, E, SW* very. *'It's het weather, varra!'.*

Varra nigh *C* very near.

Varra weel very well. Often used in relating news, etc. *'Varra weel than, I'll tell ye o'about it.'.*

Varraly *C* verily; truly.

Varry *N* very.

Varse verse.

Varst vast, a great number or quantity.

Vayper *C, N* to caper; exult; vapour. *'A vayper an'feull.'.*

Veeal *SW* veal.

Ventersom venturesome, bold daring and intrepid.

Ventersom' adventurous, rash.

Vex't *C* irritated; angry; tormented.

View hollo the cheer given when the hare is killed by the hounds.

Viewly handsome; pleasing to look upon.

Viewsom' comely; of good appearance.

Voag *C, N* repute. *'He's i'full voag noo.'.*

W'rang wrong. (seldom heard 1878).

W'reet right. (rarely heard 1878).

Wa *C* why, well. *'Wa noo than!'.*

Wa *C, E, SW* with. *'Gang wa Tom.'.*

Wa we. *'We'll gang when wa like.'.*

Waa *SW* wall.

Waad *C, SW* wade.

Waar *C* to ware, to spend. *'He nobbet waar't sixpence at t'fair.'.*

Waar *C, SW* to expend.

Waar beware; worse.

Waareld *C, SW* world.

Waaw *C* see Wawwl.

Wabberthet Wabberthwaite.

Wabble wobble or waddle; to rock sideways in walking.

Wad *C* blacklead.

Wad would. *'Wad ta like to len'me a shillin'?'.*

Wad eater *C* India rubber.

Wad n't cud dea't *C, N* could not do it.

Waff puff of wind; quaff or drink largely or luxuriously.

Waffish weakly, feeble.

Waffle to waver; to be undecided; to talk incessantly, much of which maybe nonsense.

Waffler an unsteady person; one not to be depended on; one who waffles.

Waffy weakly, feeble.

Wag by t'wo' *C* an old-fashioned clock without a case, and having the pendulum swinging exposed.

Waggle to shake; to be unsteady.

Wah *C, SW* with.

Waik weak.

Waintit *N* see Wentit.

Waistrel a person of vagabond life; an idle wanderer.

Waits outdoor Christmas musicians.

Wake *C, E, SW* weak.

Wale *N* see Weal.

Walk mill place where cloth was fulled. (see Walker).

Walker a fuller of cloth - a task once performed by trampling on the woolen cloth with the feet.

Walking a mason or quarryman's method of moving a flagstone on its end.

Walla *C* weak; faint from want or illness; tasteless; insipid.

Wallet a long bag open at the middle and closed at the ends for conveying marketing on horseback. (out of use 1875).

Wallop *C, N* to beat; to dangle loosely.

Wammel to walk with a rocking motion. *'Wammelan' like an eel.'*.

Wan won, did win. *'Lowden wan t'belt at Grasmere sports.'*.

Wan *N* having wound; did wind.

Wand *C, E* having wound; did wind.

Wand the one year old shoots of the willow.

Wandly *C* gently, quietly.

Wandy *C* slim and flexible as a willow wand.

Wankle weak or feeble. *'Poor Jemmy! he's varra wankle.'*.

Wannel *N* lithe; agile; flexible.

Want to deserve or require. *'He wants a good skelpin to mak him behave his sel.'*.

Wanter *G* a marriageable person.

Wanty deficient; imperfect or defective.

Wap *C, N* to wrap or enfold; a bundle of straw; a lap.

War were. *'War ye ivver at Whitehebm.'*.

War'nt to assure; warrant. *'Aa's war'nt ta it is.'*.

War-board *C* a shop's counter - ie. ware board.

Warang wrong. (seldom heard 1878).

Warble the larva of the *Cestrus bovis* fly which breds in the backs of cattle.

Ward award.

Wardays the six work days of the week.

Wardle *C, SW* world.

Ware *N* to expend.

Wareet right; rarely heard.

Wark ache; work. *'It's slow wark to sup buttermilk wid a pitchfork.'*.

Wark fwok labourers, workers or work people.

Warl *N* world.

Warld *C, SW* world.

Warm to beat. *'Aa'll warm tha.'*.

Warmness warmth.

Warn *C* to bid to or give notice of a funeral.

Warn see War'nt.

Warnin' *C* the circuit invited to a funeral.

Warp to lay eggs.

Warridge the withers of a horse.

Warrishin' *C* a great deal; abundance. *'A warrishin' o'sooins an' yal.'*.

Warse worse. *'Warse and warse like Worki'ton clark.'*.

Warse ner git out *C* excessively bad; something worse than being ordered out of the house.

Warsen to grow worse.

Warst. C worst.

Wart grass *C* sun spurge, the plant *Euphorbia Helioscopia*.

Warton *NW* the village and township of Waverton.

Was ter? was there; were there.

Wasdal *SW* Wasdale.

Wasdal Heid *SW* Wasdale Head.

Waster-ledges *N, E* the *Polygonum bistorta* plant, a common ingredient in traditional herb puddings.

Wasterledges *C* See Easter-mun-jiands.

Wastle *SW* Wasdale.

Wastle Heead *SW* Wasdale Head.

Wath a ford through a stream.

Watna *N* do not know. *'I watna what it is.'*.

Watter water.

Watter ask a newt or water-lizard, the small batrachian lizard.

Watter brash *C, N* a gushing (emitting copiously) everflow of saliva.

Watter crashes *C* water-cress, *Nasturtium officinale*.

Watter draw see Watter shed.

Watter dyke *NW* a ditch or sowe wide and deep enough to form a fence.

Watter gwoat *C* a place in a stream across which a rack or pole is placed to prevent cattle trespass; and the rack or pole itself; a floodgate.

Watter jags *C* one of the forms of varicella or chicken pox.

Watter jaw't *C* potatoes left too long in the water after boiling are watter jaw't and spoilt.

Watter kesh *C* the plant *Angelica sylvestris*.

Watter pyet *C* the water ousel.

Watter shed an area within which water gathers towards an outlet.

Watter stang a pole fixed across a stream in lieu of a bridge or fence.

Watter thistle *C* the *Cnicus palustris* plant.

Watter yet a heck (a gate or door) hung below a watter stang or pole, to act as a fence. (see Watter stang).

Watterey like appearance of rain coming; watery or well diluted. *'This pents varra watterey like.'*.

Watterey lonnin *C* a neglected lane where water is allowed to run along.

Wattles *G* the gill appendages of a game cock.

Wattertwitch the *Agrostis vulgaris* plant.

Wauddent *C* would not.

Waugh *B* a weak unpleasing scent. When meat begins to decay it gives out a *'waugh'*.

Waugh the bark of a pup or whelp.

Waww *C* see Wawwl.

Wawwl *SW* infant's wail. *'Waawlan like a cat.'*; silly talk.

Wax to grow larger; to swell out.

Wax end *C* a shoemaker's waxed and bristled thread.

Way *G* used as expressive of comparison or degree. *'It's a lang way better to gang that way, for it's faraway t'bainer way.'*; direction or area. *'He leevs someway out Wigton way.'*.

Way *N* woe; to be sorry.

Way *SW* see Wey.

Way betyde ye *N* You'll be getting into trouble.

Ways me! exclamations of lament.

Wayster a waster; a thief or excrescence in the candle.

Waze *N* a milk maids cushion for the head; a ring cushion to place on the head for carrying weights upon. (See Boss).

Wazes me! see Ways me!.

Wazzant *C* was not.

We *N* with. *'Gang we Tom.'*.

We's *SW* we shall. *'We's ga'to Wastle Heead.'*.

We't *E, SW* with it.

We-ans *C, N* children, little ones.

Wea *N* see Way.

Weage *N, E* wage.

Weaky *SW* moist, juicy.

Weal *C* to select; to pick out.

Weamm the womb; body.

Wear *N* to turn or stop cattle or sheep.

Wear *N, E* wore.

Wearin illness *C* consumption.

Weary *C* tiresome; monotonous. *'It's a weary rwoad to Warnel fell.'*.

Weast *C* waste; the waist.

Weather go *C* the end of a rainbow as seen in the morning in shower weather - the sailors warning.

Weathered a term for hay etc., having been exposed to wet weather.

Weay *N* woe; pity. *'I's weay for them, poor things!'.*

Weayd *N, E* wade. (from Robert Anderson's dialect poetry).

Weayst *N, E* waste; the waist.

Webster *C, SW* a weaver of webs or cloth by hand.

Wed't *N, SW* wedded.

Wedder weather; wether.

Wedder cock a weather vane or cock.

Weddin *C* Wedding, marriage.

Weddiners a wedding party.

Weddit wedded.

Weder weather; wether.

Wee *C, N* little or small. *'Wee Jack cud nivver reach the dresser top.'*.

Wee see Wo.

Wee an' *N* a small one, a child.

Weeage *SW* wage.

Weeal *SW* see Weal

Weeat *SW* wet, rain.

Weedsticks *N* tongs for pulling up weeds.

Weeer wear.

Weef an' stray *C* cattle, etc., gone astray, the owner not being known; vagrants without house or home; waifs and strays - odds and ends; a homeless or neglected child.

Weekiness moisture.

Weeky *C, N* moist, juicy.

Weel well. *'He stack up weel for t'lass.'*.

Weel cum't *C* highly bred; of good lineage.

Weelish off well off, in easy circumstances. *'Oor lasse's family is weelish off, but neabody expects owt.'*.

Ween't *C, E* will not.

Weet *C, N* wet, rain. *'It weets fast.'*.

Weet yer whissle *C, N* take a hearty drink.

Weeze *N* see Waze.

Weft *C* to beat. *'Aa'll give him a weftin' some day.'*.

Weg horned *C* horns unequally elevated.

Well *C, E, SW* weld.

Well ink *C* the *Veronica Beccabunga* plant.

Welsh *C, SW* insipid; watery; tasteless.

Welt *C* to beat.

Welt *C, SW* to overturn; to upset; to turn under, eg. with a flashing in construction.

Welts *C* the *'rig and fur'* parts of the tops of stockings.

Wend *C* to turn round.

Went on continued. *'Thee brother an' sister went on fratchan at a parlish rate.'*; talked or chatted ceaselessly. *'She went on at a parlish rate.'*.

Wentit *C* just turning sour. *'Thunnery' weather wents milk.'*.

Wents *C* narrow lanes in Cockermouth, Workington and other towns.

Werren *E* Wren (surname).

Wescwoat *C* waistcoat.

Wesh *C, N, E* wash.

Wesh dub *C, SW* a pool where sheep are washed.

Wesh foald *C, SW* the sheepfold near the washing-pool. (see Wesh dub).

Weshers *C, B* the inside works of a barrel churn used in buttermaking.

Weshins the dish water in which greasy dishes have been washed, once used for pigs food.

Wet shod feet wet in the shoes.

Wey *C* well, why; notes of assent or dissent. *'Wey, yes.' 'Wey, no.'*.

Wey see Wo.

Weyd *NW* wide; wife; wile or deceive; wine.

Weydness *NW* width.

Weyf *NW* wide; wife; wile or deceive; wine.

Weyl *NW* see Weyf.

Weyn *NW* see Weyf.

Weys beam and scales; weighs.

Weysh *SW, NW* wash.

Weyt *C, SW* a tambourine-like vessel, used for lifting grain in the barn and made of a sheep's skin covering a wooden hoop.

Weyya *C* see Wey.

Weze *N* see Waze.

Wezzan *C, SW* the gullet.

Whaa *SW* who.

Whaa-ivver *SW* whoever.

Whaar *E, SW* where.

Whack a blow, thwack.

Whacker a large one.

Whaff see Waff.

Whain *E* to rub or stroke in the direction the hair grows. *'He whain't his dog down t'back.*

Whain to fawn. *'She com whainan' and wantan' help.'.*

Whaker *C, N, E* a quaker.

Whale to cudgel or beat with a thick stick.

Whalin' a beating with a stick.

Whamp *C* the wasp. *'Keen as a whamp.'.*

Whang to throw; to hit; a leather shoe-tie; a strap used in stitching a cart-harness; a thong; a lump or large piece. *'A whang o'cheese.'.*

Whanger a large one.

Whap a blow.

Whapper a large or remarkable one, a whopper.

Wharl *C* a stone quarry; a disused quarry. (seldom heard 1878).

Whart *N* quart. (see Quart).

What'n? *N* what? *'What'n clock is 't?'.*

What's matter? *C* what is the matter or reason?.

Whate see Thwaite.

Whatsomivver whatsoever.

Whaup *N* the curlew, *Numenius arquata.*

Whay feasst pale countenance or complexion.

Whe *N* who.

Whedder whether.

Whee *N* who.

Whee-ivver, *N, E* whoever.

Wheea *N, E* who. *'Wheea's that?'.*

Wheelstrake a portion of the iron rim of a wheel, formerly applied in six lengths to each wheel.

Wheem *B* quiet of manner, whim. (see Whim).

Wheem *E* silent; quiet in speech or action; running smoothly.

Wheen *N* an undefined number; a few. *'A whun sheep.'.*

Wheer *N* where.

Wheezle to breathe with difficulty. *'He wheezles like a pursy horse.'*

Wheezy breathing thickly or noisely, chesty.

Wheg *E* a lump or thick slice. *'A wheg o'cheese.'.*

Whel *C* until, *'Stay whel I come back.'.*

Whel *E* while, whilst.

Whelk *C, N* to beat or thump.

Whelker *C, N* a large one.

Whelt *C* to beat.

Whemmel *C* to overwhelm; overturn.

Wheren't *C* milk overheated makes the curd and cheese hard and *'wheren't'.*

Whets *C* flashes of wit. *'Sec whets we hed tudder neet.'.*

Whettan *C* to sharpen a blade etc., such as a scythe, using a stone.

Whew *C* haste. *'Sec a whew he's in!'.*

Whew! *C, B* an expression of contempt.

Whewt *E* a thin flake of snow. *'A few whewts o'snow.'.*

Whewtle *C* a low modulated whistle.

Whey aye *N* yes, of couse.

Wheye *N* heifer or young cow.

Wheyle *N* until.

Wheyles *N* sometimes. *'Whiles he's here and whiles he's theer.'.*

Wheyte *NW* to whittle or cut a

stick so that it is made white; white; quite.

Whick quick; alive. *'Git yeamm whick else yer miss her.'.*

Whick'nin' *C* quickening; a small quantity of yeast sufficient to set a baking of bread to ferment.

Whick't *C* fly-blown.

Whickflu *C* whitlow - a disease of the feet in sheep; an inflammatory sore around the finger nails in humans.

Whicks *C, N* roots of couchgrass; young thorns; maggots.

Whidder to shudder; shiver; tremble.

Whidderer a very large or powerful one.

Whiet quiet.

Whiff *C* smell, *'I just gat a whiff of t'reek.'*; discover a secret or tale, often through hearing a rumour.

Whiff a transient view or glance. *'I just gat a whiff on't.'.*

Whiff quiff.

Whig whey kept for drinking. *If it became sour, aromatic herbs are steeped in it.*

Whigmaleery *C* anything showy and useless.

While *C* until, *'Stay while I come back.'.*

Whiles *C* see Wheyles

Whilk which.

Whilkan' *C* which one?. *'Whilkan' will she wed?'.*

Whillimer cheese *C* the poorest and hardest of cheese, though to originate in the township of Whillimoor, but once common over the county.

Whim *C* see Wheem.

Whim wham *C* a fanciful trifle.

Whimmy *C* given to whims and fancies.

Whimper *C* a low whine or cry. *'Git away to bed barns, and nivver a whimper.'.*

Whin *C, SW* the gorse or furze

plant, *Ulex europœus.*

Whin *N* few.

Whin cowe *C* a whin stem or branch.

Whinge to whine.

Whinner *C* to neigh.

Whinny *SW* to neigh.

Whintin *C* a dark-coloured slate found on Skiddaw. When struck it gives out musical note. The celebrated 'musical stones' at Keswick are made of it.

Whir *C, E* old and curdled buttermilk.

Whirl bent *C* the *Juncus squarrosus* plant.

Whirlgig *B* a small shining beetle that disports itself on the surface of water, constantly circling round and round, diving if disturbed.

Whishin cushion.

Whishin dance *C* an old-fashioned dance in which a cushion is used to kneel upon.

Whisht *C, SW* hush; listen; quietly. *'As whisht as a mouse.'.*

Whisk *B* a slight cleaning. *'She gev't a whisk an' a kengeud.'* (see Whick).

Whisk to move quickly. *'She com whiskan' bye like a fleean' thing.'*; a game of whist.

Whisk whist.

Whissel *C, E, SW* whistle.

Whissenday *C, E, SW* Whit-suntide.

Whissle *C* whistle; the mouth. *'Weet yer whissle.'.*

White white; quite; to require or requite. *'Od white ta!'* - God requite thee.

Whitefish *C* flattery.

Whitehebben *C* Whitehaven.

Whither *N* to strike or throw forcibly. *'He girn't an' pick't his beans wid his teeth, and than he whither't them onder t'grate.'.*

Whither away? *C* where are you going to?.

Whittle a knife.

Whittlegate *C* Formerly clergymen and schoolmasters had the privilege of eating (using their whittles) at the tables of their parishioners. (This custom prevailed till 1864, and ceased with the death of the school-master of Wasdale Head).

Whiz a hissing sound like the cooling of hot iron in water.

Whizzer a glaring untruth or lie. *'That is a whizzer!'.*

Who-ivver *C* whoever.

Whoar *C, E* where.

Whoaraway *C* where. *'Whoar away hes to been?'.*

Whol whole; hole.

Whop *C* to whip or strike.

Whopper a big lie. (see Whapper).

Whopt *C* hoped.

Whorn horn.

Whun *N* an undefined number; a few. *'A whun sheep.'.*

Whun *N* see Whin.

Whun cowe *N* see Whin cowe.

Whunner *N* to neigh.

Whup *C* see Whop.

Whup whip.

Whup hand the advantage.

Whup-while *C* as frequent as the strokes of a well-applied whip. *'Iv'ry whup-while.'.*

Whurlygig *B* see Whirlgig.

Whurry *C* wherry.

Whush *N* see Whisht.

Whushin *N* cushion.

Whusk *N* see Whisk.

Whussel *N, E* whistle.

Whussenday *N* Whitsuntide.

Why *C, SW* see Wheye.

Why-i! *C* to cry out like whipped dog.

Wi *C, E, SW* with.

Wi'am *SW* with him.

Wi'awte *SW* see Wid-out.

Wi'ma *C, SW* with me.

Wi'ya *C* will you, *'Wi'ya ivver see us agin or is yer gean for good.'.*

Wicker *E* a twig or small branch.

Wid with.

Wid'am *C* with him. *'Oor lass said she's gangan wid'am.'.*

Wid-out *C* without; unless. *'He'll hev to gang wid-out her efter aal.'.*

Widder wither.

Widderful *C* peevish; irritable.

Widdle *N* to fret; to complain.

Widdup *C* Wythop, between Keswick and Cockermouth.

Widdy *C* withy; a band of platted willows in hanging gates. (often used in former days 1878).

Wide geattit *C* walking in a straddling manner; bandy legged.

Wideness *C* width.

Widness *C* width.

Wife day *C* On a birth occurring the neighbouring wives assemble at the house for tea, etc., as soon as the mother is able to receive company.

Wild like *C* threatening wild weather.

Wile *C* to lead or entice. *'Tak a reap o'cworn wi'ye. An' wile her heamm.'.* - from an old song.

Wilk *C* the bark of a young dog when in close pursuit.

Will to bequeath. *'He will't his money to t'dowter.'.*

Will n't *C, E* will not or won't.

Wills *C* doubts. *'Aa's i'wills whether to gang or nit.'.*

Willy *C, SW* the sweet willow - *Salix pentandra.*

Willy lilt *C* the common sandpiper, *Tringa alpina.*

Willy wands *C* young shoots of the willow.

Wilta? *C, E, SW* wilt thou?.

Wima *C, E, SW* with me.

Win in *N* to secure the crop.

Win' *N* wind; to wind.

Winch *B* a vice or iron screw.

Wind *C, E, SW* wind; to wind; the time occupied in drawing the breath. *'Dick could swallow a quart at a wind.'.*

Wind egg *C* an egg dropped before the shell is hardened.

Wind row *B* peats or turves set up in a long row, being the second process in drying.

Winda window; the placename Winder, near Arlecdon.

Window leuker the inspector of lights when the window-tax was levied.

Windy noisy; talkative. *'Mair wind nor woo' like clippin' a swine.'.*

Windy bags an incessant talker. *'Oor Mary's sec a windy bags.'.*

Wine berries *C, N* red currants, *Rubes rubrum.*

Winje! *C* a gladsome exclamation of surprise or wonder. *'Winje wife, what a berry pudding!'*; winge or whinge, to complain frequently or habitually.

Winkers *SW* see Blinders.

Winna *N* will not.

Winnel strea the stem of the couch grass. *'As waik as a winnel strea.'.*

Winnet *C, E* will not.

Winnick *N* anything diminutive. In playing at pitch and toss with button tops the small ones are winnicks and the larger ones slaters.

Winsh *C, E* wince.

Winskealls *C* Winscales.

Winsom' *N* lively and pretty; of winning manners.

Winter to live through winter. *'T'oald horse 'll hardly winter ageann.'*

Winter prawwd *SW* winter wheat in too forward a state of growth.

Winter proud *C* Winter prawwd.

Winter wood *C, SW* deciduous trees which should be cut down in winter and not peeled.

Winteridge winter eatage in the field.

Wipe a hint. *'She gives him many a wipe about it.'.*

Wires *B* the frame work on the spindle of a spinning wheel, with crooked wires to guide the thread to the bobbin.

Wise like *N* wise and prudent.

Wish washy weak; worthless.

Wished on *C* recommend a person to another; foisted on or upon.

Wisk *C, SW* a light and short shower.

Wisp *C, SW* a handful of hay or straw.

Wissel weasel.

Witchwood the mountain ash, *Pyrus Aucuparia.*

Wittin' knowledge, intell-igence. *'I dud t'best o'my wittin'.'.*

Wizzan *N* the gullet.

Wizzel weasel.

Wizzen't lean or thin, withered or wizened.

Wo halt, a horse-drivers term.

Wo' *C, N, E* wall.

Woa see Wo.

Woast hoose *C* an inn; a kiln to dry hops.

Woat leather *B* see Woatin'.

Woath *N, E* oath.

Woatin' *B* a band of leather nailed around a clog to fix the leather upper to the wooden sole.

Woats *N, E* oats.

Wob *N* web.

Wobster *N* a weaver.

Woe betyde yer you'll be getting into trouble.

Wokan awaken, waken.

Woke-rife *N* sleepless.

Wol *N* weld.

Wole-eyed *C* a horse and dog having one or both eyes nearly white; wall-eyed.

Woo wheel a wheel on which wool is spun.

Woo' wool.

Wooshat *E* the woodpigeon or woodchat shrike, *Lanius rufus.*

Wor *N* were.

Worchat orchard.

Worde *C, N, E* order.

Wordy worthy.

Woremest foremost.

Workan' by girt *C* working by contract.

Worki'ton Workington.

Worniment *E, NW* ornament.

Worriment harassing annoy-ance.

Worts *C* see Orts.

Wostler *N, E* ostler or stableman at an inn.

Wotchat *E* orchard.

Wots *B* knows; is aware of.

Wots *E* see Orts.

Woy see Wo.

Wramp *C* a sprain.

Wramp *C* see Ramp.

Wrang wrong. *'It's wrang to wrang ennybody.'.*

Wreat *C, E* wrote.

Wrecklin' the smallest of a litter.

Wreyt *NW* write.

Wrought *C* rode. *'They wrought at heart's wind o't'day.'.*

Wrout *C, E* wrought.

Wrowt *C* rode. *'Ah wrowt wid 'im ower to Cockermuth.'.*

Wu'ma *N* with me.

Wud *N* mad; with (used before an h or vowel).

Wud'am *N* with him.

Wuddy *N* see Widdy.

Wull *N* will.

Wullent *N* will not.

Wulls *B* wills; will. often a bargain was closed on a bystander by saying, *'Come ov his wulls.'.*

Wully wans *N* young shoots of the willow.

Wulta? *N* wilt thou?.

Wummel an augur or wimble.

Wun *C* woollen.

Wun *N* wind; to wind.

Wun' *C, N* wound. *'He wun'up his watch.'.*

Wun' *N* to dwell. *'He wuns ayont yon hill.'.*

Wunder *C* wonder.

Wunna *N* will not.
Wunsom *N* neat, pleasant.
Wunz! *C* an oath or exclamation.
Wur *N* were.
Wurd word.
Wurl *N* world.
Wurn *E* Wren (surname).
Wurn *E* see Wurren.
Wurren *E* the surname of Wren. *'Jo' Wurren of Ondercrag.'.*
Wusk *N* see Wisk, Wisp.
Wusp *N* wisp.
Wussel *G, not E* wrestle.
Wusset worsted for knitting.
Wut *N* wit.
Wuth *N* with.
Wuvver *B* however; indeed.
Wuzzel *E, B* weasel.
Wyke *C* a narrow opening between rising grounds; the corners of the mouth.
Ya *C, SW* one.
Yaad *SW* old mare.
Yaak *C, SW* oak.
Yaap *SW* to whoop; to shout.
Yabble *C* able.
Yaddearn *B* talking much.
Yaddle *C, SW* to speak quickly and unwisely; to earn.
Yadwands whips or rods used in driving horses. *(rare by 1878).*
Yage *G, not E* age.
Yage *N* to grow old.
Yah way or anudder *C* One way or the other.
Yak *C, E, SW* oak.
Yak cubbert a large oak cupboard once built into the internal walls of old farmhouses (dating from the mid 17th century).
Yakker *C, E, SW* acre, an area of land equivalent to 4,840 sq.yds or 0.405 hectares.
Yakker spire *E* The state of the barley when the malting process is not controlled, both root and sprout are visible.
Yakkeridge *G, not E* acreage.
Yal *C, E, SW* ale.

Yal-jaw't *C* sickened by drinking ale, drunk.
Yale *C* ale.
Yalhoose inn or public house.
Yalla yellow.
Yalla yowderin *N* the yellow-hammer or bunting, *Emberiza citrinella.*
Yalseal *SW* wholesale.
Yammer *C, N* to talk in a rambling-like manner.
Yam *B* ham.
Yan *C, SW* one.
Yan-day *C* one day (a common retrospection). *'It was ya-day last week.'.*
Yananudder *C, E, SW* one another.
Yance *C, E, SW* once. *'I'll try it just yance mair an nivver ageann.'.*
Yance to bed *B* said when a person begins to yawn.
Yap *C* a mischievous lad; a little dog.
Yar *N* hair; harsh; sour.
Yarbs *C, N* herbs..
Yark to strike furiously or fiercely, *'as hard as he could yark.'.*
Yarl *N* see Yerl.
Yarls *C, N* money given to confirm a bargain.
Yarr see Hear.
Yarr *N* hair; hare.
Yas ace.
Yast *SW* yeast.
Yat *C, SW* a gate.
Yat *SW* hot.
Yaup *C* to whoop; to shout.
Yawer *SW* your; the udder of an animal.
Yawl *SW* to weep.
Ye *C* You. *'Hoo ur ye?'.*
Ye'r *SW* your; you are.
Yea's *SW* you shall. *'Yea's come, ye'r like.'.*
Yeas *C* ease.
Yedder *C, SW* a long rod used in hedging; a binder.

Yek *N, E* oak.
Yel *N, E* ale.
Yelberry *N* ale boiled with bread, butter and sugar, once given at funerals for dinner.
Yella yellow.
Yella yowderin *N* the yellow-hammer or yellow bunting.
Yems see Heams.
Yems *B* homes. *(see Heamm).*
Yen *N* one.
Yenaither *N* one another.
Yenanither *N* one another.
Yence *N* once.
Yer your, *'Behave yer sel.';* you are.
Yers *W* you, *'Where yers gaan.'.*
Yer sel yourself. *'Help yer sels to minsh pies.'.*
Yer'l *C* you will or you'll. *'Yer'l git it on Setterday.'.*
Yerb puddin' a dish of early spring, composed of young nettles and every wholesome vegetable that the garden then affords, mixed with groats, oatmeal or shilled barley, and boiled in a bag in broth. The great art in compounding this dish is to have much variety with no predominating taste.
Yerbs *C, N* herbs.
Yerd yard.
Yerdfasts large stones fast in the earth, and near the surface.
Yerl *C, E, SW* earl. *'Yon's t'yalla yerl fray Whitten castle.';* a fast water course.
Yerls *C, N* see Yarls.
Yern *N* yarn.
Yernest earnest.
Yerth earth.
Yerthful *C* greedy as the earth.
Yest *E* yeast.
Yet *N* a gate.
Yet stoop *B* gate post.
Yether *N* a long rod used in hedging; a binder.
Yetlin *N* a pan with a bule or bow.

Yigga *N* ague or cold fit which preceeds a fever.

Yiglet *N* aglet; tag.

Yik *N* oak; to ache.

Yikker *N* acre (see Yakker).

Yin *N* one.

Yis yes.

Yist *C, N* yeast.

Yister *C* Yesterday, sometimes seen as *'Yister neet'* - yesterday night.

Yisterday yesterday.

Yit yet.

Yither *N* see Yether.

Yoad *C, N* old mare.

Yod *C, N* old mare.

Yoller *C, N* to shout; to halloo.

Yon over there.

Yooar *C, N, E* your; udder.

Yooer *C, N* the udder of an animal.

Yool *C, N* weep and cry.

Yope *C* to whoop; to shout.

Yope A constant talking in a loud voice.

Youngermer *N* young persons.

Youngfwok's neet *C* similar to Oaldfwok's neet, usually held a night or two later. (1878)

Yowe *C, N, E* ewe.

Yowe chin't *C* having a ewe-like chinned; chin retiring.

Yowe locks *C* locks of wool taken from the udder of the ewe to enable the newly-born lamb to find the teat.

Yowe neck't the arch of the neck bending downwards.

Yowe yorlin *C, N* the earth nut, *Bunias flexuosum.*

Yowe yornel *C, N* see Yowe yorlin.

Yub'n steann *C* the stone used to close the oven's mouth.

Yucks *N* itches; is tickled.

Yuk *N* the itch.

Yule *N* Christmas.

Yuly yuly *B* a call to bring geese together.

Yungest *N* youngest.

Yungster *C* youngster.

Yur *C, SW* the corn-spurry plant, *Spergula arvensis.*

Yurl *B* earl. *(see Yerl).*

Yurth *N* earth.

Zookers! *C, SW* an exclamation of surprise or admiration.

Zukkers! *C, SW* see Zookers.

Design n' Prent'd in Worki'ton, Cummerlan by Pages n' Pages. 1.01